Gotti's
Boys

Also by ANTHONY M. DESTEFANO

TOP HOODLUM:
Frank Costello, Prime Minister of the Mafia

THE BIG HEIST:
The Real Story of the Lufthansa Heist,
the Mafia, and Murder

MOB KILLER:
The Bloody Rampage of Charles Carneglia,
Mafia Hit Man

KING OF THE GODFATHERS:
Joseph Massino and the Fall of the
Bonanno Crime Family

Gotti's Boys

The Mafia Crew
That Killed for
JOHN GOTTI

Anthony M. DeStefano

CITADEL PRESS
Kensington Publishing Corp.
www.kensingtonbooks.com

CITADEL PRESS BOOKS are published by

Kensington Publishing Corp.
119 West 40th Street
New York, NY 10018

All Kensington titles, imprints, and distributed lines are available at special quantity discounts for bulk purchases for sales promotions, premiums, fundraising, educational, or institutional use.

Special book excerpts or customized printings can also be created to fit specific needs. For details, write or phone the office of the Kensington sales manager: Kensington Publishing Corp., 119 West 40th Street, New York, NY 10018, attn: Sales Department; phone 1-800-221-2647.

CITADEL PRESS and the Citadel logo are Reg. U.S. Pat. & TM Off.

ISBN-13: 978-0-8065-3913-3
ISBN-10: 0-8065-3913-5

First Citadel hardcover printing: August 2019

10 9 8 7 6 5 4 3 2 1

Printed in the United States of America

Library of Congress CIP data is available.

Electronic edition:

ISBN-13: 978-0-8065-3915-7 (e-book)
ISBN-10: 0-8065-3915-1 (e-book)

CONTENTS

Gotti's Boys

The Mafia Crew
That Killed for
JOHN GOTTI

INTRODUCTION

During the mid-1980s the big news in the world of organized crime was the rise of a once unknown gangster from Queens named John J. Gotti to head of the Gambino crime family through the bloody elimination of the former boss, Paul Castellano. In a move that took much of world of law enforcement by surprise, Gotti, a little-known hijacker and compulsive gambler, engineered the murder of "Big Paul," as Castellano was known, as much as a method of self-preservation than anything else. Castellano was finally wise to the way Gotti's crew in the crime family was dealing drugs and apparently was getting ready to break up the group and possibly have some of its members killed for violating the Mafia rule against drug dealing. To protect himself and his friend, Gotti struck first. Castellano was gunned down on December 16, 1985, outside Sparks Steak House on East Forty-sixth Street in Manhattan.

With the rise of Gotti to leadership of the Gambino family, one of the five Cosa Nostra groups in New York, the public was subjected to a barrage of superlatives about the man who had the daring to kill a major crime boss. "The Most Powerful Criminal in America," and "Al Capone in an $1,800 Suit" were just some of the ways Gotti was described. He was handsome, ambitious, ruthless, the journalists told us, all of which was decidedly true.

The newspapers and television news reporters developed a cottage industry in stories about Gotti, chronicling his every public move and speculating on all of the crimes he and his crime family were involved in. His nightlife, including Manhattan forays from his home in Howard Beach, Queens, to nightspots like Da Noia and Club A made for sensational film clips, even if Gotti said nothing of substance. And don't forget his clothing. From wide collar, pattern shirts and tight trousers that made him look like a refugee from the film *Saturday Night Fever,* Gotti graduated to a better style of high-priced couture as he needed to keep up appearances for what he called "my public." He even took to daily haircuts and trims at his favorite social club, the Bergin Hunt and Fish in Ozone Park where a barber chair had been installed.

Gotti relished the gangster life, and by doing away with Castellano and becoming a boss he had risen to the top of his world. He became something of a folk hero and years after his death occasional visitors to his old club location on Mulberry Street were said to kiss the tile floor in homage. Gotti clearly reveled in the trappings of his status, and as boss made millions in tribute and other payments from the crime family rackets in the construction and garment industries, as well as labor racketeering. This was money one old friend said he was generous with to a fault. Some estimates placed the illicit yearly gross income of his borgata at $500 million and Gotti was getting his piece of it and amassing a fortune that reportedly hit between $20 million to $30 million, the latter amount not inconceivable given that his friend and Bonanno boss Joseph Massino had $10 million in assets he had to give to the government when convicted of racketeering in 2004.

Gotti once predicted that if he was able to have a good run as boss that the crime family and La Cosa Nostra would be around for a hundred years. But his glorious mob century lasted only about seven years. The gravy train essentially began to sputter in 1992 when Gotti and his underboss Frank Locascio were convicted in stunningly rapid fashion on federal racketeering charges, which happened to include the murder of Castellano as well as complicity in several other homicides. Gotti died in June 2002 while serving a life sentence in a federal prison.

Gotti's undoing was mainly brought about by the testimony of his former close associate Sammy "The Bull" Gravano—who did double duty at various times as his underboss and consiglieri. Gravano was one of the crime family leaders arrested with Gotti in the massive December 11, 1990, roundup, which nabbed Locascio as well as Thomas Gambino, the scion of the crime family. Faced with the prospect of a life in prison and after learning that Gotti had badmouthed him, Gravano decided to cooperate with federal prosecutors and testify against his old boss.

In fact, Gravano became an ally of Gotti late in the game, having earlier been more aligned with the wealthy and business-like associates of Castellano than the blue collar, thuggish Howard Beach clique Gotti represented. While most of Gotti's crew from Queens kept the faith and never turned on him, Gravano turned out to be a devastating witness against him. Sentenced for the rest of his life to the federal penitentiary in Marion, Illinois, Gotti found it increasingly difficult to run the Gambino family, forced as he was to rely on the haphazard visits of some lawyers and his family members, serving as conduits for communication.

Gotti appointed his son, John A. Gotti, known as "Junior" to the position of leadership in the hopes of keeping control. But that move only helped weaken Senior Gotti's position in that some in the crime family deeply resented the nepotism and believed—correctly as it turned out—that the son just didn't have the stomach or commitment for the job. With federal prosecutors building upon their successes and fortified with a host of cooperating witnesses, the Gambino family underwent years of trials that weakened it considerably.

Other crime families were also targeted and suffered, notably the Bonanno, Colombo, and Lucchese families. Ronald Goldstock, the former head of the New York State organized crime task force, once said that Gotti turned out to be a disaster for the mob. Given the way he brought attention to the crime families by his flamboyance and in-your-face attitude toward police and the FBI, Goldstock's assessment seems on point.

Gotti has been dead for close to two decades, and many books and countless articles have been written about him. *Mob Star: The Story of John Gotti, The Most Powerful Criminal in America* and

Gotti, both by Jerry Capeci and Gene Mustain, were among the first to hit the market decades ago. *Gangster: How the FBI Broke the Mob* by Howard Blum and *Underboss: Sammy The Bull Gravano's Story of Life in the Mafia* by Peter Maas, largely dealt with the FBI investigation that specifically targeted John Gotti through 1992. The latter tome, done with the collaboration of a well-known writer and expert on the mob, turned out to be an important work in that Gravano's words fleshed out much of the story with inside information.

In 2015, Gotti's son John authored an e-book with a forward by Peter Lance titled *Shadow of My Father*, which explored the relationship between father and son in the mob world and delineates some of the history of the crime family. The film *Gotti,* inspired by *Shadow of My Father* and starring John Travolta as Gotti, was released in 2018 after a private screening at the Cannes Film Festival. It received terrible reviews, vacillating as it did between being a gangster film and a hagiography about Gotti. Even Gotti's daughter Victoria penned *This Family of Mine: What It Was Like Growing Up Gotti* in 2009. A more critical assessment, *Gotti Rules: The Story of John Alite, Junior Gotti, and The Demise of the American Mafia*, was written by veteran Mafia writer George Anastasia, with the assistance of one-time Gambino crime family associate and admitted murderer Alite. *Gotti Rules* attempted to knock down the Gotti mystique, showing how his hubris and greed led to his own downfall, a thesis that sparked a very public and acrimonious social media debate between Alite and Gotti's son John.

So, with so much already written about John J. Gotti what more could another book reveal? Plenty as it turns out. For a start, FBI archives about a variety of public figures, notorious or not, have become available since the 1990s. I discovered how useful those files could be while doing *Top Hoodlum: Frank Costello, Prime Minister of the Mafia,* which was published in 2018. The FBI materials dealing with Gotti proved useful in showing little-known details from his early life—he was a persistent draft delinquent—to fleshing out the inside story of how the FBI was able to zero in on him and his coterie of killers. As the twenty-first century turned, new Mafia trials detailed testimony about Gotti and his crew, revealing particulars of the historical story line that were unavailable to earlier writers about the mob. Once secret government files and documents were also made available to me, they proved extremely helpful in enabling me see the interplay of events that brought about Gotti's demise.

Reading through these materials, both new and old, it became clear that there was more to discover about the men who bonded with Gotti from the start of his career, killed for him and propelled him to the top of the Gambino family. Without this band of criminals, Gotti would have never made it to the top of organized crime. It was these men whose stories provide the spine of this book, *Gotti's Boys: The Mafia Crew That Killed for John Gotti*. They were made men like Angelo Ruggiero, John and Charles Carneglia, Salvatore Scala and Vincent Artuso, as well as Sammy Gravano and to some extent his own brother Peter Gotti. Along his bloody path to power Gotti also relied on key associates like Joseph Watts, a unique criminal who while not of Italian ancestry earned the same kind of respect and power in the Gambino family as any made man. There was also Frank DeCicco, whose tenure as underboss under Gotti was decidedly short-lived when he was snuffed out by a bomb in April 1986, an assassination attempt originally aimed for Gotti. There were also troubled, homicidal associates like Anthony "Roach" Rampino, a drug addict and dealer who could be relied upon to kill when necessary but quickly fell by the wayside with a prison sentence and died a broken man.

When Gotti's twelve-year-old son Frank was killed in a car accident on the streets of Howard Beach in March 1980, Gotti and his family were awash in grief and depression. His wife Victoria would roam the streets at night and go to baseball fields in a vain attempt to find her dead son, so unbalanced had she become. The couple had four other children—Victoria, Angel, John, and Peter—but were consumed with grief over the loss of Frank. The man who drove the car that struck and killed little Frank was neighbor John Favara and in July 1980 as he left work at a carpet store on Long Island, a group of men abducted him. He was never seen in public again.

Law enforcement officials believe Gotti was impelled by his own and his family's grief to have ordered Favara's death. Another theory is that one of Gotti's close associates like Angelo Ruggiero took matters into their own hands and had Favara killed. There is some evidence for Ruggiero's involvement in the latter, along with suspicion that the late mob associate Richard "Red Bird" Gomes was among the group of men who abducted and killed Favara. When interviewed in prison by FBI agents in 2003 about the Favara case, Gomes said he was a good friend of Gotti but didn't want to talk about Favara. In 2009, federal officials developed evidence that Favara's body was dissolved in acid after he was killed. Witnesses told federal officials that the man who disposed of Favara's body was Charles Carneglia, brother of John and operator of an auto junk yard in East New York. Court documents stated that after Favara's remains were dealt with, Carneglia dropped some of the dead man's finger bones in the soup of Angelo Ruggiero as he ate at the popular Lindenwood Diner. It must have ruined Ruggiero's dinner.

Those men were among the core group that proved important to Gotti. He relied upon Gravano, John Carneglia, Rampino, Scala, Artuso, as well as Ruggiero, to be what investigators said were the key actors in the murder of Castellano. As boss of the Gambino borgata, Gotti had hundreds of other members and associates through which he earned money and projected his power. This group included Gotti's son John, Charles Carneglia, Robert DiBernardo, Edward Lino, and Jack D'Amico, to name just a few. Gotti had other brothers involved as well, notably Richard V. Gotti and Vincent Gotti, the latter a man who was troubled by drug dealing and volatility and played only a marginal role in the crime family. But many of them became important to Gotti in the years after he became boss in late 1985 and while they played their own roles in family dealings, the group that seemed to matter the most were those who were there for the *coup d'état* Gotti engineered to depose Castellano.

But history showed that the very men who helped Gotti grab power were those responsible for events that ultimately sent Gotti on his train wreck of a crash with destiny. It is well known that the bosses of the Mafia had a long-standing prohibition against drug dealing by their members. One story in mob history was that the bosses like the exiled Charles Luciano, along with Frank Costello, Joseph Bonanno, Joseph Profaci, and others met in Havana, Cuba, in 1946—or 1947, the date is the subject of some speculation—and among other business decided to ban narcotics dealing. But Bonanno's son Salvatore, in his book *Bound by Honor: A Mafioso's Story,* said that his father told him that the real anti-drug edict came during a secret conclave in a yacht off Miami. Some of the more liberal members of the Mafia ruling Commission like Vito Genovese and Thomas Lucchese wanted to get into drugs while another faction, led by Joseph Bonanno wanted to stay away from narcotics, according to Bonanno's son.

In any case, the drug ban was really a sham. Mafiosi became involved in "off the record" drug deals almost at will. While Luciano was at the Havana meeting where the drug ban was said to have been discussed, he turned out to be a major narcotics trafficker working as he did from his new home in Italy—or so American officials suspected. Leaders of the mob seemed to turn a blind eye to the trafficking, so long as they got their share of the proceeds. The federal Bureau of Narcotics and Dangerous Drugs listed hundreds of Mafiosi and their associates as being involved in narcotics. The list—which was open to dispute on some of the names—included Luciano, Genovese, Carlo Gambino, and some of his associates including the DiPalermo brothers. Some names seem thrown in just to pad the list. But Genovese himself would be convicted in the 1950s for being part of a major drug conspiracy and would later die in prison. Despite the ban, just about every Mafia family had members who dealt in drugs, knowing full well the consequences if caught.

Gotti's avowed public stance, as publicized during his final trial by his attorneys, was that he was against drugs and had devoted his life that way. But as Judge I. Leo Glasser said after presiding at that trial and listening to FBI tapes and hours of testimony, the notion that Gotti devoted his life against drugs "can only be described as cynical at best and downright false, at worst." History, as described in this book, would illustrate Glasser's point. In the 1980s, some in the Gambino family, notably Angelo Ruggiero and his crowd, saw the potential for making big money with heroin. After all, his brother Salvatore had been doing it for years as a fugitive. The result was a heroin operation run by Angelo that, while lucrative, ultimately put himself and John Gotti in conflict with Castellano, who wanted everyone to hew the line on the narcotics ban.

But fate played a major part in what happened next in this mob saga. Salvatore Ruggiero and his wife Stephanie died when a Learjet they were passengers in crashed in May 1982 off the coast of Georgia. The tragedy set in motion a series of events and investigations that would have ramifications for years to come. The immediate result was that Angelo Ruggiero, Gene Gotti, John Carneglia and others were indicted for heroin trafficking as they tried to take over the heroin business Salvatore had established. When that happened, Castellano knew he had some bad apples in his crime family and that John Gotti bore some command responsibility, as leader of the crew, for their actions. What is more, Castellano knew that any activity by Gotti's crew could come back to haunt him since prosecutors were always willing to try and link a Mafia boss into the illicit dealings of his associates.

As it turned out, Castellano did fall victim to Angelo Ruggiero and company's dealings but not the way he might have feared. The FBI investigation that ultimately led to Ruggiero's indictment in 1983 triggered a probe of Castellano, complete with ingenious FBI surveillance of his palatial home on Todt Hill in Staten Island. The resulting tapes from Castellano's house led to his indictment in 1984, something he well knew stemmed from the errant Gotti crew's activities. The tapes also caused legal woes for many other gangsters both inside and outside of the Gambino family. Fearful of Castellano and what he could do if definitive evidence surfaced about Angelo's flaunting of the drug edict, Gotti struck first with the boss's assassination.

Gotti's Boys is a book that, as the title implies, involves more than just a story about Gotti himself. At times, Gotti often did not play any significant role in events, particularly in the Ruggiero drug operation. As a result, the narrative is sometimes absent of any noteworthy mention of Gotti. But as the 1980s progressed, Gotti assumed more importance as the need for money, his survival and that of his crew became paramount. With the assassination of Castellano and in those few brief years afterward when he controlled the Gambino family, Gotti and his men were major players in New York City's organized crime world.

Back in 1978, a popular PBS television series *Connections,* featuring science historian James Burke, showed us the progress of history in a unique way: how various events, decisions, and discoveries were built upon to influence history. In thinking about the significance of a book like *Gotti's Boys,* Burke's series comes to mind. The story of *Gotti's Boys* describes a path that is similar to what we saw in *Connections.* Sometimes random events, like the 1982 plane crash, sparked a reaction within Gotti's clique that led to the development of massive drug dealing, which in turn put them in conflict with Castellano. The end result was the brazen conspiracy to kill Castellano. While the murder of Castellano might seem like one way to end the story, it wasn't. Gotti took over as crime boss and it was then that his own decisions and actions led to his demise, as well as the downfall of many of his associates. The offensive against the mob that followed Gotti's rise to power had an impact that we are still feeling today in the way the Mafia has been marginalized and forced to reinvent itself. The theme of *Connections* is a relevant and new way of looking at the Gotti story and everything that happened in his brief rise to the top.

There are numerous characters whose stories are contained in *Gotti's Boys.* But I made a decision to focus on those men who were important in Gotti's early years, those who helped him in his rise through the Gambino crime family and were instrumental in the engineering of Castellano's assassination, as well as the consolidation of power that followed. Gotti's son John played something of a role in the leadership of the crime family—he was made acting boss by his father after his old man was sent to prison in 1992—but his role in those early years was not as important as that of people like Ruggiero, John Carneglia, Gene Gotti, Joe Watts, and others. It is for that reason that Junior Gotti occupies in my mind a lesser importance in this story, along with the fact that his own book and the 2018 film *Gotti* tells his side of things.

Gotti's Boys is not intended to be an encyclopedia of the history of the Gambino crime family. The borgata traces its roots back to the aftermath of the fabled Castellammarese Wars of the 1930s, when Vincent Mangano assumed the mantel of what would eventually become the family that bears Carlo Gambino's name. To show the danger associated with the position of boss, Mangano disappeared in April 1951 in a power play by Albert Anastasia, who himself was assassinated in October 1957 as he was getting a shave. Over the years there were a number of leaders who had control of the family, and hundreds of men gained membership, controlling hundreds more associates willing to do their bidding. Many of those names don't make it into this story. But there are plenty more contemporary characters, like the members of the Corozzo clan, who played a role in some of the later events and in some ways pushed back at Gotti's tattered legacy.

Although Gotti's bold move established him at the pinnacle of mob power, he handled things in a way that guaranteed he would not last long. While he could be charming and funny to journalists and had charisma the public loved, Gotti was a brutal, thuggish boss. He liked the trappings of power and the publicity he received through the press. He was a gangster through and through, and that was all he wanted to be. Reporters were only too happy to embrace a figure like Gotti, who in some ways was a throwback to a time when gangsters were always good copy.

But Gotti made strategic mistakes. Among them was his blindness to the power of the FBI and police and their ability to find ways to penetrate his world. For years, federal agents and cops cultivated crucial informants within Gotti's inner circle who provided information that was devastating. Gotti also underestimated the technical savvy and ingenuity of the FBI, which taped him and his associates over many months, gathering evidence that provided the *coup de grâce* when it came time to prosecute the so-called "Teflon Don," the moniker he gained after he beat a number of prosecutions. Gotti once seemed impregnable to law enforcement but now we know that in at least one instance it was because he and his minions worked to corrupt jurors. Given an anonymous jury that was shielded from tampering, Gotti was quickly convicted in April 1992.

As a Mafia organization man, Gotti made major errors that made the FBI's job a bit easier. By demanding his captains pay him homage weekly at the Ravenite social club on Mulberry Street, Gotti virtually assured that crime figures once under the police radar would suddenly garner unwelcomed surveillance. In his own book done with famed writer Peter Maas, Gravano said he knew that attendance at the Ravenite would be trouble and he was right. While other bosses avoided the limelight, Gotti flaunted his celebrity. Reporters relished a figure like Gotti, who harkened back to the days when mob figures like Frank Costello and Lucky Luciano provided the fodder for an army of reporters and writers like Damon Runyon. But Gotti was not a criminal like Costello. Gotti got his power from the street as the boss of the blue-collar wing of the Gambino crime family. Gotti ruled through fear. Costello strived for respectability and almost achieved it, associating as he did with judges, politicians, and celebrities of all stripes. Gotti didn't care whether he could pass as legitimate. He wanted to be a gangster and nothing else.

In the end Gotti rose to power with the help of his old Fulton-Rockaway boys, the working-class street gangsters from Brooklyn who stayed loyal to him throughout his days. Their missteps in a sense forced Gotti to grab power to save his skin and take over as boss. Ironically, it was through them, and his own failings, that Gotti lost it all.

CHAPTER ONE
"Any Survivors?"

THE MORNING OF MAY 6, 1982, George Morton was greeted by a clear sky and pleasant temperatures as he walked to the Learjet parked on the tarmac at Teterboro Airport in suburban New Jersey. At the age of thirty-eight, Morton had accumulated 7,000 hours flying time, with about 150 in the particular kind of jet he was to shepherd through the sky this very morning, a time of day that meteorologically had conditions for flying that were nothing short of ideal.

Morton's boss, an animated go-getter named Al, wasn't at the airport but then again he didn't need to be since he hired the pilots who could do his bidding. Alfred Dellentash, as Al was known in his eclectic business world, loved planes. He learned to fly at the age of sixteen while growing up across the Hudson River in Westchester County. But it wasn't just the thrill of being airborne that gratified Dellentash. He had a knack for the aviation business and by hook or crook, sometimes one step ahead of his creditors and the sheriff, cobbled together a small transportation business that had it own special edge.

What distinguished Dellentash's company was the fact that with sheer bravado and self-promotion it took on risky flying jobs. He soon became a darling of the heavy-metal rock groups who could count on Al's discretion as he flew them around on the shortest of notice to do tours, vacations, and get dope. In fact, drug smuggling was another element of the Ibex Corporation company business model, and the supply of mind-altering substances that Dellentash's company had made the company a favorite for a certain slice of the music scene.

It was no secret that Dellentash and Ibex Corporation had cornered some of the lucrative and very high-profile rock transportation gigs. *People* magazine noted that Dellentash was in the music business himself, managing the group Meat Loaf, with whose lead singer Marvin Lee Aday he had what for a long time was a stormy relationship. In one legal hassle Dellentash won an order of attachment that prevented the rock star from selling or mortgaging his home and a condominium in Connecticut. But aside from such occasional business disputes, Dellentash still had a good reputation running Ibex. He and his planes, which were leased, were reliable, and while the entertainers would get high, have sex, and otherwise overindulge, Dellentash made sure that his pilots and crew members kept a professional distance. Dressing down for the flight crews in blue jeans like some bass guitarist was forbidden. Pilots in particular had to wear white shirts and ties. Dellentash insisted on that.

So, when George Richard Morton took command that May morning of aircraft N100TA, which was a plane leased from Air Capital Service Inc., based out of Wichita, Kansas, he was attired in the obligatory freshly pressed white business shirt and red tie. His co-pilot, a woman named Sherri Neubarth Day, twenty-four, had just over 1,700 hours flying time, less than Morton but had about as much experience as he did with the Learjet. Day, dressed in similar business attire, had been flying since she was sixteen, having been trained by her father.

Their only passengers this day were a married couple from Franklin Lakes, an affluent New Jersey township some twelve miles to the west of the airport, who were going to take a trip to Florida. Morton had previously flown Steve Teri and his wife Stephanie, both of whom were friends of Dellentash, for years. In fact, it was just a week earlier that Teri and his young son had flown in the plane down to Disney World in Orlando. Stephanie didn't make that particular trip and had stayed at home with the couple's daughter. This particular day, the

children remained with family in New York. Steven Teri had a briefcase he kept close to his side once on board the aircraft although
since they were the only passengers such cautiousness seemed ex-
cessive. But Teri was always a secretive man—he used other names
when necessary—and his true identity was known only to family
and childhood friends back in his old home neighborhood in
Queens, New York.

Flight records are kept in detail, and the notations on May 6
showed that Morton and Day taxied down Teterboro's runway and
after clearance from the control tower took off at about 10:20 A.M.
The flight plan called for the aircraft to reach a cruising altitude of
41,000 feet and head due south, skirting the East Coast of the
United States, passing over Hilton Head, South Carolina, before
dipping down to Florida airspace. The trip was expected to take
about two hours, and the Teris would be in Orlando in time for
lunch. The plane had nearly four hours flying time with the fuel in
its tank. On the return, Morton would be going up to his mother's in
New Hampshire to celebrate her graduation from college at the age
of sixty-four.

Captain Sherman I. "Moose" Helmey was at his fishing charter
boat *Miss Jerry* well before the Learjet was ready for takeoff that
morning. In fact, Helmey was an early riser because his business—
taking tourists out on fishing trips in the bountiful waters south of
Tybee and Wassau Islands—required that he be ready to compete
with all of the other charters trying to provide a unique angling experience.

Some of the best fishing was some twelve or so miles off the
coast of Georgia. It was a locale where old wrecks and discarded debris such as M60 battle tanks provided excellent hiding places for anything from sharks, cobia, fluke, red snapper, king flounder, amberjack,
and the strange looking trigger fish that was shaped like an oval. You
could fish to your heart's content on Helmey's tours. He knew the
best spots for fishing, particularly around the L-Buoy and the
nearby reefs. Of course, Helmey wasn't alone in knowing the se-

crets of the reefs. The charter boat business was very competitive so he couldn't dawdle in getting his customers out for some good fishing.

Running fishing charters off his native Georgia was Helmey's second chapter in life. He had come from a Georgia farming family, but Helmey knew early in life that there was no keeping him down on the farm. Helmey may not have liked the plow but he did show an aptitude for cars, and after he left home, he convinced a local Savannah auto-repair shop owner to give him a job. The rest was history. Saving his money and with a fair amount of hard work Helmey's Garage in Savannah became a thriving business—doing better still when he made the acquaintance of a so-called "shoe salesman" from Chicago who asked Helmey to modify some General Motors vehicles with special compartments to hold cargo. The salesman, so the Helmey family story goes, was Alphonse Capone, mobster and bootlegger extraordinaire, and the cars with the special compartments where taken to Wilmington Island to await a special shipment—not of shoes—but of booze smuggled from places up and down the East Coast.

The smugglers would sometimes off-load booze from a vessel off shore and put the loads in boats that were small enough to slip under the back of a building housing Greens speakeasy on Wilmington Island. There, off-loading crews would pull the merchandise up through a trap door in the floor and get it ready for shipment in Helmey's vehicle. The endeavor helped line Helmey's pockets and burnished his reputation as a folk hero of sorts in that part of Georgia. It didn't hurt that he had ties with Capone.

Helmey sold his auto business in the 1950s and after his first wife left him and took with her their daughter, a child named Merceles, he married again. But when his second wife Jerry died at the age of thirty-nine in terrible traffic accident, well, he needed a change. Helmey also needed to support his other five-year-old daughter, Judy, as well as try to raise her with the help of her aunt. The charter business's main asset was a fishing boat christening *Miss Jerry* and Helmey took his daughter out on charters because she loved the sea and because it was a good way to keep an eye on her. Father and daughter were inseparable. In time, Judy would become certified as a fishing boat captain as well. Her boat—to no one's surprise here—was known as the *Miss Judy.*

The morning of May 6, the *Miss Jerry* and *Miss Judy*, left their berths on the Wilmington River, on the very outskirts of Savannah and proceeded as they always did south toward the open waters. Such trips through the sinuous ribbon of river took about two hours to reach the good fishing spots. Once clear of the mainland and on the correct bearings, Sherman Helmey took the *Miss Jerry* due south toward the L-Buoy and its ripe fishing ground. Judy Helmey followed in the *Miss Judy* at a short distance and was inshore of her father's location.

In the sky above, Morton and Day were having an uneventful flight and at about five minutes to noon were cleared by the air traffic controllers to descend to 39,000 feet, although it took about a half minute for the Learjet to begin that altitude change. This would have been the gradual descent to Orlando, which at this point was some 230 miles to the southwest. Two minutes after the controllers had radioed the descent instructions, co-pilot Day hurriedly radioed that the aircraft was "descending now." The controllers also heard in the background what sounded like a warning horn, the kind that normally alerts the pilots to a sudden drop in altitude. The noise, which would later be the subject of much speculation, prompted the controller to radio "say again" in an effort to clarify what Day had meant. There was silence.

"One hundred tango alpha I've lost your transponder, sir, reset it again on code thirty-three twelve," the controller radioed to the Learjet. The time of that transmission would later be fixed at 12:01 and 14 seconds.

Sherman Helmey was well underway with *Miss Jerry.* At about noon he was between the L-Buoy and the "CCC," another prime fishing area. He was piloting the boat and knew what to do to find the best places to fish. The *Miss Jerry* might be an old vessel but she still pulled her weight and if anything happened to her mechanically Helmey would have only the *Miss Judy* as a back-up to handle the business and make money to cover any repairs.

Making about sixteen knots on his way out from the buoy, Sherman Helmey suddenly heard a crashing sound—an expensive sound to an old mariner—and some strange vibration. It all didn't sound right and made him think that something terrible had happened to the *Miss Jerry* and that his bank account would be drained for repairs. Helmey throttled back on the power and turned to go back to the stern so that he could lift the engine cover. He and his passengers, who had only wanted nothing more that day than some honest-to-goodness fishing, couldn't believe their eyes with what they saw next. There, no more than fifty feet astern of *Miss Jerry* and sinking into the azure waters, was the tail section of what looked like an aircraft. Steadying himself from the waves that hit the boat from the impact of the aircraft, Helmey was able to spot the tail letters N100TA just before they disappeared from sight.

Helmey wasn't the only boat captain to witness the crash, although he was the closest and by the grace of God just missed being struck by the Learjet debris as it plunged into the water. A minor deviation in his route, a moment's hesitation with the throttle, could have put the aircraft debris right on top of *Miss Jerry*. His daughter Judy wasn't far away either, and she and other boat captains raced to the scene where a geyser of water had fixed the location of the crash. The radio traffic between the boats was excited and frantic. Sherman Helmey was immediately on the ship radio to the Coast Guard reporting the accident.

"Any survivors?" the Coast Guard asked over the radio.

Helmey saw just small bits of debris on the water. Some unrecognizable pieces of the aircraft floated but the remainder had sunk. He knew the aircraft and the lives on board were completely lost.

"There is no way anybody could have survived this crash. There couldn't be any survivors," Hemley said with certainty.

Sherman Helmey was a man who didn't trust airplanes. Something always happened whenever he got on them, which on that day had been exactly three times in his life. After the third uncomfortable flight he decided to stay away from planes. Looking at debris in the water, Helmey must have wondered what those lost souls had gone through in those final moments. He knew then that he would never, ever, get close to boarding a plane again for the rest of his life.

Once informed of the crash, the Coast Guard sent out a vessel for a quick survey of the scene. On board was Bill Walsh, a former U.S. Navy diver who lived on Tybee Island, about two miles off the coast of Georgia. He saw for himself how little was left on the surface after the Learjet had crashed. Anything else that was to be salvaged or recovered would require a dive. There was one grim reminder of the human cost of the tragedy: a headless body of a man, seemingly drained of blood, was floating like some dismembered mannequin. It seemed like the torso of a man, more or less fully clothed. There was enough of the lower jaw left to hold some teeth. Around what had been the man's neck was a red necktie, the same kind George Morton had been wearing

It took four days for a shrimp boat to be chartered for the recovery operation, and Walsh, along with some other divers, jumped into the water. The crash site was only about sixty feet deep, but the water was murky until the divers got close to the bottom. The Learjet—or what was left of it—emerged from the muck and appeared to have gone straight in on a nose dive, and as a result the mangled debris was confined to a compact area about fifty feet wide. The tail section was the largest intact piece as were the wings. Much of the rest was shattered and scattered

The impact of the crash had done grievous damage to the body of the plane's occupants. As Walsh and his fellow divers worked the bottom, they found very little of what had been human beings. There were some bones, mostly devoid of flesh since the fish and the sharks had a field day picking over the remains. Walsh found a man's foot wearing a sock and shoe. Two hands were found: one of the hands bore some rings and was later identified as that of Stephanie Teri. The local coroner said the other hand was that of her husband Steven. Morton's headless torso was the largest body part found, and the coroner was able to determine from the teeth that remained that the corpse was that of the pilot. The body of co-pilot Sherri Day, who was on her way to becoming a full-fledged commercial pilot, was never found.

The crash had been the biggest news in a while for the charter-boat industry, and the local *Savannah Morning News* feasted on the story for days. The mystery was a good one. What had happened to the aircraft and who were those on board? Was there any truth to the rumors that it carried a fugitive or that its cargo was money being laundered from Atlantic City? One theory was that the fugitive never really got on the aircraft and instead arranged for a fatal malfunction to make it look like he was dead.

For about three weeks after the crash, accident investigator Archibald Crittenden and his staff, working from a barge, swept the ocean floor with trawling equipment in a search for debris. Although the initial searches right after the crash found some major debris in a small area, the scouring of the sea bottom uncovered aircraft parts over a wider area of several square miles, recalled Crittenden's son Edward years later. That about 70 percent of the aircraft was recovered over such a widespread debris field raised some thought that the Learjet may have broken up during its descent. If that were the case, there would have been no hope for the crew and the Teri family.

It would take a year for the National Transportation Safety Board to finish its investigation of the May 6, 1982, crash. The Learjet had no flight data recorder or cockpit voice recorder—none of which were required by regulation at the time. The NTSB posited a few theories about what caused the crash: possible clear air turbulence, a pitch up problem, a malfunctioning trim system, or maybe a sudden air cabin decompression. In the end, the mystery wasn't solved.

"Because the airplane was destroyed and critical flight-control system components were either destroyed or not recovered, the possibility of a control system malfunction could not be eliminated," the NTSB stated, adding that severe clear air turbulence could have played a factor.

But the NTSB had no definitive answer to what happened to Learjet 23 N100TA that fateful day when it carried the Teri family and the crew to their doom. The agency gave the probable cause as an "uncontrolled descent from cruise altitude for undetermined reasons," a finding that didn't really say very much.

However, it was clear right after the crash occurred that some people—they weren't from the area and had no interest in aviation—were extremely interested in finding out who and what might have been on board. After Sherman Helmey took the *Miss Jerry* back to the dock on May 6, he started getting telephone calls, lots of them.

"They weren't from this area," Judy Helmey remembered about the men who had called.

"What made it even more fishy," Judy recalled, no pun intended, "was that they not only wanted the coordinates of the crash site but they also wanted to pay someone to take them out."

As it turned out, the onboard GPS system of the Helmey boats gave the precise location of the crash some thirteen miles southeast of Wassau Island. For the callers who wanted to desperately get out to the site, cost would have been no object to them. No questions were to be asked. Fishy indeed. But Sherman and Judy Helmey had survived by their wits in the business for decades—Sherman had escaped unscathed from his dealings with Capone years back—and weren't about to do something he was uncomfortable with for strangers.

In the days after the crash, Sherman would kick back with a few drinks and talk about how crazy those wise guys from New York were who had called. "And they thought they could just ride out to the crash site and just scoop up the money," he said to Judy with a touch of incredulity. Wise guys, Sherman said, always had it in their heads that they were right. Of course, going out to the crash was impossible, and he told them so. It didn't matter what an old mariner told them though. They insisted they could get the money.

CHAPTER TWO

The Fulton-
Rockaway Crowd

JUDY HELMEY HAD NO IDEA who the people with New York accents were who had called her father and insisted on knowing where to find the wrecked aircraft. But back in and around Howard Beach, Queens, there were plenty of people with a sudden, intense interest in the demise of the Learjet, its passengers, and, more important, any of its cargo.

In particular, anyone watching the scene on May 6, 1982, in front of a house on Ninety-second Street in that neighborhood in the minutes after the Learjet plunged to its doom, would have seen two men in earnest conversation as they sat in a black Mercedes-Benz. One of the men was John Carneglia, a neighborhood gangster and street tough who was a member of the Gambino crime family. Carneglia wasn't known to many people in New York City. But in this particular neighborhood he was known as one of those men not to be trifled with although usually he acted like a gentleman, particularly when women were around.

Carneglia did have a legitimate business, an auto junk yard in East New York he owned with his younger brother Charles and their white-haired mother Jenny. Charles was not cut from the same cloth as his brother. He seemed to be constantly striving to be tough and had a bad temper, not the best attribute for an aspiring wise guy. Charles had his demons of drugs and alcohol, which made his temperament more suspect to those who controlled access to the ranks of the Mafia. But Charles was loyal to those he knew could help him get credence in the gangster life.

The other man with John Carneglia in the Mercedes was a younger, handsome fellow of Jewish background named Mark Reiter. Around the city Reiter seemed like a man with varied and mysterious business interests who sometimes posed as a wealthy garment manufacturer, natural gas entrepreneur, and playboy. A former auto chopshop guy who also had a small cocaine operation, Reiter stood out because he was tall—six feet two inches—and with blue eyes and a head of wavy dark hair had pretty boy, movie star looks.

The story was that Reiter wasn't born a Jew but had been the offspring of an unwed Italian mother and later adopted by a Jewish family. The gangster set liked him because he had a knack for making money, knew how to enjoy life, and flaunted his wealth with a high-rise apartment on Sixtieth Street on Manhattan's East Side in the shadow of the Queensboro Bridge. There was grudging affection for Reiter, which showed in the way the Italians referred to him with a touch of condescension as "The Jew" and "Jew Boy."

The house outside of which Carneglia and Reiter conversed was owned by the Ruggiero family, another Italian-American household that had escaped its more modest roots in working-class neighborhoods of Brooklyn and elsewhere to move up to the relative affluence of Howard Beach. Reiter lived upstairs in the house since he had been a friend of the family for years. Carneglia knew not only Ma and Pa Ruggiero but also their eldest son Angelo, a corpulent man whose thick, dark eyebrows and scowling face gave him a menacing quality, an attribute that fit him well in his position as another member of the Gambino family. The one problem he had was that his mouth was as open as a faucet; his incessant talking seemed compulsive and would later play out in a bad way.

Angelo Ruggiero's steady rise to mobster status was closely aligned to the fortunes of one of his more infamous street friends, John J. Gotti Jr, the fifth of thirteen children of John and Fannie Gotti. Growing up in a working-class household led by a tempestuous and sometimes cruel father, Gotti had to learn to fend for himself, particularly at school where he would show up for class with

mismatched shoes and become the butt of jokes and bullying. Gotti
learned to fight back and in time earned respect on the street, particularly from those like the Ruggiero boys. Gotti was lost by the city
educational system after he dropped out of Franklin Lane High
School and started to live by his wits. He and the Ruggiero brothers,
as well as the Carneglia brothers became the nucleus of the Fulton-
Rockaway Boys, a loosely organized street gang named after a
street intersection in East New York. Gotti's brother Gene rounded
out the group, which included a rag-tag cluster of other street guys.

FBI records show that Gotti had an arrest record dating back to
1958 for burglary and was adjudged at the age of seventeen as a
"wayward minor" in the equivalent of Family Court. From 1959
through 1965, Gotti notched up additional arrests ranging from ma-
licious mischief, bookmaking, burglary, and auto larceny. In his
youth, Gotti lost two toes on his left foot in a mishap with a garbage
truck, an infirmity which gave him a peculiar gait which to some
seemed jaunty.

To say Gotti's family life as a young man was dysfunctional is
being kind. In 1964, after he got a draft notice from Local Board
225 in Brooklyn, Gotti ignored it and was declared delinquent for
failure to report for induction into the Army on November 22, 1963.
Once-confidential FBI records, recently made available, show that
Gotti's father, when questioned by officials about where his son was
said he didn't know and had not seen him for over six months. The
Selective Service officials kept re-interviewing Gotti's parents and
got the same answer: they didn't know where he was. Eventually, by
August 1964, the parents admitted to officials that they had a
"falling out" with Gotti since he got married about two or three
years earlier. Who was the wife? The FBI records didn't identify her
but noted that an informant had alleged that the woman—possibly
meaning Victoria Gotti—had previously been married. (In her
book *This Family of Mine*, Victoria Gotti, the daughter of John J.
Gotti, reported that her mother Victoria had a brief marriage with
an eighteen-year-old boy named "Willie." There was no mention
of a child.) Gotti's family said that the couple had a total of three
children.

Gotti remained elusive when the Selective Service searched for him, going back and forth to various bars he reportedly worked at on Evergreen Avenue in Brooklyn. Finally, Gotti was arrested by the NYPD on October 12, 1965, for grand larceny auto charges and told cops his draft delinquency wasn't willful. After being read his Miranda warnings, Gotti said that he didn't realize he was supposed to serve in the Army because he was married with two kids (there was no mention of a third child) and had an arrest record, which as it turned out went back to June 1958 when he was arrested for burglary and adjudged a "wayward minor" at the age of seventeen. Gotti concluded his statement by saying he was willing to abide by the Selective Service law and serve in the Armed Forces.

Federal prosecutors, according to FBI records, decided not to prosecute Gotti for draft dodging since his delinquency didn't appear to be willful. Instead, the government was willing to forget about the whole thing if Gotti reported for induction, which he did on November 12, 1965, at the famous induction station at 39 White-hall Street in Manhattan. Then, fate intervened in Gotti's favor. His Selective Service records couldn't be found. Gotti again bounced around different apartments with his wife and children and some-how avoided being found by the Selective Service system.

Around the time Gotti was ducking the draft (and skipping out on a city hospital bill for the birth of one of his children) he and the Fulton-Rockaway gang members were pulling themselves together. By 1965, the group's toughness came to the attention of the local Mafia street bosses. The mob was always on the lookout for new talent to do its bidding, be it dishing out a beating of a recalcitrant debtor or running numbers. This was a period where the local Cosa Nostra families had a relatively free hand, thanks to a generally in-effective Federal Bureau of Investigation and corruption of the po-lice. Two bosses of East New York, brothers Carmine and Daniel Fatico had come up through the ranks decades earlier with the late Albert Anastasia, and had dabbled in the making of illegal alcohol for which Daniel did nine months in prison. The Faticos took the Fulton-Rockaway group under its wing as the elder Mafiosi them-selves rose through the ranks of the Gambino family.

* * *

There was another son in the Ruggiero household, Salvatore, a dark haired Italian-American who unlike his brother, was thinner and had a full head of black hair. Salvatore was Angelo's younger brother, but he had not been seen around the old neighborhood for a long while, many years in fact. That is because Salvatore "Sally" Ruggiero had been in the wind, a fugitive, on the lam, because of all sorts of serious legal troubles. Angelo had been in contact with Sal in that period of his absence and knew pretty much what his sibling was up to. But on this day in May 1982 and for all time hereafter there would be no more contact with Sal for the simple reason that he was dead. Sal, otherwise known as Steve Teri, and his dutiful wife Stephanie, were, in fact, the dead passengers on the Learjet that almost creamed Sherman Helmey and the *Miss Jerry* as it spiraled into the Atlantic just hours earlier.

Carneglia and Reiter knew to go to the Ruggiero house because Al Dellentash, the crashed plane's owner, had called over to Carneglia's East New York junkyard as soon as the Federal Aviation Administration informed him of the fate of the aircraft. The news created a special burden for Reiter who had to tell his wife and young son Greg about Salvatore and Stephanie's death. The Reiter family had been close to all in the Ruggiero household, and the news of the accident was especially crushing.

Carneglia, the Ruggiero brothers, Reiter, and others were not just some guys from the neighborhood. They had been on the radar of federal investigators for months in a widening investigation of the Gambino crime family. The case in its early stages was looking into the usual mob stuff: gambling, loansharking, hijacking, all bread-and-butter things for the group. Although Carneglia and his cohorts didn't know it, the FBI was in the early stages of a racketeering investigation into the borgota. The sudden death of Sal Ruggiero, and all of the furtive telephone conversations and meetings, including the scene outside the house on Ninety-second Street, would give the FBI a bird's eye view into crimes—mainly heroin smuggling and obstruction of justice—that they hadn't quite expected. It would also have more important consequences to play out years later in the Byzantine struggles of the Mafia.

If truth be told, Sal Ruggiero, while he was the smarter of the brothers, wasn't a member of the Gambino family. Angelo, older by some ten years, had been inducted into the family about 1973, after taking the fall for a homicide ordered by then–crime boss Carlo Gambino, a case that involved John J. Gotti, more of whose early years will be discussed in due course in this story. But in these particular days of May 1982, he was not much of a factor. In fact, Gotti showed up hardly at all during the myriad surveillances the FBI watchers were conducting. Angelo had one major idiosyncrasy which aggravated his friends but which was a godsend to the FBI: he talked too much. Angelo had an insatiable need to gab, so much so that he earned the nickname "Quack-Quack" and at times was called by Gotti "radio station," a sobriquet laced with a peculiar irony the way things would play out in his life thanks to the marvels of electronic surveillance.

Unlike his older brother, Sal Ruggiero was known for being an enterprising man with a head for business, either legal or illegal. It was the latter that caused Sal problems and that had prompted him, and his wife Stephanie, to take on new identities as fugitives. Everybody familiar with the Mafia knew of the strict rule set down in the 1940s and 1950s about not dealing with narcotics, although in fact many Mafiosi were involved, "off the record" as they would say. Anybody with access to the files of the federal Bureau of Narcotics and Dangerous drugs would see hundreds of names of Mafiosi who were listed—sometimes incorrectly—as dangerous narcotics violators.

Sal Ruggiero wasn't particularly worried about the no-drugs rule, and, after paying his dues doing some hijacking in East New York, gravitated into the heroin business. In April 1973, Ruggiero was grabbed along with over sixty others, including a diminutive sixty-year-old Jewish woman from the Lower East Side named Cecile Sperling and her son Herbert, who federal investigators said were part of a ring importing 220 pounds of heroin a week into the city.

Ruggiero, twenty-seven at the time, was charged in only one count of taking about two pounds of heroin from one of the other smugglers on a street corner in South Ozone Park in August 1971.

The case against Sal was so weak that during the trial the judge in May 1973 directed that he be acquitted. Herbert Sperling was a different story. Sperling's reputation was that of a tough guy from the Lower East Side in Manhattan, long an incubator for Jewish gangsters. As James Hunt, the Drug Enforcement Administration's New York special agent in charge remembered him, Sperling was involved with some of the old Italian Mafiosi from the Prince Street area, notably Charles and Joseph DiPalermo, the so called "Beck Brothers." In the 1973 case, Sperling was convicted as the ring leader and got a life sentence, for which he cursed the judge and never tired of telling anyone who would listen in later years that he got a raw deal. Sperling's mother Cecile and another woman who had been arrested were acquitted.

Sal didn't learn from his first brush with federal narcotics investigators. In the fall of 1975 he was charged in another federal heroin conspiracy case. Then, in 1976, he was charged with being part of a Brooklyn armed hijacking ring led by the infamous Daniel and Carmine Fatico, two brothers who took the nickname "Wagons" and functioned as the mob mentors for the Ruggiero brothers, as well as Gotti. In 1977, Sal and Stephanie were charged with federal income tax evasion and at that point the couple decided to head for the hills, leaving their home in the Five Town section of Long Island and fleeing to the suburban splendor of New Jersey as well as a home in Florida to make it as fugitives living under new names. (Ironically, all thirteen of the defendants who went to trial in the 1975 heroin case were acquitted.)

While life as a fugitive could be stressful and difficult, with the help of his brother, other friends in Howard Beach, a crooked lawyer named Michael Coiro, as well as the assistance of Al Dellentash and his aircraft, Sal was able to prosper. He started a shipping company, took a piece of a music business with Dellentash and bought real estate in Florida, New York, and New Jersey with the help of nominees who took title under his name and did the necessary financial transactions. Sal could have gone legitimate but with all of his pending legal issues he had to stay underground. In 1980, lawyer Coiro put out feelers with the federal government to see if he could arrange a way for Sal to surrender, but the negotiations proved fruitless.

In the meantime, Sal continued to move heroin when he could. He also did marijuana deals with Dellentash, who had been his partner in the weed business ten years earlier. Dellentash didn't particularly like the heroin business so he more or less stayed out of it with Sal. But Dellentash did know a lot about Sal's varied business deals and of course where he lived in New Jersey.

So, on May 6, 1982, after calling Carneglia at the junkyard, Dellentash quickly drove to the Franklin Lakes home where Salvatore Ruggiero had been hiding in plain sight as fugitive for the better part of eight years. Dellentash wasn't sure what he would find. Maybe money, maybe drugs, maybe crucial documents detailing where Ruggiero hid everything. There was a lot of money at stake, not to mention the potential problems the stuff could cause if law enforcement got to it all first. Dellentash had to get there and find whatever it was before the FBI did or else he and a lot of people would be in deep trouble.

That night at the Franklin Lakes home, Dellentash was joined by some other Howard Beach characters whose presence would eventually let the FBI know how big a Mafia operation they were watching. Showing up were Carneglia, Gene Gotti who was the brother of the still-absent John Gotti, Angelo Ruggiero, and a couple of associates of Dellentash. The group went over the house as thoroughly as possible. Angelo took his brother's—and Stephanie's—jewelry and other valuable items. Carneglia grabbed any documents, particularly those that showed names, addresses, and telephone numbers, stuff that could prove to be very damaging if law enforcement got its hands on it. But what they didn't find were drugs and large amounts of money. Sal was rumored to have half a million dollars on hand but the searchers found none of it.

The next day, May 7, Dellentash had to come clean with the FAA. He told the agency officials that the dead passengers on the

Learjet weren't Steven and Stephanie Teri but rather Salvatore and Stephanie Ruggiero. (He didn't tell them about the possibility that another reputed drug dealer named Oscar Ansourian might have been aboard, although Ansourian never did board the aircraft.) It took about a week before word of Ruggerio's fate made it to the newspapers. When the FBI learned of that, a lot of disparate activity the agents had seen over the past day—the visits to the Ruggiero house included—took on an important meaning. A day later, in a gesture of cooperation with the FBI, Dellentash, who was listed as the lessee on the Franklin Lakes house, allowed FBI agents to search the home. But with Angelo and his friends having picked over the place two days earlier, the agents found nothing of importance. Give them time though and they would.

CHAPTER THREE
"Never Mention Drugs"

THE TIME OF THE DEATH OF SALVATORE RUGGIERO was more than four years before Howard Beach gained national notoriety with the death of a black man named Michael Griffin the night of December 20, 1986. It was then that Griffin and three of his black friends had their car break down on Cross Bay Boulevard and had to walk about three miles north to try and get help. Along the way they stopped for some pizza at the New Park Pizzeria and were confronted by some young white men from the neighborhood. During the ensuing fight, Griffin fled and ran on to a nearby highway where he was struck by a car and killed. Griffin's death, the subsequent trial of several white men, and the heightened racial tensions that resulted gave Howard Beach—a locale with an almost entirely white population—a bad reputation for years.

But long before the racial incident, Howard Beach had its own special reputation as a haven for a number of the city's up-and-coming top Mafiosi. Old timers might like their old haunts in East New York, Ozone Park, or Williamsburg. But this slice of land on the south shore off the Belt Parkway attracted the younger men aspiring to rule the street. John Gotti lived in a house on 85th Street, while John Carneglia made his home on 163rd Avenue. His brother Charles lived with their mother just a few blocks away. Joseph Massino, an up-and-coming power in the Bonanno crime family had a spacious Georgian manse with a redbrick façade on 84th Street. Even some non-made members of the mob like Jimmy Burke, the architect of the infamous Lufthansa heist of 1978, had a house in the area. Howard Beach was attractive not only to the Mafia bosses but also to a large Italian-American community, which liked the neighborhood for its relative safety, closeness to Long Island, and the old areas of Brooklyn and Queens from which many families had originated.

For the mobsters, Howard Beach gave them a special proximity to each other. Street corner meetings were easy to hold, and the wetlands to the south and west with their tall weeds—a place some called the "Baja"—provided a nice place for walk-and-talk conversations. Any unusual vehicle—such as an FBI car—would be very conspicuous near the weeds. In the case of John F. Kennedy International Airport, the gangsters had a lucrative hijacking and stolen cargo target literally in their backyards.

In some ways, Howard Beach was a cloistered village where everybody knew everyone else, where outsiders (i.e., police and FBI) where easily spotted. Once in the neighborhood, families tended to remain, passing homes down to children and grandchildren. When somebody got arrested or took flight as a fugitive, the street provided its own grapevine and spread the word.

Around 1982, Sal Ruggiero was not the only fugitive from the area. Joseph "Big Joey" Massino, also known in FBI reports as "Messina," had taken to parts unknown, leaving his wife and daughters in advance of a possible federal arrest. Five of Massino's criminal associates in the Bonanno family had already been arrested, and Massino himself began to fear that the FBI would tie him into the murder of three Bonanno captains in May 1981, killings which were part of a power struggle in which Massino and his faction came out on top. Massino was getting antsy and around Christmas 1981 he asked his neighbor Angelo Ruggiero if he thought all of the federal subpoenas and FBI surveillance would die down.

"It ain't going to be any better," Ruggiero told him ruefully.

Not long after that conversation, Massino took off with a wad of money and clothes for the relative quiet of the Pocono Mountains in Pennsylvania.

We know how Ruggiero and Massino commiserated over the telephone because for months before the FBI had been listening into Quack-Quack's conversations over his telephone at his home on 88th Street in Howard Beach. It was on November 9, 1981, that the FBI got a warrant from a federal judge in Brooklyn to begin wiretapping Ruggiero in an effort to find evidence of crimes he, John Gotti, Eugene Gotti, and others had been committing for many months. The main focus was on the way Ruggiero, Gotti, and others, including Gambino crime family underboss Aniello Dellacroce, may have been involved in the gangland murders, robberies, gambling and narcotics dealings of Massino's crime family. Although the FBI didn't know it at the time, Gotti, Ruggiero, and others in their family had actually played a role in the disposal of the bodies of the Three Captains who were slain in May 1981 at Massino's behest.

It actually turned out that there was more implicating Gotti and Ruggiero to the Massino investigation than the burying of the bodies. Not long after the Three Captains were slain, Gotti and Ruggiero were driving along a city highway and noticed they were followed by a car believed to contain a cop. When the car pulled up to Gotti's, the man inside pointed a gun and was getting ready to fire. Gotti and Ruggiero were able to make the highway exit and get away, but not before they recognized the would-be assailant as Anthony "Bruno" Indelicato, the son of the murdered Alphonse Indelicato, one of the Three Captains.

An informant told the FBI that the threatening action of Bruno Indelicato stemmed from the fact he believed Dellacroce, a key leader of the Gambino family, had sanctioned the killing of his father and the other two captains. That made anyone connected to the Gambino family fair game for Bruno Indelicato's revenge, said the informant. Faced with such a threat, Gotti and Massino had joined forces to find and kill the younger Indelicato before he struck first. That alliance between Gotti and Massino, who already had shared in the proceeds of a Chinatown gambling operation, was enough to justify wiretapping not only Massino's telephones but also those of Gotti and Ruggiero.

Ruggiero turned out to be the focal point of the wiretaps, apparently because he had maintained contact with Massino by the time the latter had fled to Pennsylvania. But no sooner had the wiretaps been put up on the Ruggiero telephones in Howard Beach than they had to be taken down when he decided to move to a new home in Cedarhurst, Long Island, a more suburban upscale community. FBI agents learned that Ruggiero's new domicile with his family was a two-story frame house on a large corner lot. The neighborhood was residential, which created challenges for the agents in their search for a place that was inconspicuous enough to allow them a vantage point to monitor the house. It was a task for which FBI agent Joseph O'Brien had the background to solve.

Tall, lean, and handsome, with alert eyes, O'Brien was an FBI agent who looked the part of the quintessential hard-charging fed, something which set him apart physically from his peers, some of whom may not have been so energized. What also set O'Brien apart was his loner attitude. Simply put, O'Brien liked to work by himself on the street, living by his wits and coming up with off-the-wall ideas to get under the skin of mobsters. One of his favorite tactics was to gather the addresses and birthdays of Gambino crime family members and then, in a gesture of friendliness and extreme *chutz-pah,* send them birthday cards, enclosing his business card. If he learned they had received a promotion in the mob hierarchy, O'Brien would send them a congratulatory note as well. Sometimes he would slip in a dollar bill as a token of good luck. The mobsters went ballistic when they got the missives, since they feared others in the crime family would think they were cooperating. O'Brien had his laughs, but maybe, just maybe, the notes would entice someone to cooperate. Time would tell.

O'Brien found himself in the organized-crime section because his old assignment in the counter-intelligence group had come to an end. Working under supervisory special agent Bruce Mouw, O'Brien and the other agents on the Gambino squad used an FBI office on Queens Boulevard as their base in the Rego Park section, a locale that was close to the mob havens of Howard Beach and Ozone Park, where

Gotti, the Carneglia brothers, and Ruggiero hung their hats. With Ruggiero now a target on the wiretap probe, the FBI needed to quickly set up an observation post close to his new home in Cedarhurst. For that, O'Brien harkened back to his old days as a spy hunter.

Ruggiero's new home had a number of telephone lines. But as it turned out, he decided to use a Princess phone used by his daughter from which to do some of his shady business, so the agents got permission to tap not only the daughter's telephone but also the main house phone, subject to the restriction that any private conversations Ruggiero had with his wife wouldn't be taped. Aside from the taps, the FBI knew that Ruggiero was meeting with numerous people at the new Barnard Avenue address. Those meetings required the placement of two bugging devices in Ruggiero's home for which the FBI needed a nearby location to not only photograph the visitors but also listen in on the chatter the bugs picked up.

Sizing up the neighborhood, O'Brien saw that a house across the street from Ruggiero's was in an ideal location. It had a clear view of the Ruggiero driveway and side streets. To gain access to the home owner, O'Brien knocked on the door and told him that he was from the FBI and that it was believed that Russian spies might be working out of the home across the road. The property owner was appalled. Appealing to his sense of patriotism, O'Brien said the investigation was such a priority that the FBI really wanted to use his home for an observation post, all very hush-hush. The man agreed, and for months beginning in April 1982 cameras on the second floor of the house photographed any suspicious characters at Ruggiero's place while other equipment recorded conversations he was having with his visitors.

The visual sightings began to bear fruit as soon as the agents turned on their cameras and recorders. But from May 6 to May 7, 1982, the crucial time around Sal Ruggiero's plane crash, the court didn't renew the wiretap and bugging order for those two days, so the FBI didn't have any audio from the house on Barnard Avenue. But the cameras still worked from the secret surveillance post, and it would later become clear that Ruggiero and company became enmeshed in frantic activity to take over his brother's drug business and gather his plentiful assets.

The surveillance-post agents saw a lot going on at the Barnard Avenue address early on the morning of May 7. Pulling up to the house were Dellentash, his brother Robert, and friend Wayne Debany. Already inside were Ruggiero and his lawyer Michael Coiro, who made the trip from his home a few miles away in the town of Bellmore, as well as John Carneglia and Eugene Gotti. Although there was no active bug that day, the FBI eventually pieced together the conversation. Dellentash told Ruggiero that his brother Sal had made well over a million dollars in marijuana sales. Knowing full well that even knowledge of drug dealing could get him in trouble, Ruggiero nervously shifted the conversation away from marijuana, telling Dellentash they could talk about that later—presumably out of the ear shot of others.

More important was the need for everyone to concoct a story so that the FBI wouldn't think Ruggiero had secretly harbored his fugitive brother. Angelo had always been in touch with his brother and assumed—correctly as it turned out—that the FBI had tapped his telephone so they might somehow know that he had been in constant contact with Salvatore. What should they do? Coiro, who should have known better about what he would say next but didn't, advised Dellentash to make up a story that would shield Angelo from trouble if agents asked how he came to visit his dead brother's home in New Jersey. The cover story was fairly simple: Dellentash would tell the FBI if agents asked that he had found a note Salvatore had left titled "in case of emergency." The instruction in the fictional note was that Dellentash should call Salvatore's parents and Angelo and tell them about the younger man's death and have Angelo go to the house in Franklin Lakes.

It sounded like a plan. Later, in view of the hidden FBI watchers, Angelo and Dellentash walked outside the house. It was then in another moment of candor, Dellentash brought up the fact that Salvatore's marijuana business had been lucrative. Ruggiero gave Dellentash a withering look.

"Never mention drugs in my presence," Angelo remonstrated. "I don't use or deal in drugs. I only want to know what my brother's assets were when he died, not how he got them."

Angelo had to put up that front of ignorance about drugs because he didn't really know Dellentash very well. For all Angelo knew he could have been working with law enforcement. Besides, the top echelon of the Gambino family, namely boss Paul Castellano, didn't want anyone dealing in narcotics, so Angelo had to be extremely careful, least he put his own head on the block. The official line of the mob was that any made member caught dealing in drugs would face harsh penalties, including death.

Dellentash was quick enough to realize that the subject of drugs should be dropped. Taking his cue from Angelo, Dellentash listed what he knew about the dead man's business world. Salvatore owned a diner in Flushing, Queens; some stocks; a home in Pennsylvania; several homes in Florida as well as a boat. Dellentash didn't have the full picture on Salvatore's assets but there was also a shipping company, a horse stable, and a card store in Brooklyn that was losing money. While lesser men living life as a fugitive might have had trouble keeping afloat financially, Salvatore Ruggiero had done very well, living as well as if he had never become a fugitive in the first place. It helped that he had friends like Dellentash and others to front for him when needed.

Dellentash and his brother made another run through the house in Franklin Lakes to make sure they didn't miss anything. Once they were certain the place had been gone over, they turned their attention to finding a man who might have known more about Salvatore's business empire and heroin dealings: Oscar Ansourian. Over the years, the FBI had long suspected Ansourian, known as "Big O," of being a drug trafficker, and there was evidence that he was intimately involved with Salvatore's operation and made some trips to Florida with him.

Evidence from an informant showed just how big Salvatore's and Ansourian's dealings were. Barely three weeks before Salvatore died, a New Jersey state trooper talked to Dellentash and asked him—why he did so is unclear—about the Learjet and pilot George

Morton. The trooper then told Dellentash that the aircraft was being watched. The conversation spooked Dellentash who immediately called Salvatore, who happened to be in Disney World, with Ansourian, for what was turning out to be regular travel to Florida. The trips to the Sunshine State were part of the entire heroin pipeline Salvatore had set up, and Ruggiero had been in the middle of a fairly significant heroin deal when he got the heads-up call from Dellentash about the state police visit.

New Jersey officials apparently didn't know about Salvatore's connection to the plane, but Dellentash warned him about flying because there was simply too much law enforcement heat. Why bother getting caught in the aircraft if it could be avoided? The recommendation was that Salvatore should drive or take the train back to New Jersey. Boldly, Salvatore decided to throw caution to the wind and fly back to Teterboro. Nothing happened. If the cops were watching the aircraft, they didn't move on it. However, Ansourian, who happened to be in the company of about twenty-five pounds of heroin, prudently drove back to the New York area.

The sudden interest of police in the aircraft appears to have prompted Salvatore in late April 1982 to think about constructing a private airfield—he had that much spare cash—which could handle Learjets. It was to be an ambitious idea. He needed about 7,000 feet of runway space and a parking area. The price, said a builder Salvatore knew in Florida, would be about $150,000. Salvatore seriously thought about it.

Salvatore Ruggiero wasn't a made member of the Gambino family, so strictly speaking the Mafia prohibition on drug trafficking didn't really apply to him. But his brother Angelo, as a made man, knew better than to violate the protocol, especially with a crime family boss like Paul Castellano. If Angelo needed a reminder about how serious a violation peddling drugs could be, he only had to look at what had happened in recent weeks to Peter Tambone, another member of the Gambino borgata. Known as "Little Pete" the sixty-three-year-old Tambone had his own heroin racket and appeared to be supplied by none other than Salvatore. But, the problem was that while the Tambone-Ruggiero connection was off-the-record and hidden, others in the Gambino family got wind of Little Pete's pushing drugs and told underboss Aniello Dellacroce. The unsettling news also, it seems, was passed along to boss Castellano.

It was on April 24, 1982, that John Gotti's brother Gene was seen entering Angelo's home. The FBI bugs picked up what they talked about. Gene Gotti was the one to tell Angelo about Tambone's problem with heroin being known to the bosses. Angelo, who liked Tambone as a friend, knew that the old man could face the ultimate penalty of death. Since Tambone was a made man, Castellano couldn't unilaterally have him killed for violating the drug rule. The case had to be presented to the ruling Mafia commission, composed of the bosses of the other families.

While Tambone's fate was being deliberated, Angelo wanted Tambone spared and thought about asking that he not be killed as a favor. It was a heavy lift to ask for such dispensation. Castellano and Genovese boss Vincent Gigante were in favor of killing Tambone. The other two bosses, Persico and Anthony Corallo, were not so sure. The commission was deadlocked. Angelo figured that if things were to go bad, it was likely Gotti's crew that would have to kill Tambone. Another complication was that if Angelo was somehow to convince the bosses that Tambone's life be spared then he couldn't ask for any more favors, particularly if people like Mark Reiter and Arnold Squitieri, at that time considered by the FBI to be a Lucchese crime family associate but later considered a major figure in the Gambino family, got caught dealing drugs. Another possible problem was that Angelo believed that others might suspect he himself had been in on Tambone's drug dealing.

The best thing for Tambone to do was to lay low. Angelo had a suggestion, picked up on one of the FBI bugs.

"Pete, listen to me like a brother," said Angelo. "I'm telling ya', worse comes to worse, get your wife and take off."

Tambone's situation was unsettling for weeks. At his house, Angelo talked intently with Gene Gotti about the fate of drug dealers who get caught. Angelo naturally wanted Tambone spared and would continue to stand by him. Gotti thought the mob faced a conundrum. The Gambino family needed to be consistent about drugs, said Gotti. Either the ban on drugs should be abandoned—which in reality it was, given the amount of off-the-record deals being done in the mob—or Tambone should be killed. There should be no "passes" for those who dealt in narcotics because hypocrisy was a sign of weakness, opined Gotti.

From what the FBI was hearing about the Tambone situation from such discussions in Angelo's house, it was clear that the old gangster was on very thin ice that was about to break. Agents confronted Tambone and told him that there was a contract out on his life. This was standard procedure, to approach a potential homicide victim, whenever the FBI learned of an imminent threat of violence. Shaken, Tambone drove to Cedarhurst and told Ruggiero about the agents' visit. Ruggiero repeated his advice: take your wife and leave town for a while. Both men met again on May 5, and Angelo said he would try to do what he could to save Tambone but that he should think about a long vacation. The next day Salvatore Ruggiero and his wife were killed in the plane crash. Whatever was decided about Little Pete wasn't so terrible. He survived. But Angelo Ruggiero had problems of his own.

CHAPTER FOUR
"Angelo, Keep Your Mouth Shut"

PANIC WAS NOT WHAT ANGELO RUGGIERO FELT in those early days after his brother died. A sense of urgency was more like it. Although he was in constant contact with his brother, there was much he didn't know about Salvatore's dealings. There was missing money, missing documents, and things he just didn't know about. Time was important also because the FBI was trying to do a deep dive in Salvatore's activities, although that seemed frustrated for the moment because of the way the house in Franklin Lakes had been picked clean. One thing Angelo did know was that his cavalier attitude toward *babania*, as heroin was known, could blow up in his face. The cops were one thing but crime family boss Castellano and his willingness to kill anyone who pushed narcotics was quite another.

Castellano was a boss not from the world of Ruggiero, the Gottis, the Carneglias, and everybody from their crew. Castellano was a businessman, a fairly successful one who ran a meat and poultry operation on Staten Island that made him a wealthy man. His house on Todt Hill, the highest point on the island was palatial and was dubbed the "White House." He prided himself on being above the average street gangster like the blue-collar crowd of the Gottis and Ruggiero. The Gotti crew referred to him derisively as "The Pope" for his exalted sense of self-importance.

Castellano, who became the Gambino boss with the death of his cousin and family namesake Carlo in 1976, was interested in amassing money along with the power of being boss. His avarice knew no bounds: he took bundles of cash with both hands from his various captains and didn't care where it came from. Stolen-car operations, construction rackets, labor unions, garment factories and trucking companies: they all paid a share to Castellano. Maybe even drug money was among the hundred-dollar bills in his wallet, who knew. His bankroll grew and naturally, so did the contempt the Howard Beach crowd felt for him. But that was something for another time.

The odd thing about the way the underground drug operation was run was that even Tambone facing censure or death didn't stop things. Even before his brother died, Angelo had been involved in heroin deals. He tried to be careful, telling people not to talk over the telephone. But he didn't know that his house was bugged. So, when Canadian gangster Gerlando "George From Canada" Sciascia, a member of the Bonanno family wing from Montreal, paid him a visit at the Barnard Avenue house, Angelo felt quite comfortable talking about the fact that he had been in contact with his brother and that heroin was on everybody's mind. Sciascia was in the market for the stuff.

"I got thirty things of heroin," said Sciascia, "that is why I am here."

Sciascia, a handsome Canadian with white hair, wanted to know how much of the stuff Salvatore Ruggiero needed.

"I got to speak to my brother at 1:30 today," Angelo said.

"How about forty kilograms?" Sciascia asked.

Sciascia was no neophyte in the heroin trade. He had been on the radar of the FBI since early 1980. Agents suspected he was tied to a Canadian import-export firm that had been watched by investigators for a long time. The clincher came in Sciascia attendance at the November 16, 1980, wedding reception of Giuseppe Bono and Antonino Albino at the Hotel Pierre in Manhattan. The FBI would later obtain photographs of virtually all of the guests. Along with Sciascia, a number of the members of the Bonanno crime family from Montreal and New York were in attendance, as well as some Sicilian crime figures the FBI suspected were major heroin dealers.

Angelo was also paid a visit by another trafficker named Edward Lino, who lived farther out on Long Island. Lino had been a mob associate for years and had, according to informants, become involved in the heroin trade with Gambino associate Carmine Consalvo but didn't want to become a made member of the Gambino family and told Ruggiero as much. But what he did want to do was move some heroin with Angelo.

"Could you do anything if I got H?" asked Angelo.

"Yea, I got a few good guys . . . handling poppy," answered Lino.

"Call my brother, call him collect," said Angelo in a whisper, unaware that the bug was picking up even his *sotto voce* remarks.

Two days later, on April 30, 1982, Lino and Angelo talked about an impending heroin shipment. Angelo was clearly interested but warned Lino about using planes to move the product because the federal government had begun using AWACs aircraft to interdict drug operations with some success.

"Listen to me," warned Ruggiero, "forty-five hours, forty-five hours and they [government] made ninety pinches. You cannot beat them. They know the planes are going low. You cannot beat them. I'm telling you now, if you are putting up any money."

"No, no, not a dollar, not a dollar," stressed Lino.

Other things Angelo and Lino talked about showed their concern about the way Mafia bosses felt about drugs. Both men were heavily involved in moving heroin, and it seems that the mob-governing commission was split over what to do with people who wanted to be initiated but had a drug bust in their past. Lino was an aspiring gangster at this point, so he was interested now in the politics as Angelo explained things.

"Anybody that was pinched with drugs from 1962 on never, never gets straightened out," explained Angelo.

"Is that, is it official?" Lino asked.

As explained by Angelo, the ruling commission was split 2-2 on the drug issue. The Gambino and Colombo families wanted the ban but the Bonanno and Lucchese families voted against it. The Genovese family was uncertain, although acting boss Anthony Salerno had always held mobsters who pushed junk in disdain. The bosses also seemed to be continually suspicious about someone who once dealt with drugs.

"'The guy got pinched with junk, and he is out of it now? What do they got, a fuckin' rat?'" Angelo said as he paraphrased the paranoid thinking of the old timers.

"That kills me, isn't that sickening," said Lino.

Angelo said on the recording that he got arrested once for drugs, although it is not clear what he meant by that. Lino's reply to laughter was "Who says nice guys can't work?"

In the days before Salvatore Ruggiero died, the FBI bug was picking up a lot of tantalizing and incriminating conversations about the drug dealing of the Gotti crew, including conversations with some members of other crime families. When told that Lino had some cocaine for a good price, Gene Gotti said, "Angelo, I want it."

Salvatore Ruggiero's death radically changed the nature of things. Angelo was on a frantic search for assets. He also set out on a mission to keep his brother's drug business alive. So, when friend Joseph Guagliano visited the Barnard Avenue house about a week after Salvatore died, Angelo made it clear what he needed to do.

"For us, continuing my brother's thing, I have to," said Angelo. "I, you know, I have to keep doing it."

There seemed to be no lack of associates who were willing to help Angelo take over what had been Salvatore's business. To hide some cash, Angelo turned to lawyer Michael Coiro, a loyalist who had been a close friend and integral part of the crime family activities. Coiro had handled wise guy cases for years and felt honored to be part of the mob world.

"You're not our lawyer, you are one of us as far as we're concerned," Angelo told the attorney.

"I know it Gene, and I feel that way," the not-so-esteemed member of the Bar answered.

St. Helen's Church in Howard Beach is a mainstay, even to this day, of the largely Roman Catholic community. Baptisms, First Communions, Confirmations, and weddings keep the parish busy. On May 14, 1982, the church was the scene of an unusual funeral, unusual because there was no body in the casket for mourners to grieve over. The service was for Salvatore Ruggiero, whose mortal remains were part of the aquatic world some twenty-five miles south of Hilton Head in the waters off Georgia. A cousin of the deceased who happened to be a priest presided. The casket was empty because the medical examiner in Savannah was still trying to identify the pitifully small pieces of humanity retrieved from the ocean floor. Eventually, Salvatore's hand would be sent back to New York for burial.

Such a death rattled Angelo to no end. His brother, his partner in crime, had simply disappeared with hardly a trace left of him to mourn. On one bugged conversation, Angelo lamented how incomprehensible his brother's death was: "If he would have been shot in the head and . . . found in the street—that's part of our life. I could accept it. Next week, the week after, we would have got even. Whoever did it, we would have accepted it. Not this way."

Those who filled the church pews were those of the criminal class who had been part of Salvatore's world. There was his brother naturally, along with Gene and John Gotti, John Carneglia, Al and Robert Dellentash, as well as Wayne Debany. Two Canadian gangsters, Gerlando Sciascia and Joseph LoPresti, another heroin dealer, were in attendance, as well as Gambino crime family member Salvatore Scala. Mark Reiter also showed his respects. Watching the scene was FBI agent Andris Kurins, who catalogued a list of attendees that read like a Mafia's *Who's Who*. (Stephanie Ruggiero's family had a memorial service a day earlier at the home of her mother Dorothy Rubin.)

The funeral mass was a depressing affair. The mourners stared at a casket devoid of any piece of Salvatore. One mourner later said it only contained one of Salvatore's suits. Angelo knew that what had been his brother was now literally sleeping with the fishes. The horror of that death grated on him, which is why when he became angry later he threatened to feed people to sharks in a swimming pool. The service over, the mourners went to Emma Ruggiero's house on Ninety-second Street for what was to be a large Italian buffet.

Based on what had been overheard on the surveillance devices planted in Angelo's Cedarhurst manse, the agents knew that they were gathering significant evidence of drug dealing within John Gotti's crew of the Gambino crime family. They weren't close to making a case—there had not been any significant seizure of drugs yet, although in time there would be. Angelo's dealings were, as he had feared, bringing him closer to serious legal trouble. He sensed it, particularly after a New Jersey newspaper wrote about Salvatore's connection to, as Angelo put it, "this narcotics shit."

"They are going to think . . . the empire was turned over to me . . . now I'm taking over," Angelo told Coiro and Gene Gotti at one point.

"Angelo, keep your mouth shut," Gotti cautioned him. "And if everybody keeps off the telephone, they might not say anything."

But Angelo and the others couldn't keep their mouths shut. They may have been careful about using the telephone but the bugs in the Cedarhurst house and some critical leaks to the FBI later showed that the crew was scheming to not only take over Salvatore's old heroin network but also to concoct elaborate cover stories to protect Angelo from charges he harbored his fugitive brother.

While mourners on May 14 congregated downstairs in Emma Ruggiero's home the day of the funeral, Angelo and some of his buddies went upstairs. Seated at a table was Angelo and John Carneglia. Gene Gotti stood nearby. Coiro, his mind working to bend the group's plans to fit the law, paced nearby. Salvatore died without a will, and Coiro listed what had been discovered about his assets. The value was more than anyone first thought. There was even an offshore company known as the Iberian Corp. On top of that some $250,000 to $500,000 in cash remained unaccounted for. Perhaps it went down with the plane in a briefcase.

For Angelo, the real problem was all of the contacts he had with his fugitive brother. As the day of the funeral wore on, Angelo told his friends that he would face a great deal of trouble if the FBI could prove he had visited Salvatore. The brothers had been careful about their visits when Angelo traveled to Florida and New Jersey. They didn't even take photographs in case the agents raided their homes. Telephone calls between the two men were very carefully done.

"Sal would never call my house," said Angelo. "He would call a certain number and then the person would tell me to go to an outside booth, 'He is going to call you.'"

The truth of the matter was that life as a fugitive had become very wearing on Salvatore and his family. They had been in the wind since around 1975, always keeping a watch for suspicious strangers and constantly requiring trusted friends to take care of their finances. Stephanie was getting disgusted with all of the intrigue and wanted to come back to New York where her mother, father, and sisters lived. Coiro said that he was going to try and secure a house for Salvatore very near his brother in Cedarhurst. It seemed, said Angelo ruefully, that his brother was on one level looking to get arrested, to end his life on the run.

Stephanie's family was also causing Angelo problems. In particular, her mother Dorothy seemed to be concerned with nothing more than some bank books that contained $5,000. To rid himself of her nagging Angelo turned them over to her. But the real issues had to do with the growing federal investigation targeting Angelo for harboring his brother. Now, three days after the funeral, reality was setting in and a sense of panic finally began to envelop Angelo and some of the others, including Stephanie's mother and sisters who were feeling more pressure from the FBI.

One of the sisters, Estelle, had an added concern because her husband was a New York City police sergeant and feared he could lose his job or pension if it came out that he was related to Salvatore and Stephanie, if only by marriage. Agents had also tried to scare her, telling her that Salvatore was mob connected and that there had been as many as four gangland homicides in recent weeks, including that of Lucchese crime family member Anthony Stabile. The FBI visits unnerved Estelle because it seemed that the agents were linking Salvatore's death to the earlier killings

The agents' remarks caused Angelo and Coiro to speculate that maybe the federal government was actually investigating the gangland murders and not so much the actions of their crew. He still thought he was smart enough to avoid being arrested and started plotting to armor himself and keep his dealings secret. To protect his legal position, Angelo not only fabricated his own story about how he came to know about Salvatore's home in New Jersey but tried to persuade his dead sister- in-law's family to stay calm and not answer any questions from the FBI.

For dyed-in-the-wool gangsters like Angelo, the Gotti brothers and others, fending off government investigators was something that was in their blood. They were not above lying or dancing around the truth, as well as having a lawyer fight for them. But Coiro sensed that Stephanie's family could cave in under pressure and told her sister Estelle to get a lawyer who could be trusted to protect them, even if they thought about lying. But Estelle and her mother seemed to want to try and get their own legal counsel which they apparently did. Sensing the women wanted independent attorneys, Angelo began to tell them how to answer questions about whether they had visited Salvatore and Stephanie in New Jersey.

Rubin and her daughter thought the FBI knew they had traveled to New Jersey to see the dead couple. But Angelo said that was impossible.

"They don't know that," said Angelo. "They don't know that unless you tell them that. They'd not even know. You got a call from Sal, somebody came to pick you up and brought you there [to New Jersey]."

Despite the tragic deaths of Salvatore and Stephanie, their families were in the midst of bickering about not only money but also the couple's two orphaned children James and Danielle. As it turned out, according to government records, Stephanie's family signed a document relinquishing any custody rights to the children to Angelo, reserving the rights of visitation on weekends and Jewish holidays. Even with Dorothy Rubin getting her daughter's bank books from Angelo, he believed the in-laws could still be trouble.

"You sure these people aren't wired?" Gene Gotti said at one point to Angelo, raising the specter that the Rubin family might be cooperating with authorities to save themselves.

"They gonna get their heads cut off," was Angelo's reply to that possibility, the government records showed.

That possibility soon loomed fresh. On May 22, 1982, the FBI bug in the Cedarhurst house picked up Angelo in an agitated state, talking with Coiro and Anthony Moscatiello about some very disturbing news. His dead brother's in-laws had talked to a lawyer of their own choice who told them to cooperate with the FBI and tell the agents the truth about everything. This was a disaster on a number of levels for Angelo, particularly since a friend of his named Joey who had driven the in-laws to visit Salvatore while he was alive could be in trouble as a result. Angelo was panicked and angry and told Coiro as much.

"I warned you, Mike. I told you, Mike," a frustrated Angelo yelled at Coiro. "'Let's get them a lawyer, let's get them a lawyer.'"

"I will probably shoot someone," Angelo said.

The group talked about finding a way to approach the in-laws to persuade them to tell them not to follow their lawyer's advice about cooperating with the government. One thing was certain. Coiro didn't want Angelo doing it: the FBI would look upon any approach he made as coercion and probably arrest him for witness tampering. But in the end, they came up with no useful ideas about what to do. Things had taken a decidedly bad turn, and both Coiro and Ruggiero discussed more about finding out just what the FBI was looking for by using their various corrupt law enforcement sources. As an added protective measure, Coiro suggested Angelo disconnect the telephones at the Barnard Avenue house—as if that would do any good. The bugs didn't rely on the telephones anyway.

Feeling the pressure from a federal investigation they didn't know the extent of, Angelo, Coiro, and the others used what they called "the quiet before the storm" to dispose of Salvatore's assets. They believed, incorrectly in some ways, that the IRS would go after everything for back taxes Salvatore owed, leaving his children with nothing, particularly if their grandmother Dorothy Rubin cooperated. (Neither Rubin nor her daughters were ever accused of wrongdoing.)

What was left of Salvatore's remains—a solitary hand—was returned to Angelo who had the grim task of committing it with some kind of ceremony on June 15. Before he did that, Angelo met with Sciascia at the Cedarhurst house and talked about the fact that the crew in Montreal had some heroin and wanted to move it to New York. But before anybody did anything, Montreal wanted to know what the profit might be, said Sciascia.

"We'll take thirty," said Angelo, referring to the quantity of the drugs he was willing to take.

After talking business, Angelo told Sciascia about the upcoming interment for his brother's remains at St. John Cemetery later that day. Sciascia seemed like he wanted to attend the service, but Angelo told him it was best to stay away. In the end, only Angelo's immediate family and three of the men closest to him—John Carneglia, Gene Gotti, and his brother John—attended.

While there was hardly anything left of Salvatore after the crash, his assets were spread out over several states, which complicated things for his brother. With Coiro giving legal advice, Angelo told friends like Moscatiello to "get rid of anything and everything right away," even if they had to take a beating on the sales price, according to law enforcement records. As for Joseph Guagliano, who had driven the in-laws for visits to the fugitive Salvatore, Angelo told him to "pack a little bag and . . . go away for a while."

What Angelo and Coiro couldn't find out immediately was that just days after their anguished meeting together, Salvatore's sister-in-law Estelle walked into the Brooklyn Organized Crime Strike Force office on Cadman Plaza and talked to one of the attorneys. She admitted visiting her sister Stephanie in Florida in 1981—the first time she had seen her in six years. Estelle also told the prosecutor about the meeting after Salvatore's funeral with Angelo and Coiro but denied anyone told her what to say. Asked why she and her sister surrendered custody of Salvatore's children to Angelo, she said the "flavor" of the Ruggiero family reputation convinced them not to challenge Angelo.

Estelle testified a short time later before a Brooklyn federal grand jury, one of a number of people who had been subpoenaed. There was no question now that the FBI was ramping up its investigation, and Angelo would be a sitting duck if they started looking into all of the money and assets he was accumulating from his brother's demise, as well as his drug dealing. The drug dealing in particular, was getting uncomfortably close to Angelo's group.

Angelo, Gene Gotti, John Carneglia, and others had been picked up on bugs and wiretaps for months talking about drug deals, even well before Salvatore and Stephanie were killed. Some of it was in coded, cryptic conversations that could be rolled into a drug-conspiracy case. Actually, catching the group moving drugs would take more work, including extensive surveillance.

It was Father's Day, June 20, 1982, that the Barnard Avenue bug picked up Angelo talking with William "Sid" Cestaro, an associate of the Lucchese crime family who had a long-standing hankering for drug deals. His brother, Philip Cestaro of Queens, was a close associate of John Gotti and over the years had operated a bar in Queens for Gotti, all the while doing occasional drug deliveries. Philip's brother William had gone to Angelo's house to talk about a nice two kilograms (about 4.5 pounds) of heroin deal planned for a couple of days later. The drugs were, according to investigators, destined for Mark Reiter.

There was plenty of reason for the FBI to believe that Reiter was handling heroin, much of it very pure. As would later be discovered in some federal criminal cases, Reiter became a major supplier to some of Harlem's big traffickers who had taken over from Nicky Barnes after he was imprisoned. It was actually Herbert Sperling, Barnes would later allege to federal investigators, who made the connections and introductions between the Harlem network and Reiter, who by 1980 had graduated from small cocaine deals to heroin. With the Bergin crew doing its own heroin operation, Reiter had connections between the Italian mob and the black ruling council of Harlem, which Barnes had once controlled. It would be a while before the federal investigation got into the extent of Reiter's involvement in the heroin trade which over time would become more far reaching and important than that of Ruggiero.

If Angelo was getting nervous about the FBI being on to his drug operations, he didn't seem the least bit concerned as he talked with Sid about the heroin deal, even whispering as if that would defeat the ability of the bugging device to pick up the conversation. The agents heard almost every word, including Angelo's alacrity in closing the deal.

"We take it down. Nine- thirty Tuesday," said Cestaro.

"Yeah!" replied Angelo.

Actually, the deal went down on the next day, Wednesday, June 23. That was when FBI agents followed Cestaro to his home on Juniper Boulevard South in the Maspeth section of Queens. After a short visit inside, Cestaro exited the building with a shoulder bag that he placed in the trunk of his car. Cestaro was followed by the agents to the Palace Diner, an eatery Salvatore Ruggiero once had an interest in, for a short visit to the men's room after which he drove to an intersection in south Queens where he made a telephone call.

Ten minutes after Cestaro made the call, things got interesting for the agents watching him. It was then that a man named Salvatore Greco, who worked in John Carneglia's junkyard in East New York, drove up in front of Cestaro's vehicle near the pay phone where he had made the call. Cestaro blinked the headlights of his car on and off. Then Cestaro got out of his car, as did Greco, and both men conversed briefly both returning to their respective vehicles. Both men drove to Ninety-first Avenue near Eightieth Street were Cestaro took two bags from the trunk of his car and Greco took a white bag from his vehicle. The pair then exchanged bags and got back into their cars.

Bam. The FBI team moved in and arrested Greco and Cestaro before they could drive away. The bag Cestaro had given Greco contain about $145,000 in cash. But the bag Greco had given Cestaro held the real pay dirt for the agents. It contained two kilograms of heroin with a purity of 97 percent. Greco also had a piece of paper on which were written some cryptic words, including the phrase "200 1 Plus." The paper also contained another tantalizing clue: a fingerprint of Reiter, the Gambino associate who had been spotted outside the Ruggiero house with John Carneglia the day Salvatore and Stephanie died in the plane crash.

The captured heroin was significant. But the problem for the FBI was that if Cestaro and Greco were prosecuted the government would have to tip its hand that a big investigation was underway and perhaps screw up the probe of Angelo and his many associates. It was too big a risk for so little gain. The case was getting closer to its conclusion, but the government needed to keep the Gambino crew guessing. So, after Greco and Cestaro were arraigned on a federal criminal complaint for possession of heroin, the case was dismissed on a court motion by the government. Both men were freed. The heroin and the cash stayed with the government.

But news of the arrest traveled fast to the Howard Beach crowd, and Angelo knew things were heating up. The bug in this Cedarhurst house picked him up telling Gene Gotti that "They might start grand juries" and that "We're gonna be involved." When an associate stopped by, Angelo told him to stay away because the house was being watched. Then, from June 27 through July 4, the conversations picked up on the bug became of little value, likely because Angelo wasn't having any visitors to whom he could shoot his mouth off.

Mark Reiter, according to federal court records, also sensed that things were "getting hot," and around this time started to tell one of his workers, Salvatore Corallo, to "lay low" and be careful about his actions. Reiter had known Corallo for a couple of years and once tried to persuade him, without success, to accompany a shipment of heroin from Italy back to New York. For the most part, Reiter used Corallo to deliver heroin to customers, the court records stated. To compensate Corallo, Reiter agreed to take care of his associate's loan-sharking debts and, according to investigators, would compensate him $500 for every kilogram of heroin delivered to a white customer but upped the price to $2,500 for each kilo delivered to a black customer—such was the size and more lucrative nature of the drug market in communities like Harlem.

Although John Gotti had once made a show of chasing Reiter from the Bergin crew because of his drug dealing, the act seemed to be just that—a show. Even veteran heroin supplier Herbert Sperling knew it was a fake move on Gotti's part and in prison told Nicky Barnes that was the situation. Reiter continued to keep close ties with Gotti's men and allegedly kept the flow of drug money going back to the 101st Avenue club house. At one point, according to investigators and court records, Reiter, accompanied by Corallo, delivered $500,000 in cash proceeds of heroin sales to John Carneglia. One mob informant, John Alite, would later tell the FBI—as well as the author—that he was present at his apartment in Manhattan when Reiter allegedly gave Gotti $100,00 in drug money. But one former law enforcement official expressed skepticism about Alite's account of that transaction since he would have been about twenty-five years old at the time and part of a much younger group of Gambino associates. One former Gotti associate, who wanted to remain anonymous, flat out denied that such money was ever paid to the Gambino boss.

The next visitors of consequence to Angelo's house on Barnard Avenue the summer of 1982 were people he didn't want to see but had been expecting for quite some time. On July 7, 1982, an FBI team armed with a search warrant, raided Angelo's home. If he had any doubts about the investigation, Angelo quickly learned from the warrant that he was the target of a drug and racketeering investigation. His suspicions about a probe had been well founded. But as it turned out, the search, which was witnessed by attorney Michael Coiro while Angelo was out of the house, uncovered nothing of value. There was one exception to the latter: the agents removed the bugging device that had been so fruitful in gathering evidence

CHAPTER FIVE
"Take Care of Him, Nino"

JOHN GOTTI HAD KEPT A VERY LOW PROFILE with all of the drug dealing going on with his crew. The wiretaps and bugs picked up nothing that implicated him directly in what was happening. He did show up for the funeral and interment of Salvatore Ruggiero but that was out of respect for his family, and it would be a stretch for the government to make anything more out of it.

While not directly involved, Gotti likely benefited from the trafficking from the money his crew kicked up to him. He had to know that Angelo was dealing off the record with heroin: Gotti's own mob intelligence was fairly well-tuned to give him that information. But Gotti's approach was kind of a mob "don't ask-don't tell" when it came to probing too deeply about the narcotics money. At one point, Gotti made a big show according to one informant of expelling Mark Reiter from the Bergin crew because of drugs. But the ban wasn't enforced because, as the informant said, Ruggiero and Reiter still dealt in drugs.

Gotti's so-called chasing away of Reiter seemed rather halfhearted. According to Andrea Giovino, who as a young and pretty Italian woman from Bensonhurst gravitated to some of the big mob characters of the day, she claimed to have partied often with both Reiter—with whom she said she had a relationship for about a year—and Gotti in early 1985 at the trendy Club A in Manhattan.

Party night for Gotti and his capos at the club was usually Tuesdays and Thursdays.

A spitfire when provoked, Giovino recounted in her book *Divorced from The Mob: My Journey from Organized Crime to Independent Woman* how she pummeled another woman in the club with a liquor bottle and got Gotti's stunned admiration. Again, an associate of Gotti who asked to be unnamed, disputed her recollection and contended she never partied in Gotti's presence. In the summer of 1987, DEA agents and NYPD detectives surveilled Reiter visiting Gotti's base in Ozone Park, the Bergin Hunt and Fish Club. The incidents show that Gotti didn't keep his arm distance from drug dealers like Reiter, although he was never linked to drug trafficking.

"Either he had to be the dumbest boss alive or he was involved," was how government witness John Alite, once a Gambino associate, viewed possible explanations for Gotti's behavior. But others were not so sure that Gotti had any direct involvement in drug trafficking but he simply took what was given to him.

"I think he was just a profit taker," opined Jim Hunt, years later about Gotti's relationship to the drug dealing. "Guys around him had money—Eddie Lino, a wealthy guy, John Carneglia, a wealthy guy, they were the movers and shakers, they were his guys. There is no way he [Gotti] was not getting some kicked up."

Looking back, Hunt believed that the drug dealers in the Bergin crew never told Gotti the money he got was from heroin deals. If they were kicking up enough cash to Gotti, he knew it wasn't from bookmaking or the other crimes. Gotti's refusal to talk openly about drugs, either on the telephone or in person, is why he wasn't ensnared in the indictment, said Hunt. A former FBI agent who took part in the Ruggiero drug probe also told the author that there was no evidence that Gotti was involved in drug deals.

But at the very least, Gotti had a *willful blindness* to what was going on. It was the same sort of behavior that decades later officials would allege about some of the big investors with Wall Street scammer Bernard Madoff who were viewed as surely having to know that all of their fantastic brokerage-account returns were too good to be true—and thus ill-gotten gains. That sculpted ignorance made them in some sense complicit in Madoff's crimes. As a legal concept, willful blindness is defined as involving conscious avoidance of the truth and, as the dictionary says, gives rise to an inference of knowledge of the crime in question. Knowledge of a crime is not the same in a legal sense as participating in it, and on that score there is no evidence Gotti trafficked in drugs.

To put it another way, Gotti, given his shrewdness about what his men were doing on the street, could take a position like police Captain Louis Renault, the Claude Rains character in the film *Casablanca*. Renault expressed shock and horror that gambling had been going on in Rick's Café, yet he really knew what was going on in the casino since in the next breath he gladly accepted his winnings from playing the roulette wheel. Money was what the mob was about, and frankly Gotti wouldn't have cared where it came from as he stuffed it into his pockets.

Beginning with Angelo Ruggiero, the drug men in the Gambino heroin trade were all people Gotti had grown up with on the street. They had shared a lot together, and it wouldn't have been easy for Gotti to turn his back on them. The men in Gotti's crew had a long, common history through his steady, fortuitous rise to a position of power.

Gotti's old Fulton-Rockaway crowd migrated with their Gambino crime-family mentors, the Fatico brothers, to a new social club on 101st Avenue in Ozone Park: The Bergin Hunt and Fish Club. But by 1972, Carmine Fatico, the more powerful of the brothers, had a series of legal problems, notably a loansharking indictment on Long Island, which hobbled his ability to attend to business at the Bergin. As journalists Jerry Capeci and Gene Mustain noted in their book *Mob Star,* Gotti was anointed to fill the leadership void at the social club in Fatico's absence even though at the age of thirty-one Gotti wasn't even a made man. As a result, Gotti had a great deal of face time with Dellacroce, who was the most powerful man in the crime family after Gambino himself.

When Dellacroce had to go away for a stint in prison, Gotti became the Bergin's man to talk directly with Gambino. At the club, Gotti relied on his brother to run the facility. According to former FBI agent Bruce Mouw, Gotti also turned to Ruggiero to work as the administrator of the crew' activities. Of Gotti: "John was not a good administrator," said Mouw. Gotti seemed more interested in being the wise-guy boss.

If Gotti impressed Gambino with the way his crew brought in money from hijacking and its other street rackets, it took something more important to solidify the young gangster's importance for the old boss: homicide. The story about the killing of James McBratney in May 1973 is one of those tales often told about Gotti so it need not be delved into very much here. McBratney was an Irish street thug who had the reckless effrontery to kidnap Emanuel Gambino, the nephew of Don Carlo himself. McBratney and his cohorts demanded a $350,000 ransom and eventually settled on $100,000 which the victim's wife paid, thinking it would secure the release of her spouse unharmed. The money went and so did Emanuel. He was dug up from a grave in New Jersey in January 1973. He had been shot in the head.

The elder Gambino, so the story goes, turned to Gotti to avenge the murder. On May 23, 1973, Gotti, Ruggiero and an associate named Ralph Galione walked into Snoop's Bar & Grill on Staten Island. It was then that the trio walked over to McBratney, who had been nursing a drink at the bar, and attempted to remove him from Snoop's. Angelo had a pair of handcuffs, Galione was armed with a handgun, and Gotti provided the muscle. All three surrounded McBratney and acted like cops, telling him to come with them. Anything that was supposed to happen would be done away from Snoop's.

But the combative McBratney resisted, and when he did Galione fired at him three times. McBratney fell dead while Gotti and company fled, but not without having been witnessed by a number of patrons inside Snoop's. The killing was done in a room full of witnesses, a major tactical mistake. It took police about two months to arrest Angelo and Galione for the hit. In Gotti's case, he had bragged about the hit in the presence of a friend who actually had been working for many months as an FBI informant. The NYPD eventually showed witnesses a photo of Gotti, and he was identified as one of the three men who killed McBratney.

It would take about a year for Gotti's braggadocio to get him arrested in the McBratney homicide in May 1973. The key evidence was information given to the FBI—and then the NYPD—by the informant in Gotti's midst, known at the time by the codename "Wahoo." Gotti, with the help of the politically connected celebrity attorney Roy Cohn, did post a $150,000 bail and promptly returned to the Bergin, where his crew continued its crimes, mainly hijacking, with some loansharking and other offenses thrown in.

Although he had tested prison previously with a federal hijacking rap, Gotti really didn't want to spend much more time behind bars. With Cohn as his mouthpiece, Gotti and Angelo got a plea bargain with the Staten Island District Attorney's Office for attempted manslaughter in June 1975. The conviction charge meant a four-year prison sentence, which in reality would work out under the sentencing scheme to about two years, give or take. Both Gotti and Angelo surrendered and were sent to begin serving their time in Greenhaven Correctional Facility, less than 100 miles north of Howard Beach, a trip that was a relatively easy ride for their wives and children to make.

Gotti and Angelo had taken one for the team, and under normal circumstances that would have meant an easy jump to Mafia membership. But Carlo Gambino was at a point in his life as boss when he wasn't making new members. The books of the Mafia had been closed, and Gambino himself was wary of admitting too many people to membership. In fact, there had been stories that Gambino believed the Five Families had become too unwieldy, with too many young turks who were hot blooded and impulsive, a description that could at times fit Gotti. In *The New York Times,* veteran crime writer Nicholas Gage said in December 1972 that Gambino had even thought about expelling certain members who had shown weakness and vulnerability to being compromised by law enforcement. Gambino also had an aversion to drug dealing because he believed, correctly as it would turn out, that it invited too much scrutiny by federal law enforcement.

In some ways, Gambino was ahead of his time in his thinking. He only had to look at the machinations of the Gotti-Fatico crew. The Bergin Hunt and Fish outfit had been penetrated by at least one crucial informant and would see at least two or three more secretly work for the government. Gotti's bragging and pugnacious behavior were potential danger signs and sources of trouble as well. So Gambino kept the books closed to membership and although he may have been grateful to Gotti for handling the McBratney matter, the old timer kept his own counsel and refused to make new members.

Gambino died of natural causes on October 15, 1976, at his home in Massapequa. His heart troubles and other ailments finally caught up to him, and after a relatively low-key funeral at Our Lady of Grace Church in Brooklyn, one surveilled by the FBI, NYPD, and other agencies, Don Carlo was interred in a crypt in the mausoleum at St. John Cemetery. The immediate speculation was that Dellecroce, the powerful family underboss, would take over from Gambino as boss. But Dellacroce was in prison on a tax-fraud case, and it appeared that prior to his death Gambino decreed that he wanted his cousin, Paul Castellano, to succeed him. The higher ups in the crime family agreed, and Castellano started running things.

Gotti was in prison on the McBratney homicide when Gambino died so he missed becoming a made member of the Mafia at the same time Angelo Ruggiero and Gene Gotti were given membership. But soon after Gotti was out of state prison in 1977, he got his button after Castellano opened up the books for new members. With Gambino gone, the Mafia ruling Commission allowed the Five Families to expand its ranks. Life was good for Gotti now. He not only was the top dog at the Bergin club (the Fatico brothers were doing time in federal prison for a hijacking charge) but his chief mentor, Dellacroce, was now out of prison and was said to have been given a free hand by Castellano to run the Gotti-Bergin crew as he saw fit. At the Bergin, Gotti was an acting captain—someone with all the privileges and responsibilities of that rank but without the official position.

Of course, the drug ban was still very much in place under Castellano, at least as far as he was concerned. Yet, there is evidence that Castellano was talking out of both sides of his mouth when it came to narcotics. He spouted the line that drug dealing among his made men was banned. But at some point during the Pizza Connection investigation, which in 1984 unmasked the Sicilian heroin connection, investigators during a surveillance operation spotted something they didn't expect to see. One day in October 1980, Castellano himself, the boss of the Gambino family, met at Martini's Sea Food Restaurant in Bay Ridge with Salvatore Catalano and Giuseppe Ganci, two of the main actors in the heroin case. Also present was Castellano's driver and faithful acolyte Tommy Bilotti. It was believed, although never proven in court, that Castellano had worked out a deal at that meeting to get a cut of the heroin profits for himself.

Years later, one prosecutor told the author that the government was never able to prove that Castellano took drug money from the Sicilians. Had that happened, Castellano would have likely been charged in the Pizza Connection. But two of the prosecution's main witnesses, undercover FBI agent Joseph Pistone and Italian criminal Luigi Ronsisvalli, testified they were told that Catalano and his drug operation did have ties to the U.S. Mafia families, the prosecutor said. Pistone, the prosecutor added, said that he learned through the mob that Carmine Galante was assassinated in 1979 because he wasn't sharing heroin money with the other families.

Although ostensibly barred by Castellano from narcotics, the Bergin crew was still unofficially doing drug deals. Even before Castellano came to power, Salvatore Ruggiero was involved in heroin, cocaine, and marijuana trafficking. Since he wasn't a member of the mob, Salvatore technically wasn't violating a mob rule by dealing in drugs. It was around this time that the FBI began to hear conflicting stories about Gotti's possible involvement in narcotics. One informant, known by the code name BQ, believed that Gotti was a major drug investor and alleged that he had some contact with

Salvatore, who at this point in time was a fugitive. Where Gotti, who was a compulsive gambler, could have found the money to invest in narcotics was unclear. Another informant, known as "Wahoo" who was in actuality Gotti's close associate William "Willie Boy" Johnson, was skeptical that Gotti was involved at all in drugs but kept open the prospect that the mobster might be investing.

While Gotti may not have been directly dealing with narcotics himself, he must have known from his own street sense and from the money that people like Angelo Ruggiero were bringing in that drugs were in the picture. As would be shown a few years later in the Cedarhurst tapes, Angelo's own drug deals were widely known among mob associates across two or three Mafia families. Gotti would have had his head in the sand not to know.

Castellano was a boss cut from a different kind of cloth than Gotti. While Gotti's men were the working-class kids who roamed the streets in athletic shoes and casual dress, Castellano fancied himself the urban businessman who had built up a poultry and meat operation. His favorite style of dress was that of the custom-made business suit that hung well-tailored on his six-foot-three-inch frame. His dark rimmed spectacles gave him the bookish look of an actuarial. His distinctive nose was as one writer described "vulturine," which was a term synonymous for rapacious or predator—given his greedy ways that seemed to be a fitting adjective.

Castellano's wing of the family also had a significant presence in the then-lucrative garment industry, primarily through the trucking and dress companies of his nephew Thomas Gambino, the son of Carlo. Both Thomas Gambino and his younger brother Joseph, who wasn't a member of organized crime, had built up a major garment trucking empire, which did tens of millions of dollars in business a year. Trucks were important to the industry for moving finished product to the retailers and between manufacturers. Over the years, allegations would be leveled that the Gambino brothers were part of a cartel that controlled the garment trucking industry, allegations that would cost them dearly in the years ahead.

Another Castellano ally was Joe N. Gallo, an elderly and diminutive gangster who would ultimately become consiglieri of the crime family. It was through Gallo and others that organized crime controlled the Greater Blouse Association, a group of manufacturers on Seventh Avenue. Three mob families—Gambino, Genovese, and Colombo—had divided power over the association and thus held sway over a significant swath of the garment industry in the city.

Yet, although he fancied himself above the blue-collar mobsters, Castellano had got his hands dirty over the years. He was believed to have controlled significant loan-sharking operations. In fact, around the time of Gambino's death, Castellano went on trial in Brooklyn federal court for loan-sharking. But when a key government witness refused to testify, even when granted immunity, the case collapsed.

In addition, a crew aligned with Castellano ran a homicidal car-theft ring, led by killer Roy DeMeo, which sold stolen vehicles to the overseas market. DeMeo, who operated under captain Nino Gaggi, was one of those men who seemed to relish killing, and the word on the street was that he was responsible for about thirty-seven murders, or 100 depending on which account was given credence. One of his victims was said to have been Castellano's own son-in-law Frank Amato, who was married to the Mafia boss's daughter Constance. When Castellano learned that Amato had been cheating on his daughter, and abusing her as well, the errant spouse was not long for this world. Castellano told DeMeo to take care of Amato, and in September 1980 he disappeared. Castellano himself didn't participate in the car thefts but instead got regular bundles of cash from the DeMeo gang, delivered to him at his large mansion, the White House, on Todt Hill in Staten Island.

As would be later described in a federal court trial, DeMeo killed those he suspected of being informants or competitors in the stolen-car racket. To dispose of the bodies, DeMeo and his associates, often gangsters Joey Testa and Anthony Senter, would take the victims and in a bathroom or the floor of a garage dismember them, boxing the pieces for disposal in a garbage dump. One time, according to a witness, DeMeo was in such a frenzy in cutting up a body that an ear of the victim went flying around a garage, only to be found and eaten by the junkyard dog.

However, at some point DeMeo's blood lust even made Castellano uncomfortable. The reason seemed to have been the increasing attention Manhattan federal prosecutors were paying to the activities of the stolen car ring. As a result, Castellano decided that DeMeo himself had to be eliminated and for that he turned to Anthony "Nino" Gaggi. An FBI bug picked up Castellano telling Gaggi to "Take care of him, Nino." So, in January 1983, DeMeo's body was found in the trunk of his abandoned car in Brooklyn. He had been shot several times in the head. Various stories later surfaced about how DeMeo was actually killed—one said he was having coffee with some of his crew members when he was dispatched. But the end result was the same. DeMeo, perhaps the most prolific and out-of-control killer in the Mafia, was gone.

While he fancied himself a businessman, Castellano didn't get to where he was by being meek. When it came time to contract out some hits, Castellano held his nose and agreed to a sit-down with leaders of the Westies, the bad Irish gang on the West Side of Manhattan. The Irishmen were a group of about two dozen gangsters and killers who sometimes kept the heads of their murder victims in freezers before getting around to disposing of them. They were successors to the tough tradition of mobsters like Mickey Spillane. Connected as he was to the politically connected McManus family, Spillane (not to be confused with the famous author) not only controlled gambling dens along Tenth Avenue but was a dispenser of jobs and other favors in the Irish community. In a sense, Spillane was the Gaelic equivalent of Carlo Gambino in his day, a man people came to see much like Don Corleone in *The Godfather.*

However, the Westies were a different breed from the Irish mob under Spillane. Led by James Coonan, the gang gained a reputation as killers and was suspected by the Gambino family of summarily dispatching a favorite mob loan shark, Charles "Ruby" Stein. At the time, one of New York's most prolific loan sharks, with some of his millions in loans financing garment-district businesses, Stein in May 1977 was lured to a West Side Irish club, slain, and dismembered. His remains later washed up on a Queens Beach.

As distasteful as Castellano may have thought the Westies were, he agreed to a meeting with Coonan at Tomasso's Restaurant, a favorite Italian restaurant in Bay Ridge, next to Gambino captain Jimmy Failla's Veterans and Friends Social Club. Castellano, accompanied by Dellacroce, Joe N. Gallo, Nino Gaggi, and some others, met Coonan and his chief lieutenant Mickey Featherstone to hammer out a deal in which it was agreed that the Irish would take hit contracts from the Gambino family. Although questioned about what happened to loan-shark Stein, Coonan swore to Castellano he didn't know what had happened to him.

Like most bosses of the period, Castellano sometimes hung his hat at a social club, his particular favorite being the Veterans and Friends on Eighty-sixth Street in Brooklyn, where Failla held sway. Failla, known as "Jimmy Brown," was one of those older Gambino mobsters who was considered part of Castellano's white-collar apparatus. Failla had become an important captain under Gambino and according to investigators had been the old boss's key liaison between Gambino and Sam "the Plumber" DeCavalcante over the use of New Jersey garbage dumps. Failla's interest in the carting industry stemmed from his involvement in one of that industry's major trade associations, the Association of Trade Waste Removers of Greater New York. As in the garment trucking industry, the mob used certain trade waste associations as the basis for a cartel, controlling which company entered the market and where it could do business.

There was another industry that Castellano had influence over and that was construction. He and the bosses of the other crime families (excluding the Bonanno family) had set up the Concrete Club, a secretive arrangement that squeezed concrete companies in New York City for payoffs. Working through Ralph "Little Ralph" Scopo of the Colombo family, the bosses extorted the payments and in return the companies were allocated contracts on building projects in the city of over $2 million. In return the contractors kicked back 2 percent of their earnings to Scopo who shared it with the four crime families. Some of the cash found its way to Castellano who was raking in cash from other construction companies through his own captains.

The avarice Castellano showed as the boss—forgetting for a moment his own legitimate businesses—soon began to build up resentment among some in the Gambino family, notably the Bergin crew. Castellano's imperious attitude had long been a sore point with Gotti and his crew. Loyal to Dellacroce, the Bergin crew nevertheless continued to earn money through hijacking, loan sharking, and gambling—along with some drug dealing—and showed their value to Castellano. But although the Bergin crew did its job, none of them had any love for Castellano.

Mafiosi in the other crime families also couldn't help but notice Castellano's greed. He just couldn't get enough of the money. In one secret recording that surfaced years later, Lucchese gangster Sal Avellino recounted to his boss Anthony Corallo how Castellano whined about getting a reduced payoff from a labor union of $25,000, down from the usual $200,000, cash Castellano called a "bone." Corallo could only express his disbelief and contempt.

"A bone, two hundred thousand dollars?" Corallo asked rhetorically. "Imagine that, he can't get enough. I don't understand him for the fucking hell of me, he didn't get enough. Imagine that, he didn't get enough money."

CHAPTER SIX
"I Could Give You Information"

WITH DELLACROCE GIVEN A FREE HAND to oversee Gotti's Bergin crew, Castellano had essentially ceded command of the Ozone Park gang to his seasoned underboss. The problem was—much as the late Gambino had feared—the younger generation that made up the Bergin club was undisciplined and reckless. The group was also riddled with informants. Among the worst of the lot was Gotti himself, who threw away money on gambling like the proverbial drunken sailor, befriended people who were working secretly for the government and, it is believed, invested in drug deals to fund his compulsive gambling.

How wanton Gotti's gambling was has been described in Mustain and Capeci's *Mob Star,* as well as Davis's *Mafia Dynasty.* By January 1981, Gotti seemed unable to catch a break with horse betting or football. One weekend Gotti lost $21,000 on football, followed by another of $16,000, Mustain and Capeci noted, adding that Gotti's forays to the local race tracks only added to his financial misery. Gotti also had a dice game in Manhattan's Chinatown that did well but even as owner, Gotti continued to lose betting with house money. His losses became debilitating to the Chinatown dice game, and his brother Gene and Angelo were overheard talking about how it might be best to close the place down.

"We don't need him in the fucking game!" Gene Gotti exclaimed when told of losses his brother sustained one night of $30,000.

Yet, Gotti's Bergin crew continued to do well in its other operations, mainly gambling, hijacking, and loansharking, kicking up proceeds to Dellacroce and Castellano. So long as the money flowed, the big bosses were happy. But no one realized how vulnerable the crew in Ozone Park had become to being penetrated by law enforcement. That was made clear by the way not only the FBI had developed informants but also how even the Queens District Attorney's Office had focused on the Bergin club house, putting in wiretaps and snaring a key informant.

William "Willie Boy" Johnson was one of those men close to Gotti who, while unable to become a member of the Mafia because of his mixed ethnic background—his mother was American Indian—nevertheless had value to the Gambino family. Johnson was part of the Fulton-Rockaway crew and was described by one writer as "sausage stuffer by day, bookmaker by night, part-time boxer and part American Indian." Johnson was tough and mean, just the kind of guy Gotti liked to have around. Johnson served as Gotti's driver, a fact that didn't go unnoticed to the local Queens detectives.

Remo Francheschini was one of the NYPD's premier investigators of the Mafia. Once wounded in a shootout and awarded the Combat Cross by the department, Francheschini had worked for a time in the Intelligence Division down on Hudson Street in lower Manhattan, the unit that among its many functions kept tabs on organized crime figures around the city. When needed, his men would team up in special undercover cabs and prowl around the city, surveilling mobsters. One detective, Jack Clarke, kept his own index-card system of surveillance reports in a shoebox, a primitive system for sure but one that would later provide critical leads to federal investigators in the Pizza Connection drug case. In 1977, Franceschini moved over to Queens where he commanded the detective squad of District Attorney John Santucci. Once a city councilman, Santucci was interim district attorney in December 1976 after his predecessor left for a judgeship. In November 1978, Santucci won the job outright in a follow-up election.

Although the Queens District Attorney's Office had over the years been looked upon suspiciously by the FBI—there were rumors that

the mob had inside sources of information about investigations—
the arrival of Francheschini changed things a bit. He got the squad
to focus on Gotti's club at the Bergin where they suspected crimes
were being committed but didn't know what. The slim reed of intelligence the Queens investigators had about the Bergin was later described by Francheschini in his autobiography *A Matter of Honor*
when he said that his investigators saw some of Gotti's men talking
on a pay telephone by the door.

"We wanted to put a tap on the line, but you can't just go in to a
judge and say, 'I know there's crime in there.' You've got to have
probable cause," Franceschini said.

Had Queens had a good relationship with the FBI and an unsul-
lied reputation in law enforcement, the office might have been able
to approach the Bureau for help and much-needed intelligence. But
the FBI was carefully keeping Johnson's role as their high-echelon
informant secret, so Francheschini had to come up with evidence on
his own to use against Johnson and Gotti. Once again luck played a
part in what happened next.

One night in 1981, Johnson was spotted by two of Francheschini's detectives meeting Arnold Squitieri, a known drug dealer, in
a parking lot outside Kennedy Airport. As described in *A Matter of
Honor,* the detectives noticed a car pull up and saw a black man take
a package from Johnson and handed him a paper bag which Johnson
placed in the trunk of his car.

"We had pretty good suspicion that we'd just witnessed a drug
dealing going down but, of course, we had no evidence," remembered Franceschini.

The detectives followed Johnson to near his home, watched him
take the paper bag out of the trunk and place its contents in an at-
tache case, and then they approached him. Startled when the cops
asked him what was in the case, Johnson blurted out, "Oh, this is
from my gambling operation," said Francheschini. Johnson apparently did have a gambling business on the side, but his admission
put him in legal trouble.

"Come with us," the detectives told him as they handcuffed Johnson for the trip to Queens, along with the $50,000 in cash.

What happened next was something out of a Grade B detective movie as it was recounted in *A Matter of Honor*. Back in Francheschini's squad room, he let Johnson stew for a while, alternating between detectives who seemed friendly and those who played the bad-cop routine. Johnson spoke up.

"Can we do some business?" Johnson said to one of the detectives.

"What kind of business we talking?" the detective asked.

"Well, who's here? The lieutenant, and I got you three guys. Uh, what about eight thousand? To let me go," answered Johnson.

One of the detectives then went and got Francheschini who, when he entered the room, was offered the entire $50,000 by Johnson.

"Well, I'm going to tell you something. You're under arrest, first of all for trying to bribe my detectives and now for trying to bribe me the fifty thousand," Francheschini told Johnson.

Panic hit Johnson. He was on probation and if arrested again would go back to jail. He played the one card left. He told Francheschini he could help him.

"I could give you information," said Johnson.

But as Francheschini remembered things, working out a deal with Johnson was not so simple. If he was arrested and put through the court system it would become quickly known that the cops had grabbed him, and his usefulness as an informant would be zero. There was also the question about what to do about his bribe attempt and the money the cops had seized. To avoid the regular NYPD channels, Franceschini worked out a plan with District Attorney Santucci in which, with the approval of a state prosecutor, the money was placed in the district attorney's safe and vouchered, Johnson indicted for the bribe attempt but the indictment itself remained sealed with the court and thus unpublicized. In effect, Francheschini had a hold on Johnson.

Meetings between Francheschini and Johnson sometimes took place by Maple Grove Cemetery in Kew Gardens, Queens, a short walk from the lieutenant's office. Johnson would be standing by a grave as if praying when Francheschini arrived. The detective carried a gun to these rendezvous because, after all, Johnson was a killer. Also surveilling the two men were other detectives from Francheschini's office. At other times, Johnson would call Francheschini in his office, where the informant was known by the simple code name "the girl."

Over time, Johnson gave Francheschini a rundown on the way Gotti ran the crew at the Bergin and the various personalities. As the cops already knew, there was gambling inside the club. No surprise there. Johnson gave the investigator a fill-in on all of the characters close to Gotti, some were useful, efficient gangsters, others were not respected, said Johnson. Gene Gotti was described as a family man with a mean streak, constantly complaining about his brother John's gambling losses while another brother, Richard Gotti, was pegged as a simple bookmaker who wouldn't really be anywhere if it had not been for his brother's stature. The eldest Gotti sibling was Peter, a city sanitation worker who was on disability for falling off a garbage truck and sometimes ran the Bergin if brothers John and Gene weren't around.

Also part of the Bergin crowd, related Johnson, were some names Francheschini didn't seem all to familiar with: Heroin addicted Tony "Tony Roach" Rampino, John Carneglia, an up-and-coming gangster, and attorney Michael Coiro, whose claim to fame was that he knew a lot of judges and some prosecutors in Queens. But of all those at the Bergin, the one man Gotti seemed closest to was Angelo Ruggiero. Angelo was also someone Johnson had nothing much good to say about.

"Angelo Ruggiero," said Willie Boy, was a loudmouth, *a cafone* [slang for uncouth]." "Always talking loud on the phone, always bitching," Francheschini would later remember in his book. "Ruggiero was a soldier, not a boss, although according to Willie Boy he acted higher than his place."

As Johnson talked more to Francheschini, he related Angelo's heavy involvement in heroin trafficking, just like his brother who still was alive at this point and on the lam as Willie Boy talked to the lieutenant. Johnson pegged Angelo as running drugs with Gene

Gotti and people like Arnold Squitieri, although as Francheschini
noted, Willie Boy said nothing at all about that $50,000 cash he was
caught with coming from drugs as the investigators suspected.

What about John Gotti, was he involved in the drug deals? Other
informants would say Gotti had invested in some drug hauls. But
Johnson wouldn't give up his boss.

"No, he said, John wasn't into drugs. He was emphatic about
that: John Gotti had nothing to do with narcotics," noted Francheschini. "Willie Boy was very protective of his boss."

Of course, all of the information Willie Boy Johnson relayed to
Francheschini wasn't enough to make any arrests since it was basically uncorroborated. So, in May 1981, Franceschini and the
Queens District Attorney's Office received judicial authorization to
wiretap the telephone in the Bergin. Undercover operatives—detectives—had made it a practice of hanging out by the Bergin and
picked up snippets of conversations about bets being placed on the
clubs's pay phone, so that helped in getting the judicial order.

As it turned out, Santucci's staff put two taps on two telephones
in the Bergin and then planted a bug to pick up conversations in the
club itself. For about a month the surveillance picked up some evidence of gambling. But soon things got interesting for the Queens
District Attorney's Office, but not in the way Francheschini or Santucci would have expected, and they only had themselves and their
staff to blame.

On June 30, 1981, FBI agents and members of the NYPD public
morals unit raided the Bergin to seize illegal fireworks. Why the
FBI would have an interest in fireworks is unclear unless it is remembered that the agency was in the early stage of its probe of Angelo Ruggiero, John Gotti, and others. As the raid was underway,
FBI agent Donald McCormick picked up the pay telephone inside
the club and was told by club denizen Jack Cavallo, who actually
ran the gambling operations, that the line was being tapped by Santucci's office. McCormick actually suspected the line was tapped
but wanted to place a call just to see what showed up. About a day
later, McCormick's supervisor, Bruce Mouw, got a call from some-

one working for Santucci to congratulate the FBI for the Bergin raid.

While the FBI discovered the Santucci bug quite by chance, its existence created problems not only for the bureau but also the Queens prosecutor. Both agencies were in danger of stepping all over each other's investigations and screwing them up. On September 2, Mouw and two of his immediate supervisors turned up at Santucci's office for a meeting with his staff, including Francheschini. At Santucci's suggestion, the group went to the Altadonna, a local Italian restaurant on Cross Bay Boulevard in Howard Beach, one well-known to mob characters. The confab was, to say the least, competitive, although Mouw would later remember that the prosecutor was cordial and expressed a desire to work together with the FBI. Santucci said his electronic surveillance had been "very successful" in obtaining gambling information but had to admit he had not found anything of value about loan sharking or homicides, two major crimes the Bergin crew was involved with. In fact, Santucci had to admit that taps on social clubs weren't that productive and that electronic surveillance should be done on the homes of mobsters.

Santucci was right that bugging residences of the Mafiosi could provide good evidence, but he was wrong about the social clubs being dry holes, as the FBI would find out in its various operations in Mafia clubs around the city, which turned up some useful tapes. In any case, Santucci agreed to back off his effort on the Bergin and let the FBI take the lead in that area. Mouw, who grew up in Iowa and hadn't dealt much with city prosecutors who came out of the political world as Santucci did, remembered feeling uncomfortable in dealing with the district attorney, although there was nothing he could put his finger on as the source of his discomfort.

About ten days later, Mouw and Santucci's staff met again to talk about surveillance of Gotti and his crew. But as Mouw would remember it, Santucci's people indicated they believed they could have a possible leak in their office and wanted the FBI's help in uncovering those who might be responsible. While it was no secret that Coiro claimed to have a hook in the local prosecutor's office and that others like infamous Lufthansa heist mastermind Jimmy Burke had very good sources there, the problem might actually have been an embarrassing slip-up with Santucci's own staff. It seems that Santucci's office had failed to put the notation "do not notify" on its subpoena to the telephone company when records of the Bergin telephone were requested. Without that notice, the telephone provider was free to—and apparently did—tell the Bergin at some point that its telephone records had been requested by Santucci. So when Cavallo told agent McCormick that the telephone in the club was tapped, he had it on the best of authority. (A few years later Santucci was further embarrassed when it was revealed in the newspapers that he had a long lunch, by some estimates as long as fourteen hours, with an up-and-coming NYPD inspector, a reputed Gambino associate named Sal Reale, and several political operatives at the Altadonna.)

In the saga of the Gotti era, Santucci's efforts were noteworthy but in the end they turned out to be small beer. The mishandling of the subpoena was an embarrassment. In June 1982, Santucci's people and the NYPD raided Gotti's gambling operation on Mott Street in Chinatown. Neither Gotti nor Ruggiero and the other big men of the Bergin happened to be present when the detectives rolled through the door. But the cops seized $100,000 in proceeds and gambling paraphernalia and made seven arrests, among them Anthony Rampino, William Battista, Peter Tambone, and Frank DeCicco. The defendants appeared in court a day or two later and, with Coiro acting as their lawyer, pleaded guilty to misdemeanor gambling charges for which they where fined $500. But it also appeared that the court papers indicated that there had been an informant involved in tipping off police about the gambling operation. If Gotti didn't realize before that his operation had been penetrated, he knew it now.

The Santucci screw-up with the subpoena wasn't the only thing that compromised law enforcement focus on Gotti, Ruggiero, and the rest of the Bergin crew. The FBI offices in Queens were in Rego Park, a busy commercial and residential neighborhood in which Queens Boulevard was the spine that ran down its center. Mouw and his agents from a suite of offices had availed themselves of the various bars and restaurants in the area. Sometime in June or July 1982, one of Mouw's agents stopped by a local bar and stayed for a while. The problem was that upon leaving, the agent left behind a folder that contained documents that happened to be the affidavit for the surveillance being done on Angelo Ruggiero. The material was a basic roadmap of the government's investigation, laying out what they suspected Ruggiero of doing and who was believed to be doing it with him. The stuff somehow got into the hands of Anthony Moscatiello, a Gambino associate of Gotti's. From there, it got back to Ruggiero.

The FBI learned that Ruggiero was also on to the agency surveillance as spelled out in the affidavit from a confidential informant. Ruggiero said that "a big guy" in another crew of the Gambino family had told him that a federal judge in Brooklyn (it was Judge Henry Bramwell) had signed the surveillance order. As Ruggiero learned, Bramwell had reviewed information provided to him by the FBI from five informants to place three bugs in his Cedarhurst house. Ruggiero also found out that it wasn't just him who was a target but also Gene Gotti, Edward Lino, John Carneglia, and Robert DiBernardo, a Gambino captain who had made his work in the pornography industry.

CHAPTER SEVEN
"You Are Pissing Some Big People Off"

It was in late March 1982, some three months before Ruggiero even saw the FBI surveillance affidavit, that he suspected he might be the object of government spying. His unsuspecting wife had let some men who claimed to be telephone workers into the Cedarhurst house. They did their work in looking for the source of a neighborhood power problem and left. Both Ruggiero and Coiro were suspicious, and, sure enough, after checking around they discovered the men weren't real telephone company employees at all. No one was really sure who they were, but Coiro suspected they were FBI agents disguised as repairmen and installing taps on the telephones and bugging the house.

Made men, if they had any sense, would always be surveillance conscious, watching for strange cars and looking in their rear-view mirrors for tails. But electronic devices were beyond their ability to do anything about. In frustration some of the regulars at a mob social club once tore down a parabolic antenna, thinking it might be spied upon by the FBI. Once at a Bonanno social club a glitch in a bug transmitted conversations and flushing toilet noises to a nearby AM radio—leading to the discovery and dismantling of the devices. However, to counter the surveillance capabilities the government could amass against them, mobsters had to call in some experts and in New York City, with the largest police force in the country, there were always retired cops willing to help out.

John McNally had worked as a special investigations unit detective and attained the rank of 1st grade, the highest. After retiring, McNally, like many who left the force, became a private investigator. In a city like New York with such a great number of attorneys working in all sorts of fields, investigators with connections to law enforcement didn't have much trouble finding work. Civil lawyers needed them for divorces, workers-compensation claims, and accident investigations. On the criminal side, investigators were the ones to dig into the backgrounds of prosecution witnesses and seek out witnesses to help the defense. So when Coiro needed an investigator on some of his cases, he had occasionally used McNally.

With Coiro suspecting Ruggiero's place to be bugged, he turned to McNally to perform an electronic sweep of the Cedarhurst house for the presence of electronic monitoring devices. Electronic sweeping is a specialty that requires the right equipment and a person who knows how to handle it. McNally hadn't really specialized in sweeping but as chance would have it had a few months earlier reconnected with an old NYPD friend who was versed in that kind of work. John Conroy was a fifty-three-year-old retired 1st grade detective who had landed a job as manager of security for Philip Morris, Inc.

Sadly, McNally had recently lost his twenty-year-old son in a car accident. Conroy came to the funeral to console his old colleague. As they chatted, Conroy let it be known that he needed extra money. Would McNally help him earn some extra money moonlighting, Conroy asked? As it turned out, Conroy had recently acquired some experience in debugging technology from working at both Merrill Lynch and Philip Morris. For McNally, that was the right connection at the right time since he often had to do electronic sweeps for clients. Both ex-cops struck a deal: McNally would give Conroy assignments to do sweeps in return for one-third of the fee the client paid, according to government records.

Over a three-month period in early 1982, Conroy got three assignments from McNally. Two of them involved sweeping the homes and offices of private executives, while the other involved a social club on Long Island. The payments were all in cash, and Conroy used his own equipment, as well as some from Philip Morris. When the time came in April to sweep Ruggiero's house, Conroy called and arranged a date for April 17, 1982, a Saturday.

As astute as Conroy and Ruggiero tried to be in arranging the sweep, the FBI was on to the plan because the bugs already operating in the house were picking up their conversations. So, when it came time for Conroy to do his sweep for bugs, the FBI agents simply deactivated them for a day. Conroy showed up on schedule and checked the house out on all three floors. There were no bugs in the house, Conroy told Ruggiero. But, he added, the telephones were indeed tapped—except for the Princess phone in his daughter's room, which Ruggiero had been using for many of his calls. Conroy would later explain his finding by telling Ruggiero that while testing his telephone lines they produced a higher than normal energy output, a sign he believed that the lines were tapped.

With his paranoia confirmed, Ruggiero asked Conroy to sweep his cars for bugs, but those also turned up negative. With advance warning, the FBI had masked the house bugs by deactivating them. After Conroy left, they could be turned back on. But Conroy, for reasons which are unclear, missed the tap on the Princess phone, the one which Ruggiero used most. Nevertheless, Ruggiero was convinced of Conroy's abilities. He asked him to perform sweeps at his friend's home and at the Lucchese crime family club The 19th Hole in Brooklyn. Ruggiero also asked Conroy if he had any contacts who could confirm if the taps were legal and which agency had placed them. Sure, said Conroy, he had a contact at the telephone company.

Angelo raised six children of his own, and at this point was ready to take care of his brother Salvatore's children should the need arise—as it would. As family oriented as he was for a heroin trafficker, Angelo had a number of personality faults. One of them was that he could be played like a fiddle by anyone who saw a vulnerability with him. In the case of Conroy, the ex-cop knew that Angelo didn't have the sophisticated understanding of how electronic surveillance worked. He thought Angelo was kind of stupid. As a man in need of money, Conroy saw how he could manipulate Angelo by giving him what he wanted—knowledge of government surveillance.

Conroy had no inside sources of information in the telephone company. But Angelo didn't know that, so when the ex-cop offered to find out if the Cedarhurst telephone lines were tapped, he jumped at the chance. The deal was that Angelo would pay Conroy $1,000: $800 was to go to the phantom telephone company employee and the rest was ostensibly Conroy's and McNally's finder's fees for $100 each, government records stated. So on April 24, 1982, Conroy told Angelo that, indeed, his telephones were tapped, "legally" tapped as he put it, pursuant to a court order signed by a federal judge in Manhattan. Angelo asked if Conroy's contact had a copy of the affidavit used to get the court order, but he made up a story that he doesn't receive them to initiate a tap.

Angelo thought he had a good thing going with Conroy and his supposed connections. The information that Conroy related about the Manhattan federal court wiretap authorization seemed to confirm Angelo's earlier suspicions that he was being watched by the FBI because of his secret contacts with both his brother Salvatore and Joseph Massino, both men who were fugitives. As far as Conroy was concerned, he *knew* he had a good thing with Angelo. The Gambino mobster was so anxious about his situation, so unsophisticated and so impulsive that he was willing to pay whatever Conroy asked for to find out information. Thousands of dollars were also paid to Conroy to check the home telephones of John and Gene Gotti as well as of John Carneglia. He even asked for more electronic sweeps to be done. Conroy was only too happy to comply. He had found a cash cow in Angelo and was going to milk him for all he could in this secret little scam.

Conroy kept this scheme going, dangerous as it was. He was conning one of the toughest street crews in the Gambino family all for his own greed. Ruggiero did get something for his money. He was able to warn the other crew members and associates that there were taps on his home phone so that they could take precautions. Their telephone conversations were more circumspect and Angelo often arranged to have people call him at public telephones at prearranged times.

Into May 1982, Conroy continued with his charade. At one point he told Angelo and a group of mobsters, including Victor Amuso, a top captain in the Lucchese crime family, that the mob social club The 19th Hole did have taps on its lines but no bugs. Conroy embellished things further by saying that he had found a parabolic microphone device installed on the roof of a building about two blocks away from the bar. The device, Conroy explained, had the ability to pick up conversations inside the bar. Angelo and the other mobsters were fascinated over Conroy's "discovery" and no questions asked, paid the ex-detective more money on the spot.

Angelo thought Conroy was something of a genius, a man with connections who could be very valuable. Since Salvatore Ruggiero had died in the plane crash, Angelo had been on a search for his assets. Could Conroy help find Salvatore's safe deposit boxes in New Jersey banks? Conroy said he could but that it would cost. To get the ball rolling Angelo gave Conroy two aliases his brother had used, "Sal Cappazzano" and "Terri D'Asato." Conroy said he would check with his contacts, figuring that he could keep this little scheme going against the unwitting Angelo.

Angelo even admitted to Conroy that he feared the FBI could cook up any charge it wanted to against him but that narcotics wasn't his game.

"Jack, they could accuse me of a lot of things and I'll probably say it happened," Angelo said in a moment when he opened up to Conroy at the gangster's home. "You know, my game is numbers, my game in shylocking, bookmaking, hey, I'll even shakedown a guy for $50,000, I'll do it."

"They start that narcotics," scoffed Ruggiero. "I got six kids."

Then, on July 7, 1982, everything started to unravel when the FBI raided Angelo's house, gave Coiro search warrant materials, and then removed the bug from the downstairs living area—the bug that Conroy had assured everyone didn't exist. To make matters worse, Coiro read in the search warrant affidavit information that listed

Conroy's name as having once done work for the federal organized crime strike force. To Coiro and Angelo, this was distressing information to learn on top of the FBI raid. Both men immediately suspected, incorrectly as it turned out, that Conroy might have actually planted the bug in the Cedarhurst house himself, working as kind of a double agent for the government.

Two days after the raid, the FBI did pay Conroy a visit, and agents gave him a rundown of everything he had done for Angelo. At that point, Conroy knew the government had a line on him and could cause him a great deal of trouble. For an old cop, Conroy knew he had few options. He agreed to cooperate and even wear a tape recorder to catch Coiro and McNally making incriminating statements.

But Conroy apparently felt a strange loyalty to McNally and agreed to meet him in secret, without telling the FBI and without wearing a recorder, investigators said in a prosecutorial memo. In one meeting McNally told Conroy that Coiro had read about his previous work for the strike force and that after the bug was removed from Ruggiero's house, the mobster suspected he had planted it.

You better be concerned for your safety, McNally warned Conroy, the memo stated.

McNally also likely started to sweat because Conroy told him that he had given up everything to the FBI: the sweeps, the debugging, the bogus telephone company contacts. Fearing the worst and trying to backpedal, McNally said he only did "legitimate" investigative work, even if it was for gangsters. [McNally was never accused of wrongdoing in the case.]

With the July raid, the FBI search warrant affidavits, and all of the things Conroy had been feeding him, Angelo knew that he was a choice target for the feds. He was becoming increasingly paranoid and concerned—with good reason. With the bug found in his house, Angelo knew that for a period of months before his brother Salvatore died and right through the time he did some major heroin deals himself, that the FBI had likely listened to his most conspiratorial conversations. He still thought he was being looked at for talking with the fugitive Massino but the drug situation was much worse.

One FBI informant inside the Bergin told agents that Ruggiero was sweating bullets about an imminent arrest. In *Mob Star,* Mustain and Capeci related a memo put in FBI files that summarized what the informant or source said about Ruggiero's predicament.

"Source advised Angelo Ruggiero is scared to death . . . because he had been lying systematically to Big Paul and Neil [Dellacroce] insofar as he constantly told them he is not dealing in drugs by himself but merely cleaning up loose ends of his brother's narcotics operation . . . (if) they learn he was (lying) it is quite likely that Angelo might be hit."

Angelo and Gotti laid low in the summer of 1982. They avoided the Bergin, which was in the hands of Gotti's brothers Gene and Peter for day-to-day operations. But Ruggiero, if he feared the FBI and his Gambino bosses, couldn't stay away from the heroin racket. With the FBI breathing down his neck, Ruggiero nevertheless on August 4, 1982, checked into the Sheraton Hotel in Smithtown, Long Island, under the name of Sal Scala, a Gambino soldier. Ruggiero would stay at the hotel for almost two weeks, his comings and goings being watched by FBI surveillance agents.

He then met on August 13 with John Carneglia, Mark Reiter, and others in the Whisper Lounge, a site with an ironic name given that the FBI seemed to have enough agents in the area to get a sense that something no good was going on. That seemed obvious when early the next morning, according to court and government records, a Gambino family associate exchanged envelopes with Reiter and then, at Carneglia's direction, retrieved the $200,000 in one of the envelopes and brought it to Ruggiero's hotel room. Within minutes of the cash exchange, Carneglia drove home, followed by FBI agents, who saw him retrieve a duffel bag from his car and bring it into his house in Howard Beach. It all meant, the FBI said, that a major heroin deal had gone down, even in the face of a major investigation. Ruggiero and the rest of the group were being nothing, if not reckless.

The long FBI look into Angelo Ruggiero and the Bergin crew was leading to more than just the heroin deals. The bugs in the Cedarhurst house, combined with informants and surveillance at the club, showed that Paul Castellano was himself involved in criminal activity and directing the crime family. But Big Paul was circumspect. He didn't dare visit the *hoi polloi* clubs like the Bergin or the Ravenite in Manhattan, rarely going to places like the Veterans and Friends club in Brooklyn, which practically speaking was not far from his White House estate on Todt Hill.

FBI agent Joe O'Brien knew Todt Hill well. A maverick of sorts, O'Brien was part of the C-16 squad put together by Bruce Mouw that targeted the Gambino crime family. Other agents had focused on Queens and places like the Bergin club, while O'Brien spent some of his time on Staten Island. The decision had been made that the top bosses in the crime families were to be targeted and for that the FBI squads did the usual surveillance activity. This was all part of Mouw's game plan: get the agents out onto the street to troll the areas where the gangsters live and work. Make connections. Dig for information. In the case of O'Brien, he started working Sundays to try and find out who was meeting Castellano on Staten Island and taking the license plate numbers of cars that visited the boss's Todt Hill estate.

As innocuous as some of the surveillance may have seemed, it got O'Brien into some tense situations, particularly with Thomas Bilotti, the man who was Castellano's driver. It seemed that Bilotti didn't like O'Brien's snooping around Staten Island but also the agent's ploy of sending the wise guys cards on their birthdays and such. One Sunday, as O'Brien was tailing Billotti, the gangster had enough. He pulled up next to O'Brien's car and started screaming.

"You and your fucking greeting card, you think you are funny?" an apoplectic Bilotti yelled. "You are pissing some big people off."

Unfazed, O'Brien said that Castellano wouldn't approve of Bilotti's tirade, since the boss tried to treat the agents with respect. To goad Bilotti even further, O'Brien quipped that some of the gangsters referred to him by the moniker "the wig," a reference to the obvious hair piece Bilotti liked to wear.

At that point, a further enraged Bilotti motioned with his arm in a gesture indicating to O'Brien that he was reaching for a baseball bat kept under his seat. Concerned that he was alone in enemy territory and about to get into a serious physical confrontation, O'Brien pulled out his service handgun. Seeing the piece, Bilotti sped away.

In terms of Castellano, it became obvious that more than just a telephone tap would be needed to get the goods on him. A tap had in fact been authorized but it had been unproductive since Castellano was circumspect about what he talked about on the telephone. Mouw decided that just as they had done with Angelo Ruggiero, the FBI needed a bug in Castellano's house. An informant, later unmasked as businessman Jules Miron, told investigators that Castellano did a great deal of his business at home in a dining alcove by the kitchen. Miron even drew agents a diagram of the setup.

With the information Mouw's agents had collected through surveillance of the garrulous Ruggiero and at the Bergin club, there was more than enough evidence for prosecutors to compile an affidavit for a warrant to authorize bugging the Castellano home. The real challenge would be finding a way to enter the mansion after having neutralized any alarms and security systems, plant the bug and then get out—all without being caught. Physically, the house made it difficult to penetrate: there was a tall metal fence surrounding it, and Castellano had two big Doberman pinschers prowling the property.

To case out the location, Joe O'Brien and another agent Wally Ticano knocked on the door of the Castellano home to serve a subpoena. They were greeted by Castellano's wife Nina and his daughter Connie who let the agents come in and use a telephone to call the crime boss's attorney James LaRossa. This was in the era before cell phones, and the family extended the courtesy of the call, not realizing that as O'Brien entered the kitchen to use the telephone that he carefully glanced around and noticed the dinette area with a highbacked chair, which he assumed was were Castellano sat. Miron confirmed that guess in his talks with the agents.

The crucial day in the bugging operation was March 17, 1983. Castellano, his maid and paramour Gloria Olarte, as well as Tommy Bilotti had decamped to the boss's condominium in Pompano Beach, Florida. The only person left in the house was Castellano's wife Nina. What happened next in the FBI operation was a masterpiece of planning, bravado and luck, all of which was later described in the book *Boss of Bosses,* penned by O'Brien and fellow agent Andris Kurins. The first issue was the fierce Dobermans patrolling the property and for that two agents, puttering outside the fence tossed two sirloin steaks laced with animal tranquilizers to put the canines into a sleep that would last about six hours. As expected, the animals started to snooze and the FBI break-in team began its business at about 1:30 A.M. the next morning.

As described in O'Brien's and Kurins's book, two FBI agents had the assignment to break in to the mansion, but there were teams of other agents posing as sanitation men in a truck to block a key road leading to the mansion should the alarm be tripped and the special security team Castellano hired to watch his systems tried to drive up to the mansion. They had to plan for everything. The penetration agents, the ones doing the break-in, even carried tranquilizer darts in case the dogs awoke from their slumber. Another FBI car was in the area to watch the house in case lights suddenly came on inside.

On a signal from O'Brien and Kurins, the team of three FBI technical experts the morning of the break-in parked about a half block from the mansion and dressed in black walked to the garage after scaling the fence. The lock to the garage was picked, and the agents found themselves among four Castellano vehicles, including a Jaguar and a Mercedes, as well as the two sleeping Dobermans. As Kurins remembered it, he gave one of the dogs a slight nudge with his foot just to make sure they were in deep slumber. They were. Using a special digital device, the black-bag squad deactivated the Castellano alarm system and entered the living area by picking another lock.

In the kitchen, Kurins and O'Brien said they made a bee line toward the dinette area. There, O'Brien took apart a lamp near Castellano's favorite chair, installed an omnidirectional microphone and a power pack, and then reassembled everything, with Kurins putting the lamp back in its proper place. To simplify the job, O'Brien substituted a new lamp base for the old one, putting the old piece of equipment in a sack he carried. Kurins made sure the lamp was put right back where it had been. The agents cleaned up any stray debris, turned the alarm system back on and left through the doors they had picked. As O'Brien and Kurins remembered, the entire job took about twelve and a half minutes. The agents walked to their vehicle and drove away.

The story as described in *Boss of Bosses* of the bugging of Castellano's mansion is a marvelous cloak-and-dagger episode. Simply marvelous. Gripping. Everything sounded like it went off like clockwork. The two men must have had nerves of steel to pull it off. At least that is what it sounded like. The problem is that, at least as far as Kurins and O'Brien's activities that night were concerned, it very likely wasn't true. As former supervisory FBI agent Bruce Mouw later revealed publically, the two agents did not and would not have done the break-in. The complex, risky job was done, according to officials, by a highly trained FBI technical team supervised by James Kallstrom. The episode described in *Boss of Bosses* appears to have been added to juice up the narrative.

But what was true was that to monitor the bug, O'Brien and Kurins had selected a location not far from the mansion and soon began harvesting the fruits of the surveillance, which turned out to be bountiful. The location was the monitoring room in a Victorian house at 1510 Richmond Road, which the FBI rented for $1,000 a month. It provided for a good vantage point from which to monitor the bug and get a sense of who was visiting the Castellano mansion.

Years later, the two agents recalled in *Boss of Bosses* how they anguished for hours as they waited to see if the bug worked. They needed to pick up any sound to make sure the device had been activated and would do the job. Failure would jeopardize the entire investigation. Their answer came in the form of Nina Castellano, the Don's wife who early that morning was overheard talking to the drowsy dogs, unaware they had been drugged.

"You're sleepy this morning. Don't even want to go outside?" said Nina. "Look at you, so lazy."

As O'Brien and Kurins remembered it, those inconsequential mutterings of the old woman was music to their ears. The bug was up and running. For over four months the device picked up 600 hours of relevant conversations from the mansion. It was another thing Castellano could thank the Bergin crew for, as well as his own neglect of his job as their boss. The bugging and taping would have gone on for longer but at some point in August 1983, it malfunctioned and died, giving back nothing but silence. Still, the material it had provided continued to feed the investigation for many months.

CHAPTER EIGHT

The Junk Crowd

As 1982 CAME TO A CLOSE, Angelo Ruggiero knew that things were getting precarious. The FBI had collected tons of information from the bug in his house. Surveillance teams were all over him and the Bergin club. His mentor and close friend John Gotti may have been running things at the club, but he was proving to be a distracted boss. Gotti was burning through tons of cash with his compulsive gambling, and had problems of his own. Around Christmas time, when Alfred Dellentash, the drug dealer and sometimes aircraft operator, went to visit him in Cedarhurst, Ruggiero walked outside with him and complained about all of the "drug heat" he was feeling.

Dellentash may have been a close friend of Angelo's brother Salvatore but he wasn't above being a bit duplicitous when it came to their drug activities. According to government documents, just before Salvatore died in the May 1982 plane crash, he had given Dellentash and his partner, Wayne Debany, about 1.5 kilos of heroin in a suitcase to hold for safe keeping in return for a fee of $2,500. Debany actually later recalled that he never even opened the suitcase until after Salvatore died and discovered five envelopes filled with the heroin. But instead of turning it over to Angelo, Dellentash and Debany kept the narcotics in Westchester County, turning down an offer of $450,000 for the batch, investigators determined.

The heroin held by Dellentash and Debany had value beyond just what it could get them on the street. In January 1983, both men were in Baton Rouge, Louisiana, to work on a deal for fifty-five kilos of cocaine, or about 120 pounds. The sellers agreed to take $120,000 in collateral and to hold about one kilo of heroin, which had been part of Salvatore Ruggiero's suitcase stash. Once the full payment was made for the cocaine, Dellentash and Debany were to get the heroin back.

The night of January 24, 1983, Dellentash and Debany turned over the heroin and the cash deposit to the sellers and expected to take custody of the cocaine. Instead, both were immediately arrested by Louisiana state troopers—the purported sellers had been under-cover officers. Dellentash and Debany had found themselves in a great deal of trouble, facing decades in a state prison.

To the rescue, sort of, came the federal government and Louisiana officials. The feds already had intelligence and a line on Dellentash through the investigation of the Bergin crew, knew he had been in close contact with Angelo and had a lot of information about the heroin ring. The proposal was simple: help the big investigation in New York and prosecutors would ask the judge to give some con-sideration to Dellentash when he came up for sentencing. So in April 1983, Dellentash entered into an agreement with the Brooklyn Organized Crime Strike Force and their federal counterparts in Louisiana to cooperate, according to government records. As an ini-tial showing of good faith Dellentash told the prosecutors where they could find the additional heroin that had been part of Salvatore Ruggiero's little suitcase stash. Back in Westchester, one of Dellen-tash's relatives took agents to an underground safe where the heroin had been kept.

The heroin taken from the ground in Westchester was tested and found to have been manufactured in Pakistan, as had the heroin seized on Dellentash in the Louisiana arrest. Dellentash was a good catch for the prosecutors. He could provide key information about some meetings that took place at Angelo's homes in Howard Beach and Cedarhurst at times when the bugging device wasn't available. He could list the participants, the essence of their conversations, and if necessary make identifications of voices heard on recordings.

Even with Dellentash and Debany on the side of the government, prosecutors still had a great deal of work to do to make a case against Angelo and to see how close they could get to the Gotti clan, including John Gotti. There were hundreds of hours of tape recordings to analyze and tons of documents to scrutinize to see how well it might all dovetail with what Dellentash and Debany could provide. This was going to be a monster prosecution.

About three months after Dellentash decided to cooperate, Brooklyn prosecutors finally put together a battle plan. In a prosecution memorandum sent to their superiors in Washington, the government attorneys, Laura Brevetti and Norman Bloch, painstakingly sketched out who the potential defendants might be and what charges they could face with the evidence in hand. The prosecutors also had to consider the defenses Angelo and the others might raise, as well as a potential problem presented by a government screw-up in sealing some of the recordings involving Bonanno captain Joseph Massino.

Aside from Angelo, the prosecutors had their eyes on indicting twelve other defendants: Gene Gotti, John Carneglia, attorney Michael Coiro, Joseph Guagliano, Anthony Moscatiello, Oscar Ansourian, Edward Lino, Mark Reiter, William Cestaro, Salvatore Greco, Salvatore Scala, and the Canadian gangster and heroin trafficker Gerlando Sciascia. Conspicuously absent from the group was John Gotti himself.

The indictment being drafted comprised eleven counts, the core of which centered around the narcotics operation. Angelo was to be a central figure in the case, as were Gene Gotti and John Carneglia. The government figured it had enough to charge them with racketeering conspiracy, narcotics conspiracy, and obstruction of justice. The main conspiracy seemed to extend from November 1981, when Angelo was first called before a Manhattan federal grand jury looking into the mob, through August 1983, when he was involved in the Long Island heroin deal.

The activity after Salvatore Ruggiero's death in May 1982, the pressure being put on his in-laws not to cooperate with the government or give false information, would be the basis for the obstruction-of-justice charges. Angelo's payments to ex-cops John Conley and John McNally to find out about sealed court orders on surveillance were to be the basis of the obstruction-of-justice charges, as was the activity of several others to hide Salvatore's assets after his death.

Angelo, Gotti, and Carneglia would likely be charged in all of the counts. But many of the others would face less exposure. For instance, Mark Reiter would only be charged with the heroin trafficking, as would Scala, Sciascia, and some of the others. Michael Coiro would have his fair share of problems in the case, and was to be charged with obstruction of justice through witness intimidation and hiding Salvatore's assets.

The case wasn't without its potential problems. In their battle plan, the prosecutors noted that, as a general rule, FBI agents monitoring the bugs in Angelo's house had a duty to minimize the amount of innocuous or non-pertinent conversations they recorded. Sometimes it was easy to discern what might be relevant—such as when Angelo was talking to his wife Marie or their children about mundane family matters. But other times when Angelo was talking about things in a cryptic way it was more difficult for the agency to decide. Sometimes, to err on the side of caution, agents didn't listen to some conversations that may have actually been relevant because they couldn't identify those talking. But in the end, the prosecutors thought that the issue of minimization was in their favor.

Another problem arose from Coiro's status as an attorney for Ruggiero. Normally, attorney conversations with a client were off limits on surveillance if they were about legal issues and representation, as well as spoken in *confidence*. But Coiro sometimes spoke with Ruggiero in the presence of others, including Salvatore's in-laws, and in those case their talks weren't protected by the privilege. A critical conversation in which Ruggiero, in the presence of others, told Coiro "You are one of us" was not only outside the privilege but pretty damning. Another problem for Coiro was that his conversations, particularly about hiding Salvatore's assets, involved criminal conduct and were also not protected. With so many taped conversations of Coiro about committing crimes, it seemed to the prosecutors that they could use them against him with impunity.

There was another issue about the tapes that was more serious for the prosecution and that could lead to some problems. Surveillance tapes have to be sealed and if there is any delay in doing that after the recordings end, the courts sometimes bar prosecutors from using them. As far as Angelo's tapes were concerned, there was one troubling forty-two-day delay in sealing some of the recordings and that the prosecutors readily acknowledged could lead to some of the tapes being suppressed by the court. But even if that were so, those tapes were found to mostly relate to Ruggiero talking with the then-fugitive Joseph Massino and weren't seen as crucial.

For prosecutors, witnesses like Alfred Dellentash, Wayne Debany, and others had their own particular baggage in that they readily admitted committing crimes and their motives for cooperating with the government might be viewed with suspicion by a jury. Salvatore Ruggiero's in-laws might also be uncooperative on the witness stand. But prosecutors believed their recalcitrance would be attributed by the jurors to their fear of Angelo. However, there were some pretty good tape recordings that could be used to work around those problems. Prosecutors expressed confidence.

"Simply put, the tape recordings alone make this a good case," the prosecution team said in its memo to Washington. "The tape recordings plus the testimony of the civilian witnesses make this a powerful and conclusive case."

The prosecution memo was dated July 8, 1983. If arrests were authorized, any subsequent trial was expected to take about six weeks. Shortly thereafter, the indictment plan was approved. For the Gotti Boys, the future was going to become unsettled very quickly. For the New York Mafia, things were going to get even worse.

The Bergin crew was bracing for some kind of indictment. Nobody knew exactly what would be in the charges, but Angelo is said to have acted nonplussed, reportedly spending $40,000 to renovate the Cedarhurst house and scoffing at the notion of an indictment. John Gotti was sweating because he knew he had been the object of surveillance as well. Lawyer Michael Coiro, for whom an indictment would be a tremendous fall from grace, was said to be drinking more than usual.

The suspense finally lifted on August 23, 1983. Teams of FBI agents fanned out around New York and Long Island and arrested eight people at their homes: Angelo Ruggiero, Michael Coiro, Gene Gotti, John Carneglia, Joseph Guagliano, Anthony Moscatiello, Mark Reiter, Salvatore Scala. A total of thirteen people were actually charged but five—Edward Lino, Gerlando Sciascia, William Robert Cestaro, Oscar Ansourian, and Salvatore Greco—weren't found by the agents and were considered fugitives. They would all eventually be arrested.

The group was charged under a federal criminal complaint, a prelude to a later indictment—and accused of smuggling hundreds of pounds of 98 percent pure heroin from Southeast Asia. In court, assistant U.S. Attorney Norman Bloch said the crew purchased its heroin from wholesalers in Florida for $150,000 a kilo and sold back in New York on the wholesale market for $200,000. Bloch told federal magistrate Shira Scheindlin that the FBI made the case through hundreds of hours of conversations picked up on bugs in Angelo's house in Cedarhurst.

"This is the beginning and not the end of what the government plans to prove," Bloch told Scheindlin.

The FBI was a bit coy in tying the case to organized crime. Thomas Sheer, the special agent in charge of the FBI office in New York, said the men were part of a number of Mafia families but didn't identify which. But anybody plugged into the intelligence networks knew that the Gambino and Bonanno families were among those targeted.

As soon as the arrests went down, Castellano and Gotti knew they had problems, although for different reasons. Castellano now realized that the autonomy he had given Dellacroce to supervise the Bergin crew had been a strategic mistake. Despite the drug ban, Gotti's crew had become major suspects in a massive heroin operation. As boss of the crime family, Castellano knew that he was at risk for being ensnared in the case if it could be shown that any of the money Dellacroce and Gotti's crew kicked up to him had come from narcotics, something that would make him part of the charged conspiracy. In Gotti's case, the charges showed that either he knew what was going on or that he was a crew leader who couldn't follow

Castellano's edict against drugs. Either way, Gotti was to be viewed with suspicion by Castellano who could if he wanted to summarily break up the Bergin crew or have some of them killed.

"John Gotti is on the carpet with Big Paul Castellano over the drug bust," one FBI agent wrote in a report after debriefing informant Willie Boy Johnson. "Paul feels that either John was involved himself, and if he was not, then he should have known his crew was involved and therefore cannot control his crew."

Gotti was called to meet Castellano at the Don's house on Staten Island and told by the boss, "Look, Johnny, you better prove that you weren't involved." Castellano also wanted to get copies of the tapes that were the basis for the indictment. If he didn't, then something would happen to Ruggiero, and Gotti might be removed as captain of the Bergin crew and assigned someplace else.

But in the Fall of 1983, the nuclear options were still in the distance. Gotti still had Dellacroce as his mentor and protector, an elder statesman who could hold Castellano at bay and convince him not to do anything to hurt Gotti or his men. At least that would be the way things could remain for a while, until the prosecution turned over tape-recorded evidence and Castellano could learn the truth about the drug dealing. In the meantime, things remained peaceful as well as tense. Ruggiero, Gene Gotti, John Carneglia, and the other defendants—at least the ones who weren't fugitives—posted bail and were able to get out of jail. In Angelo's case, he had to post a $1 million bond, secured by real estate and other assets. When the defendants first appeared at their arraignments, they all entered pleas of not guilty. Johnson also noted that Angelo tried to spin the story that he was merely trying to close out his dead brother's previous dealings with drugs. They denied the charges, and that at least gave them some breathing room with Castellano.

As DEA official Jim Hunt remembered, the cover story about Ruggiero closing out Salvatore's interests was the one used to convince Castellano that drug dealing wasn't a major operation of the Bergin crew.

"There was a lot of money on the street owed to Sal," remembered Hunt. "That was the argument . . . that Gotti said he [Ruggiero] was just, he wasn't a drug dealer, he just was trying to get money for Salvatore's kids . . . total bullshit."

The big bust was not the first indication that the Gotti crew drug dealings had publically surfaced, and if Castellano had his antenna tuned, he would have seen trouble indications as far back as April 1983. It was then that Reiter was charged with a separate heroin distribution conspiracy, this time with a successor to the infamous Nicky Barnes in Harlem. Until he was busted in the late 1970s, Barnes was the main heroin supplier in Harlem and had amassed a great deal of clout and money. In the Reiter indictment, the evidence was circumstantial but the indictment charged that Reiter conspired from January 1980 through April 1983 with a small group that included Thelma Grant, who at one time had been a girlfriend of Barnes and was suspected of taking over his operation when he went to prison in 1977. As it turned out, the government believed that old Herbert Sperling, who had been arrested with Sal Ruggiero back in the 1970s, had been doing time in prison with Barnes in Marion, Illinois, and made a crucial connection in the case. Sperling, investigators said, arranged through Barnes for Reiter and another man to supply heroin to the enterprising Grant, an attractive sex pot who, according to Barnes, would service him sexually in prison during visits.

Barnes, fed up with prison life and the prospect of dying behind bars, decided to become a cooperating witness for the government while he was arranging for Grant to meet with Reiter's cohorts on heroin deals He was also angered by the way Grant had stolen his money stash and how his fellow drug lords on the Harlem-based council kept sleeping with his old girlfriends, including Grant. Barnes turned on Grant and everyone else in the case. Since the evidence was pretty solid against Grant, she decided to plead guilty to the entire nine-count indictment. She also agreed to testify for the government in the case against Reiter. But while prosecutors believed Reiter had been the supplier of heroin for several sales to an undercover agent, Grant denied that Reiter had been part of her drug conspiracy, despite having met him in a restaurant. Grant had told an undercover agent cryptically that her source of heroin was "a

Jew" and "an Italian," which investigators believed was a veiled reference to Reiter and his friend Salvatore Corallo. But the judge
hearing the case entered a judgement of acquittal for Reiter.

With various bail packages, or in the case of Reiter a favorable
court ruling, most of the Bergin crew and their associates indicted
on the heroin case were out on the street. But the world had defi-
nitely changed for them. The indictment was serious enough, but for
Angelo and John Gotti there was the added pressure of Castellano.
After the drug charges, Castellano's suspicion ramped up. Then,
when he learned of the tapes made by the FBI bug, Castellano demanded that they be turned over to him as soon as Ruggiero's
lawyers got them in preparation for trial. Ruggiero had been indiscreet in talking about Mafia business with non-members, including
the bad mouthing of Castellano, who frankly wasn't liked by many
people in the crime family. But apart from embarrassment, the tapes
were damning evidence of Ruggiero's guilt in the drug conspiracy,
and if Castellano got his hands on the tapes he could easily order
Ruggiero—and possibly John Gotti—killed.

Castellano constantly badgered Aniello Dellacroce, his underboss and the man who had oversight over the Bergin crew, to get the
tapes. Castellano said he needed them for his own defense in the
stolen-car case and really didn't care about any indiscreet or embarrassing remarks Ruggiero may have made. Dellacroce was feeling
the pressure and did the best he could to delay and fend off Castellano but his frustration showed in one taped conversation with Ruggiero.

"I have been trying to make you get away with these tapes," said
Dellacroce, "but Jesus Christ, Almighty I can't stop the guy from always bringing it up. Unless, I un' un' unless I tell the guy [Castel-
lano] 'Hey, why don't you go fuck yourself and stop bringin' these
tapes, tapes up,' then you know, what we are gotta do then, we, we
go and roll it up and go to war."

"I don't want that," said Angelo. "No, I don't want that, no, I
don't want that."

Dellacroce tried to get Angelo to see that a fatal conflict with
Castellano was the absolute last step but that everybody should take

a deep breath and "take it easy." But there was always the chance that things could get bloody if the issue of the tapes continued to fester. Dellacroce also seemed to indicate that Angelo was being too self-absorbed and selfish.

"I ain't saying you're wrong," said Dellacroce. "Don't forget. Don't only consider yourself. You know, you got a lot of other fel— you know fellas too, that you like. And a lot of other fellas'll get hurt too. Not only you could get hurt, I could get hurt, he could get hurt. A, a lot of other fellas, could, could, could get hurt. For what? For what? Over, over because you don't want to show him the tapes?"

It was unlikely that Dellacroce knew the full contents of the tapes, which Angelo had only alluded to as being embarrassing. But there was an added complication looming. Castellano himself had been the object of a bug in his own house and while he was still months away from learning about that, once he did, his anger against Ruggiero—as well as Dellacroce and Gotti for their lack of candor and control over the talkative mobster—would rise to an unprecedented level.

CHAPTER NINE
"I Ain't Givin' Them Tapes Up"

PAUL CASTELLANO BEGAN TO LEARN just how badly he had been served by Angelo Ruggiero and the rest of the Bergin crew when on February 25, 1985, FBI agents Joe O'Brien and Andris Kurins arrested him at the Todt Hill White House in a gigantic case involving him and the other bosses who made up the Commission. The indictment was aimed at the ruling body of the New York Mafia. Charged along with Castellano: Anthony "Fat Tony" Salerno, the street boss of the Genovese family; Anthony "Tony Ducks" Corallo, boss of the Lucchese family; Carmine "The Snake" Persico who headed the Colombo family. The Bonanno family boss Philip Rastelli was the fifth Commission member but he was not indicted on some of the charges as the FBI had learned that the Bonanno group had not been sitting on the ruling panel because of past drug involvement and its previous infiltration by undercover FBI agent Joseph Pistone.

The idea of roping Castellano and the other bosses into one racketeering indictment had come from then-Manhattan U.S. Attorney Rudolph Giuliani after he read Joseph Bonanno's book *Man of Honor,* published in 1983. In it, Bonanno described the operation of the Commission, and Giuliani saw the body essentially as one big racketeering conspiracy. One particular focus of the case had been the Mafia families involvement in the so-called Concrete Club, a cartel that lorded over the ready-mix concrete industry in New York.

The crime families required that all concrete jobs over $2 million be handled through the club, which divvied up the contracts in return for a two-dollar-per-cubic-yard fee that went to the bosses of the crime families.

It turned out that the FBI learned about the operation of the club in part through the bug in Castellano's house where he often talked about the payments. Of course, when Castellano was first arrested by O'Brien and Kurins he didn't know that his own words had caused so much trouble. The two agents showed up at 177 Benedict Road, and after knocking on the door told Castellano he was being arrested for racketeering. It was actually the second federal indictment against him in the last year: Castellano had been charged in 1984 for being part of the DeMeo stolen-car racket. Leading the agents into the house, Castellano took them to the kitchen where his maid and mistress Gloria Olarte was preparing a roast beef dinner. Castellano's daughter Connie was there with her husband. Castellano's personal physician was also there for dinner. Castellano asked if he could change into a suit and O'Brien and Kurins consented. The Mafia boss returned after a short interval dressed in a double-breasted blue suit and kissed his family good-bye. Both his wife Nina and Gloria began to cry and at that Castellano decided to leave with the agents in the government car. Kurins drove and O'Brien sat in the back with Castellano for the ride. For security another FBI car drove in front. Although the agents could have handcuffed Castellano for the ride they didn't, something he appreciated.

Just before Castellano left his home, his doctor gave him a shot of insulin and gave the packet of syringes and the medication to O'Brien and Kurins. It was unclear when Castellano might be freed on bail so he needed the insulin with him. Once in the car, possibly because his blood sugar was running low from not having eaten, Castellano told the agents he felt a bit ill and asked them to get him something to eat. As recounted in *Boss of Bosses*, O'Brien knew of the diabetes condition and told the driver of the car to stop by a deli so they could get some chocolate bars. The driver at first refused: he had orders to drive Castellano straight to Manhattan where his arrest would be processed. But pulling his weight as the case agent, O'Brien insisted they stop and some candy bars were purchased and given to a grateful Castellano.

As they continued on the drive, Kurins and O'Brien didn't say a word at first about the bugging to Castellano. But as the two agents later recalled, Castellano heard about it over the car radio and the shock of the news prompted him to lean forward to listen more intently to the news bulletin. Castellano was troubled enough by the realization that the bug had picked him up discussing criminal conduct and insulting some of his colleagues, particularly the Bergin crew. But he was also concerned that the microphone had recorded his sexual escapades with Gloria. O'Brien tried to reassure Castellano that the government didn't listen to personal stuff, although it would later surface very explicitly in the agents' book published in 1992. Castellano wasn't persuaded by their assurance that they didn't listen to the salacious things he and Gloria did and as it turned out he would be right.

Actually, news that the government had taped Castellano, as well as some of the other bosses, had been revealed in *The New York Times* about a week before the arrest. Citing law enforcement officials, the newspaper said that conversations picked up by various bugs provided criticial evidence "that may result in the joint indictments of the reputed leaders of New York City's five major organized-crime families." State investigators with the Organized Crime Task Force had bugged the black Jaguar of Corallo and, as one official said, discovered evidence that rivaled anything he had heard in the past two decades. The article also referenced Castellano, saying evidence had also been obtained from electronic eavesdropping by the FBI of his home on Staten Island.

When the car with Castellano reached Manhattan, O'Brien saw the crowd of reporters and photographers around the federal building opposite the courthouse at Foley Square. It was a mob scene, of sorts, and O'Brien wanted to avoid subjecting Castellano to a press crush. To do that, O'Brien ordered the driver to go around the block and park on a grassy area by the federal building, away from the crowd. With Castellano in hand, the agents took him into the building for processing before he was taken to the courthouse.

At his arraignment the next day in Manhattan federal court, Castellano was represented by his longtime attorney James La Rossa. With the help of his family, Castellano put together a bail package of $2 million, which was on top of the $2 million he had posted in the car-theft case. It was a great deal of money to put up, although Castellano did have the property to secure the bond.

Once back home, Castellano had much to think about and much of it wasn't good. He now faced two major federal indictments. The DeMeo stolen-car ring case was put together with the help of informants and cooperating witnesses; Castellano's own greed had made him a target there. The Commission case was constructed in large measure from the bug in his house and Castellano soon learned that it was the Ruggiero tapes that had given the government the probable cause to wire-up his manse in Todt Hill. Everything traced back to the loud mouth Ruggiero and to some extent his street boss and good friend, John Gotti.

Castellano had prided himself on being discreet and careful in his telephone conversations, so the fact that his mansion, with all its security devices and the two Dobermans, was invaded by the FBI stunned him. He went on a remodeling rampage, replacing his entire kitchen, its equipment, and the dinette area. The bugging device, by that time long deactivated, was never found.

There seemed to be other problems looming for Castellano. Succession is something smart Mafia bosses always contemplated, and in Castellano's case the flurry of indictments that began in 1983 made him wonder where he could turn. Complicating things further was the fact that his aging underboss Dellacroce was steadily losing his battle with cancer, so it was doubtful that he could reliably assume command of anything if Castellano himself was convicted in any of the federal cases arrayed against him.

There was also the suspicion that Dellacroce was, like his Bergin crew, somehow dabbling in drugs through some New Jersey members of the Gambino family.

Despite his illness, Dellacroce remained a target for the federal government, and in March 1985, just a month after Castellano had been arrested on the Commission case, he was charged in *United States of American v. Aniello Dellacroce, et al.* The case was aimed at the Bergin crew, including John Gotti, Anthony Rampino, and Willie Boy Johnson. It was a contentious prosecution. The probe had been led by an earnest, if not stubborn, assistant U.S. Attorney named Diane Giacalone who was working the Brooklyn U.S. Attorney's Office. FBI agents like Joe O'Brien and his supervisor Bruce Mouw saw that Giacalone's prosecution was riddled with problems. The evidence just wasn't there, and other federal officials believed it was doomed to failure. One federal prosecutor in Brooklyn, Edward McDonald, who worked with the Organized Crime Strike Force, believed that if Giacalone's case faltered that the Bergin crew might be protected, based on principles of double jeopardy, from ever being indicted again federally.

Giacalone, a thin, tall, dark-haired woman of Italian ethnicity, was backed by her immediate superiors and persisted in pushing the case. Since the FBI was not backing her, Giacalone didn't have the benefit of the Ruggiero tapes. There were more problems looming. At the arraignment on the case Giacalone told the presiding judge, Eugene Nickerson, that Johnson had been an informant for the FBI for over fifteen years. The news was devastating. It almost seemed that Giacalone was willing to sacrifice Johnson to the mob. Not only was Johnson now outed to the mob as an informant, his utility to the FBI was thrown away. Since he didn't want to go into the witness protection program, Nickerson said he had to deny Johnson bail for his protection.

Dellacroce, getting progressively weaker, was arraigned at his bedside. Unknown to Nickerson and Giacalone, Dellacroce's home had already been bugged by the FBI. But to avoid potential problems, the FBI turned off the device for the arraignment. On June 8, 1985, Dellacroce held court at his home with Ruggiero and John Gotti to rehash the tape issue. Castellano kept pestering Dellacroce for transcripts of the Ruggiero house bug. Ruggiero was adamant about not turning them over.

"If you two never bother with me again . . . I ain't givin' them tapes up. I can't," said Angelo.

Dellacroce and Gotti tried to browbeat Angelo into turning the material over to Castellano.

"While he's the Boss, you have to do what he tell you," said Gotti.

But Angelo was not going to turn over the tapes since he knew it spelled the end for him if he did. The tapes were filled with drug trafficking evidence, and Castellano would have been justified in killing Ruggiero, and possibly Gotti.

A blood bath was a distinct possibility. It was later revealed, that by mid-1985, John Gotti, his brother Gene, as well as Angelo and John Carneglia were getting information that Castellano was thinking of cleaning house and having them killed. The source of that tidbit for the FBI was Willie Boy Johnson, who was feeding information to both the Feds and the Queens District Attorney's Office. The atmosphere for the Gambino borgata was indeed poisonious.

Aware that he might be convicted in either of the two major federal cases and sent to prison, Castellano held a conclave at his home with Gotti in June 1985 to lay out his plan for the future. For a peaceful transition, Castellano hoped, after Dellacroce died. Although there was no bug in Castellano's house at that point, other surveillance evidence surfaced in which Gotti was heard saying that the boss proposed a three-part ruling committee with day-to-day control of family split between Tommy Gambino, Gotti, and Tommy Bilotti. Three-man committees would be proposed later in the mob but as author John H. Davis observed, the situation was an organizational disaster waiting to happen for the Gambino family.

"It was an unrealistic solution," said Davis. "Although Gotti got along well enough with Tommy Gambino, he detested the impetu-

ous Tommy Bilotti, whom he once referred to as a 'fuckin lug-
headed scumbag.'"

Another Gambino gangster, Sammy the Bull Gravano, had his
own insights into Castellano's mind. Gravano, a beefy killer born in
Brooklyn who was initially part of the Castellano faction, believed
that the boss would shake things up when Dellacroce died. John
Gotti had a lot at stake in what could happen.

"I think John did give a fuck when Neil [Dellacroce] died, which
we all knew would happen sooner or later," Gravano remembered
later in conversations with writer Peter Maas for *Underboss*. "He is
going to break John down to a soldier, stick him somewhere in a
crew, maybe under Joe Butch [Corrao] . . . Without even being dead,
he is finished."

While Castellano's plans for succession involved Gotti, the
leader of the Bergin crew had actually become more powerful now
that Dellacroce was edging closer to death. Infirm and unable to
make his rounds to visit other mobsters, Dellacroce couldn't make
his way to visit his favorite club, the Ravenite at 247 Mulberry
Street. In his younger days, Dellacroce lorded over the club and if
he was having a bad afternoon would sometimes be seen by surveillance cops kicking the German shepherd that liked to sleep on the
steps. The Ravenite—the origin of its name was uncertain—was
one of those Little Italy storefronts with a large glass window at the
front. Inside were card tables, a couch, a soda vending machine and
espresso machines. Nothing fancy here. The old-time gangsters
loved hanging out there, and local people had a habit of spotting police and FBI surveillance vans.

With Dellacroce bedridden, Gotti began using the Ravenite as his
de facto Manhattan headquarters, doing the bidding of his underboss and acting as the Gambino family's big shot in Manhattan.
This was a time of uncertainty in the borgata. Castellano, facing two
major indictments and an imminent trial in one of them—the stolen-
car case—had to hunker down with his lawyers. Already a distant
boss who stayed aloof from his blue-collar crews, Castellano became

increasingly cut off from things. He apparently even stopped press-
ing the ill Dellacroce for the Ruggiero tapes—he had his own tapes
to worry about. But he also remained hungry for money, something
that continued to be a source of irritation among his own men and
some of the other Mafia bosses. Even Dellacroce had complained
about the avaricious ways of bosses like Castellano, once telling
Ruggiero about the way the ruling Commission during a meeting
over the construction industry could talk about nothing but "Money,
Money, Money."

As 1985 ground on, Castellano went on trial in the stolen-car-
ring case. The mob operation was believed to have shipped hundreds of cars to places like Kuwait for a profit of about $3,000 on
every vehicle. Castellano's cut was said to be $20,000 in a wad of
bills delivered to his house on Todt Hill each week. The list of the
other charges was ugly. Prosecutors alleged that the ring, run by the
now dead, homicidal Roy DeMeo, had committed up to twenty-five
murders. There was no direct claim that Castellano took part in the
killings. But as a charged member of the conspiracy, Castellano
could be found liable for the killings.

While his defense attorney believed he had a shot at getting an
acquittal—there was little evidence that Castellano was actively on
the scene of the auto-theft ring—that didn't prevent his name from
coming up. On November 4, 1985, in Manhattan federal court, Vito
Arena, a forty-three-year-old gangster who was serving an eighteen-
year prison term for murder and car theft, testified that he had been
reliably told a number of times that Castellano was the boss of the operation. Then, there was testimony about Castellano getting the cash
hauls once a week as his cut of the proceeds. True, the witnesses had
their own baggage and problems of credibility. But if Castellano
wanted to preserve any image he might have of being just a successful businessman, the testimony stripped away that veneer.

The witness who seemed to do the most to portray Castellano as
a mobster was another man not yet forty years old. Dominick Montiglio, thirty-seven, was the nephew of Anthony "Nino" Gaggi, one

of Castellano's key captains and one of the co-defendants on trial in the case. Testifying for the government, Montiglio recalled that on one occasion when he was acting as a collector for his uncle that he delivered a wad of $100 bills to Castellano at his meat market. Castellano, said Montiglio, was often portrayed as the boss and leader of "our organization." Yet Castellano had qualms about the brutal way DeMeo and some of the other killers did business, knocking off rivals.

Castellano's squeamishness was portrayed in a conversation Montiglio said he overhead between Gaggi and the crime boss discussing the murder of rival car thief John Quinn and his girlfriend Cheri Golden. Both were killed in 1977, and Castellano seemed upset that the woman was murdered and her body found stuffed under the dashboard of an abandoned Lincoln Continental on a street in Coney Island.

"Mr. Castellano asked my uncle why this girl Cherie was killed," recalled Montiglio. "My uncle told him she was part of the operation of Quinn and something about him going to the law and he had to be taken care of."

But like any government witness who abandons the life of crime in the hopes of getting a break, Montigilio had issues that later started to raise questions about his candor and credibility. For instance, it came out that he had waited almost two years, about till the eve of the trial, to tell investigators that Castellano was involved with the car-theft ring. To make matters worse, Montigilio admitted lying to the grand jury when he denied knowing details that would have tied Castellano to the ring. Montigilio also admitted having committed perjury two years earlier.

The questions about Montiglio came after other witnesses had created problems. Some failed to identify or misidentified defendants as being part of the auto ring. Another called a different government witness a liar. These were things that happened in complicated federal "mega trials" as these big courtroom spectacles were known. But the impact on some trial observers was that the government was having a hard time.

The morning of December 15, the headline on *The New York Times* story about Castellano's trial would no doubt have gratified him and his lawyer James LaRossa. *"Another Setback for Prosecution in Case Against Gambino Group,"* blared the headline. If you were one of the defendants, it was not a bad way to start the day.

CHAPTER TEN
"I'm Going to Blow This Motherfucker Away"

ANIELLO DELLACROCE DIDN'T NOTICE the December 15 *Times* head-line on the Castellano story for the simple reason he was not around to see it. Having checked in under an assumed name into Mary Immaculate Hospital in Queens, in late November, Dellacroce died on December 2, 1985, at the age of seventy-one. The cause was cancer. As if to foreshadow what was to come, Dellacroce's obituary in *The New York Times* mentioned his "uneasy relationship with Mr. Castellano."

Dellacroce, while alive, was the restraining hand who kept the Gambino family factions from tearing each other apart. The Bergin crew led by Gotti despised Castellano and felt threatened by him, particularly when the Ruggiero drug indictment hit. Yet, it was old-timer Dellacroce who told Gotti's people to hew the line, respect the boss, and not try any war-like moves. Although Dellacroce stalled when Castellano asked for the Ruggiero tapes, eventually the boss's attorneys got their copies in the course of normal pretrial discovery. What Castellano heard and saw of the tapes angered him to no end. Ruggiero had not only bad-mouthed him but had discussed Mafia Commission meetings with a non-member. Then there was the clear evidence that heroin trafficking had been the life blood for the Bergin crew, done more or less openly and involving numerous family members and associates.

The hate for Castellano among Gotti and his crew had been simmering for many months, and the FBI had picked up on it almost immediately, thanks to the various electronic bugging devices it had planted around town. One was inside the Casa Storta in Brooklyn where on January 26, 1983, a table bug picked up Ruggiero meeting with the acting boss of the Colombo family, Gennaro "Gerry Lang" Langella and a capo Dominick Montemarano. It became clear, in a dispute over a $50,000 construction-industry payoff, that Castellano had denied the Colombo group.

Ruggiero blurted out, "I think Paul's looking to whack Neil," referring to Dellacroce. Ruggiero said he even told Dellacroce, "Why don't you just do it and forget about it? Go in and fucking smoke him."

"What did I tell Donnie," piped up Langella to Montemarano. "After the holidays, what would happen . . . that Neil and Johnny Gotti will die."

Ruggiero commiserated that the situation within the family and Castellano's avarice was dragging things down.

"He ain't gonna get away with it no more," Langella said. "I tell you, Ange, somebody's gonna . . ."

"I know," replied Ruggiero. "Believe me. Gerry, I know."

Robert DiBernardo was one of those gangsters who had clout in the Gambino family not because he was a killer but because he brought in money. Initially considered a member of the DeCavalcante crime family in New Jersey, DiBernardo was an earner and did so through his holdings in the pornography industry, particularly around Times Square peep shows. When needed, DiBenardo traveled to California to do deals with porn merchants there. He brought in money, lots of it, and as a result wasn't expected to do work: commit murders. His home in Hewlett Harbor on Long Island was not far from Ruggiero's in Cedarhurst.

It was late in September 1985 that DiBernardo, after talking with Ruggiero, conveyed a message to Sammy Gravano. For years Gravano had been a mainstay of the Gambino family's construction rackets and so aligned with Castellano. Everyone knew that. What wasn't so clear was his allegiance to the boss. DiBernardo's message to Gravano was a request, nicely put, asking if he could visit Ruggiero and John Gotti in their home turf of Queens.

As Gravano remembered things, he went. There was no good reason not to go. But as it turned out only Ruggiero showed up. Both men talked. Ruggiero was the one to broach a very sensitive subject, one that could earn him his own death if it ever leaked to the wrong people.

"Sammy, we're gonna make a move," said Ruggiero, according to Gravano in *Underboss*. "I'm making a move on Paul. Are you with me? . . . I am gonna blow this motherfucker away."

Gravano would later recall that he sat quietly, letting Ruggiero speak and make his pitch. Since Gravano would later cooperate with the FBI, his rendition of events in this crucial period in the Gambino family is the best—and only—version of what happened since the other key participants are mostly dead or just never talked. As Gravano remembered things, Ruggiero told him Gotti was with him on the murder plot and that the conspirators were going to try and pull in another key captain, Frank DeCicco.

"Angie, I'm not going to tell you what my position is," Gravano said to Ruggiero, as related to writer Peter Maas. "But I'll tell you what I'm going to do. I'm getting in my car and going to see Frankie myself and tell him about this meeting we're having now. You got any problem with that?"

Ruggiero said it was okay for Gravano to reach out to DeCicco, telling Gravano that he needed both of them as part of the plot or, as he put it, "I'm dead without you."

At DeCicco's house both Gravano and he took a walk to toss around the idea of killing Castellano. It was something, Maas later wrote, that was almost unheard of since Vito Genovese tried to kill Frank Costello in 1957. Hits of a Mafia boss just didn't happen without the sanction of the other families.

During their three hour discussion, which took place in DeCicco's backyard, he and Gravano talked about the pros and cons of killing

Castellano. One option, said Gravano, was to just sit things out and let the Gotti faction fight it out with the Castellano group. But in the end, both men agreed that they would be part of it, assuming the Gotti group had its act together.

"' Neil's not long for this world,'" DeCicco said, according to Gravano, referring to the underboss's terminal illness. "Paul may go up [get convicted] on these cases he has."

Castellano's succession plan included having Thomas Gambino as boss and Tommy Bilotti as underboss. The prospect of those men in leadership appalled Gravano and DeCicco. While an intelligent garment center trucking businessman, Gambino was derisively considered nothing but a "dress maker" and Bilotti an abusive mob hot head. The better option, it seemed, was to remove Castellano by force and have Gotti take over, with DeCicco in the wings if Gotti screwed up and had to be killed. Both DeCicco and Gravano were prepared to get rid of Gotti if he showed he wasn't up to leading the crime family.

The next day, according to Gravano's published account, he and DeCicco summoned Ruggiero to come to Brooklyn where they told him, "We are with you." But they demanded that Gotti come down to the next series of meetings. They didn't want the Bergin crew leader to act like a prima donna and told Ruggiero that if Gotti didn't show, their offer to be part of the murder plot would be withdrawn.

Anxious not to lose key allies, Gotti showed up at the follow-up meeting in Brooklyn off the Shore Parkway with Gravano, DeCicco, Ruggiero, and DiBernardo, who was really there to be a messenger. The discussion then centered on making alliances with the older mobsters in the family, the respected people like Joe M. Gallo, the consiglieri, and Joe "Piney" Armone, a captain who held sway with the restaurant workers union. Both men were Castellano allies, so the plotters had to be careful in approaching them.

Known as "shorty"—he was five feet, five inches tall and 140 pounds—Armone was a drug trafficker himself with a federal record for narcotics, so in one sense he had a common interest with

Ruggiero. His older brother Stephen also had a narcotics conviction. He had no known job or occupation and aside from Little Italy, Armone hung out in the area of East 14th Street in Manhattan and over the years had become very respected in the family. His backing of the plotters was seen as crucial to winning over the other seasoned gangsters in the borgata. Gotti had indicated that Armone would back the plan. Gravano needed proof.

In trying to keep the planning clandestine, Gravano said he, De-Cicco, Gotti, and Ruggiero arranged a meeting with Armone in the basement of the Staten island home of Joe Watts. Long a fixture in the Gambino family, Watts was known as "The German" but couldn't become a member of the mob because his father was believed to be Welsh. He sometimes used the alias "Joe Russo." How he got to be called The German is unclear, but it didn't matter because he had earned a great deal of respect in the underworld.

Watts seemed to earn his respect because he had no qualms about violence. According to court papers filed years later in federal court, Watts allegedly had connections to numerous Gambino family homicides over the years going back to the late 1970s. It was then, according to prosecutors, that Watts lured one Anthony Miano, suspected of taking part in the kidnapping and death of a nephew of Carlo Gambino, to the Watts home on Staten Island under the ruse that he had some tires to give the victim. When Miano arrived and drove his truck into the driveway, Watts shot and killed him, according to prosecutors. (Watts was never charged with the homicide.)

Other murders laid at the feet of Watts took place in the early 1980s. In one case, that of the slaying of Nicolina and Michael Lizak for the killing of Gambino soldier Robert Russo, Castellano personally gave Watts the assignment for the homicides, prosecutors alleged. It was in early March 1982 that Watts and other Gambino family associates tortured and killed the couple in a Staten Island social club, said prosecutors, adding that the bodies were never found. In 1984, John Cennamo was found hanging from a tree in Queens and while it seemed like a case of suicide, investigators later alleged that Watts, Ruggiero, and Willie Boy Johnson carried out the murder on the orders of John Gotti. (Watts was also never charged with those killings.)

In another homicide which investigators tried to put on Watts was that of William Ciccone, who made the mistake in April 1987 of firing several shots at Gotti outside the Bergin club. According to federal prosecutors in later court filings, Watts took Ciccone to another location where he was tortured in an effort to get him to give up others involved in the plot against Gotti. Ciccone said he acted alone at which point he was killed by Watts and others, with his body being taken to the basement of a Staten Island candy store, prosecutors alleged. While investigating a burglary report, cops discovered Ciccone's body and Watts was arrested on state murder charges in the case but ultimately acquitted.

Watts was a man the Bergin crew had trusted, and his home seemed a proper place to meet in secret with Armone. For added security, the plotters asked Watts, who was still just an associate, to leave the house for a while. As Gravano remembered things, he and DeCicco in particular wanted to hear from Armone himself how he supported the plot. At one point, Gotti started to answer for Armone. But DeCicco cut him short and said, "Please, John let me do the talking now," remembered Gravano.

Armone told the group that consiglieri Joe N. Gallo wasn't on board with the plot but wouldn't do anything to oppose it. He would stay on the sidelines. DeCicco questioned Armone about whether Gallo would tip off Castellano to the conspiracy, and the aging capo answered with ice in his veins. "If he betrays us, or backs up one inch, I will kill him," recalled Gravano.

The great irony in Armone's position was that he was plotting the death of his boss, a man he once waxed philosophically with about the way the mob life could be so rewarding, if one survived, words all caught by the FBI bug in Castellano's house.

"This life of ours, this is a wonderful life," Castellano said to Armone. "If you can get through life like this and get away with it, hey, that's great. But it's very, very unpredictable There are so many ways you can screw it up."

"Yeah, Paul, you're right," replied Armone.

"Because there's just so many fucking things that can blow up on you," Castellano continued.

"Yeah, Paul, there are," Armone agreed.

"There's so many fucking ways they can get to you," said Castellano, probably referring to the FBI.

CHAPTER ELEVEN
"Fuckin' John's Crazy"

IN THE YEARS BEFORE CASTELLANO, GOTTI, AND GRAVANO were even born, life among the Italian organized crime figures was sketchy in terms of longevity. In the very early part of the twentieth century in New York City, cops were perplexed by the barrel murders. Italian criminals didn't have highly organized groups at the time, but they were noticed by cops because of the way they killed their victims with multiple stab wounds and then stuffed them in wine barrels. Even if you had clout on the street, an Italian criminal was an easy target for assassination by rivals, no questions asked.

During the early days of Prohibition, bootleggers who were largely Italians, warred with each other over territory, and bodies littered the landscape. No matter how important a criminal might be in the Italian gang landscape, he could be fair game. Death among the Italians seemed always around the corner for those who weren't vigilant. Frankie Yale, a powerful mobster in Brooklyn who controlled numerous rackets, was machine-gunned to death in July 1928 as he franatically tried to drive away from his pursuers. His death was attributed to Al Capone's anger over a stolen load of booze. Michael Abbatemarco took over for Yale and was himself slain as he sat in a car just three months later.

But in 1931, after the Castellammarese War in New York led to the killing of old boss Joseph Masseria and then later Salvatore Maranzano, those who helped engineer their assassinations set up a structure for the American Mafia keystoned by the formation of the ruling Commission. The chief architect was Charles "Lucky" Luciano, who for a variety of reasons believed everyone should cooperate in some kind of structured setting as a way of avoiding unnecessary bloodshed and making sure the spoils of crime were protected. Among the various duties of the Commission was to decide policy for the Mafia families—in this case five families in New York City—and where necessary, decree the fate of a boss who may have made some transgression. No longer could family bosses be summarily executed without an okay from the powers of La Cosa Nostra. That rule also applied to the settling of other disputes. The Commission was set in place to try and defuse potentially explosive situations by conclaves known as "sit downs," which meant exactly that: emissaries of the Five Families got together to talk over problems and make a decision about who was owed what.

The Commission's existence didn't mean that bosses couldn't be killed. In fact, in 1951, Vincent Mangano, the boss of what was to become the Gambino family, disappeared and it was widely believed that dockland tough Albert Anastasia was behind the disappearance. The members of the Commission called Anastasia on the carpet, and he explained that it was Mangano who had been plotting against him, hence the need for a preemptive strike. But in October 1957, Anastasia, who was not well liked by other mob bosses, was himself gunned down as he sat in a barber's chair at the Park Sheraton Hotel.

The lesson in all this was that if you wanted to take out a boss, you needed the approval, or at least the acquiescence, of the other Commission members. Gotti, Gravano, and the rest of the plotters against Castellano knew that they had to sound out the heads of the other Mafia families. If they couldn't call a meeting of the Commission to raise the question, they certainly could go through the backdoors and get a sense of how the other bosses felt about Castellano.

For a start, Gotti was very tight with Joseph Massino, his neighbor in Howard Beach and a powerful captain in the Bonanno crime family who was the effective street boss of the clan with the incarceration of official boss Philip Rastelli. Gotti bragged that he had

Massino in his pocket and counted on the Bonanno family support. The way Gravano explained it, since the Bonanno family had been on probation with the Commission because of drug dealing and its penetration by undercover FBI agent Joseph Pistone, the removal of Castellano increased the family's chances of getting back in the good graces with the rest of the Five Families. In terms of the tumultuous Colombo crime family, its bosses had expressed disdain about Castellano earlier to Ruggiero. Anthony "Tony Ducks" Corallo hated Castellano's greed.

Another important member of the Lucchese family, Anthony "Gaspipe" Casso, was somebody Gravano said he approached for support. How would Gaspipe feel if Castellano was no longer boss, Casso was asked according to Gravano. The reply, again according to Gravano, "he didn't give a fuck about Paul." So the Lucchese support was viewed as in the bag, at least that was the story from Gravano.

But in a biography of Casso, *Gaspipe: Confessions of A Mafia Boss*, published in 2008 in collaboration with the late writer Philip Carlo, the Lucchese mobster had an entirely different recollection. It was DeCicco, Casso said, who approached him about the Castellano plot, not Gravano. Once hearing about the idea of killing the boss, Casso told Carlo his reaction was one of shock and surprise. He told DeCicco as much.

"Fuckin' John's crazy," Casso told DeCicco as they walked near Dyker Park in Brooklyn. "This gonna do nothing but make trouble for everybody. The Chin [Gigante] and Vic [Amuso] won't sit down for this. We're gonna have to—all of us—come after John . . . not only John, but everybody involved in this."

Casso said he counseled DeCicco, who he considered a friend, to be careful. He predicted if Gotti did pull off the hit, he and everyone involved would be dead within a year. DeCicco, according to Casso's recollection, was to say nothing in reply.

As Casso had indicated, the powerful Genovese crime family was against the idea. The ties between Castellano and Genovese boss Vincent "The Chin" Gigante were too strong, recalled Gravano. There was no way that the Genovese family could be approached for its backing of the plot. In the end, the Genovese family was kept outside the loop. The plotters figured that since they were breaking the rules of La Cosa Nostra by killing a boss, they could expect the Genovese family and perhaps some others to seek retaliation. A war was possible. Yet, Gravano said, "If it comes down to it, we'll go to war with them."

On December 2, 1985, Aniello Dellacroce finally died. The one man who could have kept things calm between Castellano and the Gotti faction was gone. Whenever somebody of that stature passed away in the Mafia, it was considered a sign of respect that members and associates show up for the wake or funeral. Paul Castellano did neither. The no-show by the Gambino boss at the wake was particularly galling to the rest of the family. Castellano would claim he had to stay away to avoid the publicity and out of concern for his legal cases. But it was seen as the ultimate disrespect.

Dellacroce's casket was taken after the funeral to St. John Cemetery in Middle Village, Queens. There, in a niche within the Cloister Mausoleum, the old underboss was put to rest. The peaceful setting was amidst tasteful wood-paneled walls. Even today, the location is memorable for any who visit. Ecclesiastical music at a very low volume can just be heard in the background, lending to a contemplative atmosphere. Dellacroce is doing his eternal rest just yards away from another noteworthy niche holding the body of Frankie Gotti, the son of John Gotti who died at the age of twelve in an accident on the streets of Howard Beach.

With Dellacroce, their main buffer between them and Castellano gone, Gotti and the Bergin crew knew they had to move swiftly. For security, the plotters divided their operation: Gravano and DeCicco stayed in a basement suite in Joe Watt's home on Staten Island. Ruggiero and Gotti made their own arrangements. In this era before cell phones, the group stayed in contact by using certain land-line telephones and relaying cryptic messages, Gravano remembered.

The difficult part of the plotting turned out to be how to actually carry out the hit on Castellano. With so much surveillance surrounding him, it would be foolhardy for any attempt to be made on Castellano at his home or as he was leaving it. Again, Gravano related to

Maas that a couple of schemes were considered: Watts's family would vacate the house while plastic sheeting was put up, ostensibly for new paint, but in actuality to catch the blood and guts when Bilotti walked into an ambush he would be lured to. With Bilotti out of the way, DeCicco would call Castellano and say Bilotti was ill and that he would be his driver, pick him up at his house and then kill him, said Gravano.

"We kicked that around," Gravano told Maas. "What if Paul don't want to come out? What if this? What if that? It was too haphazard."

Another plan, according to Gravano, was to follow Castellano and Bilotti as they drove to a diner in Brooklyn they liked for breakfast. Once they settled in for coffee and eggs, an old friend of Gravano's known as Joseph "Old Man" Paruta would walk unnoticed into the diner, don a ski mask in the bathroom and then come out and shoot both men to death. Paruta was an elderly man who made his living in a grocery store and had nerves to handle the shooting. Maybe it could work. Yet it had big risks, namely that in a busy diner, things could suddenly go awry. Then, there was always the possibility that police would be nearby, perhaps themselves on a coffee break.

But, suddenly, Castellano unwittingly presented the plotters with an unexpected opportunity. Castellano asked some of his key captains—Thomas Gambino, Jimmy Fialla, Dan Marino, and DeCicco himself to have dinner at Sparks Steak House on East 46th Street in Manhattan. Gravano said DeCicco didn't know what the meeting was for but he told the plotters the date and time: December 16 at 5:00 P.M.

CHAPTER TWELVE
"He's Gone"

A GOOD MURDER—ONE YOU CAN PULL OFF without getting arrested on the spot—takes planning. The plotters knew a place and time where Castellano could be found but to ambush him in Midtown Manhattan, at the height of the Christmas shopping and party season, not to mention rush hour, presented challenges. But as Gravano remembered, it also was a great opportunity. There would be thousands of people on the street going about their business.

"The hit would only take a few seconds, and the confusion would be in our favor," Gravano told Maas. "Nobody would be expecting anything like this, least of all Paul. And being able to disappear afterwards in the crowds would be in our favor. So we decided this is when and where it is going to happen."

The assassination team would have the element of surprise, but it still needed to be an organized group, one with backup shooters in case something went wrong. The escape route had to be prearranged—nothing helter skelter. Then the disguises had to be picked to limit to the greatest extent possible that any of the shooters would be identified.

A key planning session took place a day or two before December 16, in the basement of Gravano's office building on Stillwell Avenue in Brooklyn. Gravano remembered eleven people showing up. Gotti and Ruggiero were with one group of arrivals, while Frank DeCicco and Joe Watts came together. The curious thing about the

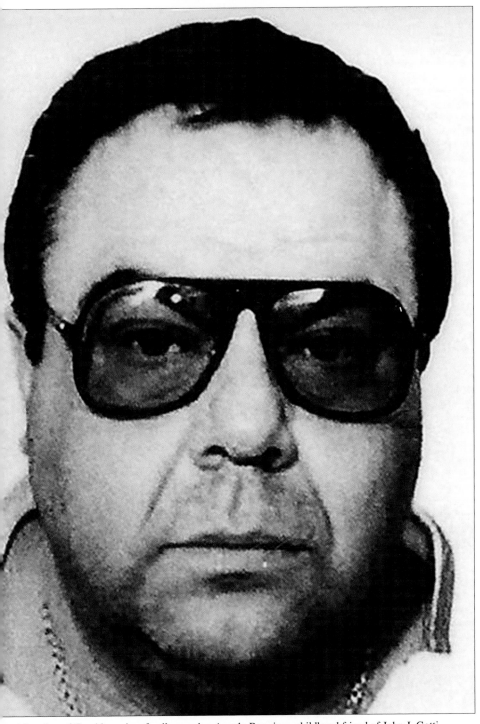

Mug shot of Gambino crime family member Angelo Ruggiero, childhood friend of John J. Gotti, whose incessant talking was captured on FBI surveillance and led to a big heroin case. Because of his illness, the case against Ruggiero was dismissed, but others were convicted. The heroin case helped precipitate events that culminated in the killing of Gambino boss Paul Castellano in 1985, leading to Gotti's assumption of the top spot. Ruggiero died in December 1989.
(Photo: Federal Bureau of Investigation)

This surveillance photo shows John J. Gotti, the Gambino crime family boss (*right*), with Bonanno crime family member Vincent Asaro circa the 1980s outside Gotti's Bergin Hunt and Fish Club in South Ozone Park, Queens. In the doorway, behind Gotti, is Angelo Ruggiero.
(*Photo: U.S. Attorney's Office, Eastern District of New York*)

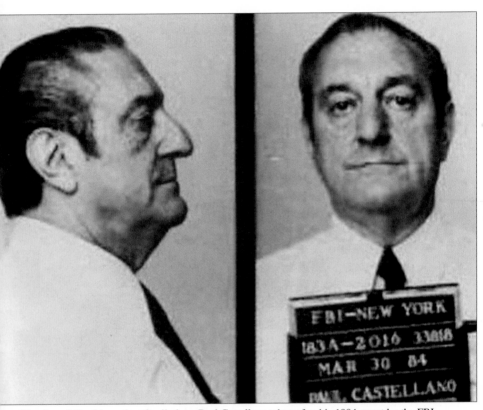

Mugshot of Gambino crime family boss Paul Castellano taken after his 1984 arrest by the FBI.
Castellano took over as boss following the death of his cousin Carlo Gambino in October 1976.
He was assassinated in a plot engineered by John J. Gotti in December 1985.
(Photo: FBI and Wikipedia)

Joseph Watts, a nonmember of organized crime who nevertheless held great power in the Gambino crime family and was close with John J. Gotti. Watts was sentenced to federal prison and was due for release in 2022. *(Photo: FBI and U.S. Attorney's Office, Eastern District of New York)*

Mugshot of Edward Lino, a Gambino captain and reputed heroin trafficker. Lino was overheard on FBI surveillance tapes talking with Angelo Ruggiero about heroin and was indicted along with Ruggiero in 1983 on heroin charges but ultimately acquitted. *(Photo: FBI and U.S. Attorney's Office, Eastern District of New York)*

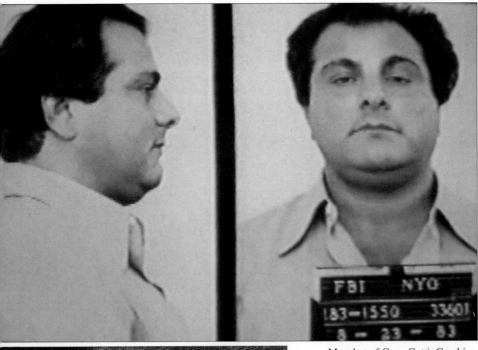

Mugshot of Gene Gotti, Gambino crime family captain, after his arrest in 1983 by the FBI. The brother of John J. Gotti, he was convicted in 1989 of being part of a heroin ring involving other members and associates of the Gambino family. He was sentenced to 50 years in federal prison and scheduled for release in September 2018. *(Photo: Federal Bureau of Investigation)*

Surveillance photo of Bonanno crime family member Gerlando Sciascia, originally from Canada. Sciascia was strongly suspected of being part of the Angelo Ruggiero heroin ring and was indicted in 1983. However, Sciascia was acquitted of the drug charges. He was slain on orders of former Bonanno boss Joseph Massino in 1999 in the Bronx. *(Photo: FBI and U.S. Attorney's Office, Eastern District of New York)*

FBI booking pho[...]
John J. Gotti following his a[...]
in December 199[...]
federal racketeering cha[...]
(Photo: Federal Bu[...]
of Investiga[...]

John Carneglia, a Gambino
crime family captain,
during a break in his federal
heroin conspiracy trial.
(Photo courtesy Newsday LLC

A. Gotti (*left*), son of
...bino crime boss John J. Gotti,
...in a surveillance photo
...ing with Gambino soldier
...les Carneglia on their way
...uneral, circa 1990.
*...to: FBI and U.S. Attorney's Office,
...ern District of New York)*

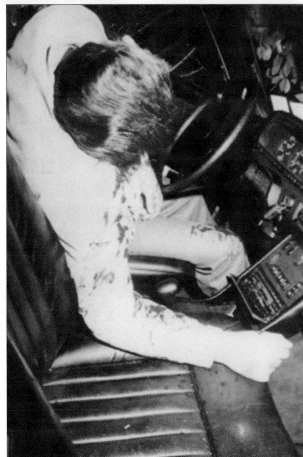

The body of Gambino captain
...dward Lino, after he was shot dead on
...road in Brooklyn in November 1990.
Evidence showed that Lino
was assassinated by the so-called
"Mafia Cops," Louis Eppolito and
Stephen Carracappa, while driving
along the Belt Parkway in Brooklyn.
*Photo: FBI and U.S. Attorney's Office,
Eastern District of New York)*

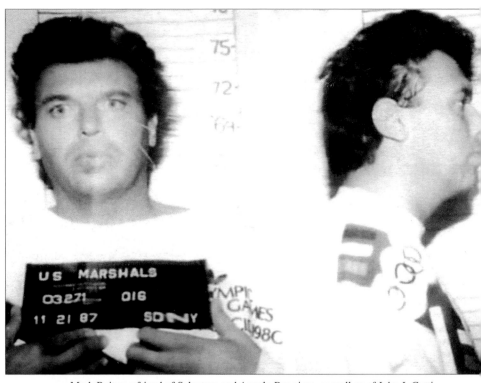

Mark Reiter, a friend of Salvatore and Angelo Ruggiero, as well as of John J. Gotti. Reiter was convicted in a federal heroin case, in which evidence showed he dealt with some Harlem-based Black drug dealers. Reiter was sentenced to life in prison. *(Photo: U.S. Drug Enforcement Administration)*

The late Michael Coiro, an attorney who was close to John Gotti and his crime family.
Coiro was convicted of laundering drug proceeds and sentenced to 15 years in prison. He died in 2003.
(Photo courtesy Newsday LLC)

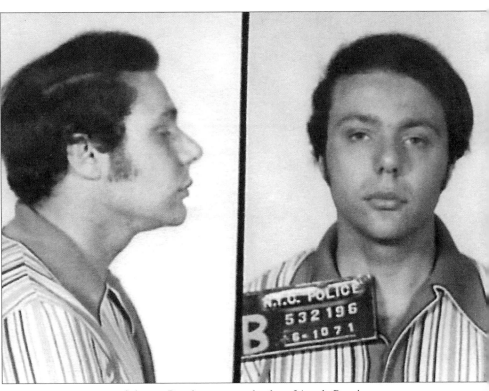
Salvatore Ruggiero, younger brother of Angelo Ruggiero.
Salvatore ran an extensive heroin operation even while living as a federal fugitive.
He and his wife, Stephanie, died in May 1982 in the crash of a Lear Jet off the coast of Georgia.
Evidence showed that his brother Angelo took over Salvatore's drug operation.
(Photo: U.S. Drug Enforcement Administration)

Salvatore "Sammy the Bull" Gravano,
a Gambino crime family underboss
and consiglieri under John J. Gotti,
shown in his FBI booking photo
the night of his arrest in December 1990.
(Photo: Federal Bureau of Investigation)

Booking photograph of
Wilfred "Willie Boy" Johnson,
a close associate of John J. Gotti
and for years a federal and
local police informant.
Johnson was assassinated on
Gotti's order in 1988 as he left
his Brooklyn home to go to work
(Photo: NYPD)

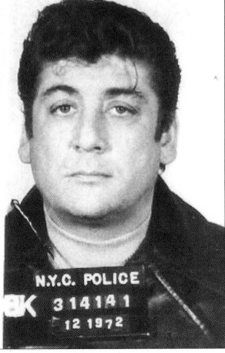

John Gotti seen in an FBI surveillance photo during a visit to Florida.
On Gotti's left is his son John A. Gotti.
(FBI photo)

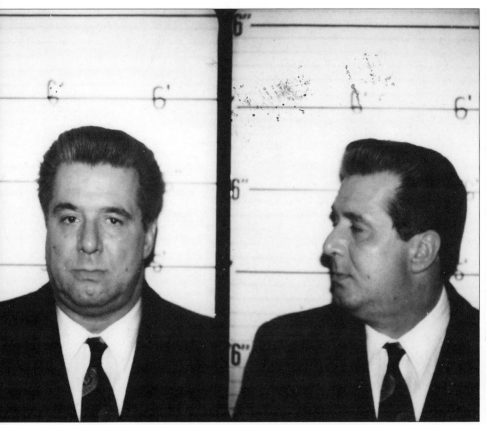

Mugshot of the late Salvatore Scala, a member of the team of shooters involved in the murder of Gambino boss Paul Castellano in December 1985.
(FBI photo)

Mugshot of Joseph Watts, a powerful associate of the Gambino crime family
who was close to boss John J. Gotti.
(FBI photo)

Former supervisory special agent Bruce Mouw, of the FBI office in New York, who led the investigation that led to the arrest and conviction of the late John J. Gotti and his underboss Frank Locascio. *(FBI photo)*

FBI mugshot of Pasquale Conte, reputed Gambino captain. Salvatore Gravano testified in federal court that he once approached Conte and asked him to revive a heroin network so that some payments could flow to family boss John Gotti. Federal investigators said there was no proof that the drug network was ever revived. *(FBI photo)*

Gene Gotti
(*foreground left*)
surrenders in July 198▮
with John Carneglia
(*middle*) to begin their
50-year prison terms
for their conviction
on a federal heroin cas▮
Both were released
in 2018.
(*Photo courtesy
Newsday LLC*)

The late Gamb▮
crime family consig▮
Joe N. Ga▮
He presided o▮
a meeting right a▮
the Castellano mur▮
where he called▮
members to be c▮
and told them ▮
the killing ▮
being investiga▮
(*FBI ph▮*

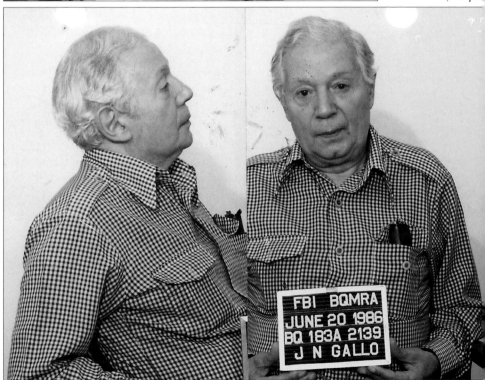

FBI BQMRA
JUNE 20 1986
BQ 183A 2139
J N GALLO

planning was that Gotti only let a handful of people—Gravano, DeCicco, Ruggiero, and Watts—know what was going on and who the target was. The others were in the dark, told only that two people were going to die and that the hit was huge.

"John tells them that no matter what, don't run, even if there are cops around," Gravano recalled. "These two guys have got to go. 'Don't worry about the cops,' he says, 'because if you run and these guys ain't dead, we will kill you.'"

It was clear that it was a do-or-die situation. The afternoon of December 16, the plotters met at what investigator Bruce Mouw said was Madison Square Park, a square patch of greenery by Twenty-third Street and Madison Avenue, within the shadow of the iconic Flatiron building. As Gravano would later tell the FBI, the designated shooters were: John Carneglia, Anthony Rampino, Vinnie Artuso, Sal Scala, and Ed Lino, the drug dealer who finally had become a made man. Gravano, who was driven to the park by Joe Watts, saw the gunmen were also dressed alike in long beige overcoats and fur Muscovite-style hats. The garb, which had been acquired by Ruggiero, was a nice way of assuring confusion among eye witnesses, Gravano thought. Gotti then told the group what everyone needed to know: the targets were to be Castellano and Bilotti.

Castellano's last day of his life started with his leaving the White House on Todt Hill with Bilotti as the usual driver of the black Lincoln town car. He lunched at a diner on Staten Island with Jimmy Failla and New Jersey mob boss John Riggi. Finished at the diner by around 2:00 P.M., Castellano and Bilotti drove over the Verrazano Narrows Bridge to Brooklyn where they went north on Route 278 to the Brooklyn Battery Tunnel—the bridge route to Manhattan was generally too slow and unpredictable with traffic. Once in Manhattan, they went north to Madison Avenue where Castellano's attorney Jimmy LaRossa had an office. The location, ironically, was just a few blocks north of Madison Square Park where Gotti was meeting with the hit team. They reached the office around 2:30 P.M. and since it was Christmastime, Castellano delivered envelopes with cash to LaRossa's administrative and secretarial staff who had been working in the back office on the stolen-car trial. Castellano and

LaRossa chatted: the trial seemed of late to be going well so they both had a positive vibe.

Having finished at LaRossa's, Castellano had some time before the meeting at Sparks Restaurant and did a little bit of shopping for perfume for a secretary. Castellano and Bilotti illegally parked and got a ticket, which they took with them and didn't discard. Then it was back in the car, with Bilotti driving, for the trip uptown and dinner.

After the final meeting in the park, the hit team, Gotti, and Gravano separated and proceeded to Forty-sixth Street. The shooters arrived separately and took up prearranged posts around the restaurant entrance, trying to look inconspicuous. As Bruce Mouw later remembered, Gravano said the shooters had definite assignments: Lino and Scala, who were brothers-in-law, were to target Bilotti, John Carneglia and Artuso were to deal with Castellano, while Rampino was on the scene as a backup. Various reports later had Ruggiero and Watts in the area as well.

Traffic and parking being what it was in Manhattan, Gotti and Gravano didn't have an easy time of it getting into position. The plan was for both men to sit in their car on East Forty-sixth Street, just to the west side of Third Avenue. The spot was about 200 feet from the front of Sparks and would, if traffic cooperated, afford them an unobstructed view of the scene. However, their first pass to the parking spot didn't work out so they had to go around the block and try again. The second time they were successful, and they didn't have to wait long for the show to begin.

Gotti and Gravano had hardly settled into the parking spot when Sammy glanced to his right and got the surprise of his life. There, perhaps three feet away was Castellano's Lincoln with Bilotti in the driver's seat of the car which was stopped for a traffic light with the interior dome light on. Gravano, trying to avoid eye contact with Bilotti, told Gotti and then got on the walkie-talkie to tell the shooters that their quarry was about to arrive. Still, Gravano said he was worried that Bilotti and Castellano might notice him and Gotti and think something was up and suddenly abandon their plan to go to Sparks. Gravano said he put his hand on this gun, thinking that he might have to waste Castellano and Bilotti on the spot. Gotti told him to be cool and let the hit team do its job. As it turned out, Gotti didn't want to be part of any shooting for the reason that he told Gravano he wasn't armed, something which stunned Gravano.

The light changed and Castellano's Lincoln proceeded with the crosstown traffic east to go the short distance to Sparks. DeCicco was in the restaurant, as was Fialla and Thomas Gambino. They were waiting for Castellano, who at this point was a bit late. The tardiness also was apparent to one of the shooters—later identified as Artuso—who a bystander overheard grumbling: "They should have been here by now."

It was about 5:30 P.M. when Castellano and Bilotti pulled up in front of Sparks, the limousine maneuvering to the right to get close to the curb. Across Third Avenue, Gotti and Gravano saw the shooters spring into action. Carneglia, as one bystander would later testify, along with Artuso approached Castellano as he opened the passenger-side front door. Carneglia fired but Artuso's gun, it was later reported, jammed and didn't shoot, although some pundits believed he simply lost his nerve. Hit six times in the head and body, Castellano crumpled to the pavement, his head by the vehicle and his mouth agape and eyes wide open. In his death spasm he clutched a pair of leather gloves in his right hand.

Bilotti had exited the driver's-side door, apparently to assist Castellano go into the restaurant, but never got any farther. Scala and his brother-in-law Lino fired at Bilotti, also hitting him a total of six times. But that wasn't all for "The Wig." A witness, Jeffrey Davidson, would later tell the FBI and repeat in court that after the first round of shots he saw a man he identified as Carneglia walk around the front of Castellano's limousine to Bilotti as he lay in the middle of Forty-sixth Street and then fire three times at him. Bruce Mouw noted that Carneglia was heard cursing at Bilotti as he shot him.

It was over that quickly. The biggest mob hit in decades went down almost as planned with Castellano and Bilotti both dead. The shooting set off pandemonium among the crowd of pedestrians on the street. A nurse attempted to give aid to Bilotti in the street, but he was long gone. Inside Sparks, a waiter approached DeCicco and Fialla and told them Castellano wouldn't be making it for dinner. Gravano later recalled that DeCicco, the fifth columnist who had betrayed Castellano to the plotters, told Failla the boss was dead and that on hearing the news Failla turned ashen since he could have been in the car with Castellano but opted instead to travel on his own to Sparks. "Don't worry, you wouldn't have been hurt," DeCicco said. Both men ran into Thomas Gambino coming into the restaurant—he must have arrived seconds before the shooting—and told him his uncle was dead and to leave quickly, which he did.

The shooters left at a brisk walking pace, not running, proceeding East along Forty-sixth Street. Gravano and Gotti, meanwhile, had seen the shooting and when it was over drove slowly past the carnage. Gravano glanced out at Bilotti's body lying in the street in a growing pool of blood and said to Gotti, "He's gone." They both then drove East toward Second Avenue to make the right turn for the trip back to Brooklyn.

As fate would have it, many in the law enforcement community were attending a lecture at New York University by Robert Blakey, who was the creator of the federal racketeering statute. As Blakey held court, beepers of the officials in attendance went off, almost in unison, a beeping and chirping call to action. Those alerted called their offices and heard the news, leaving the lecture for a long night on the street.

Police arrived within two or three minutes to the homicide scene but by then Gotti, Gravano, the shooters, and the rest of the hit team were long gone. Police seemed blindsided by the murders. NYPD chief of detectives Philip Nicastro told reporters that he didn't want to speculate as to why Castellano was killed. The department's chief spokeswoman, Alice T. McGillion, did note that it appeared that the gunmen used .380 and .32 caliber handguns. She added that the killers, there may have two or three, fled in a dark-colored car parked at Forty-sixth Street and Second Avenue. As for Castellano, he reportedly had about $3,000 cash in his pocket; Bilotti about $6,700. Neither man had any weapons on them or in the car.

"We know there were many people on the street," McGillion said, "and we hope that someone will come forward with a better description than the ones we have."

In the post-September 11 era, with the city ringed with thousands of interconnected surveillance cameras and with cops able to use license-plate readers, the fleeing killers would have very likely been spotted on video and their cars tracked to wherever they were going. Assuming the cars all converged at Gravano's place in Brooklyn, the license plates would have been tracked to Stillwell Avenue and the car owners immediately identified. The case could have been broken quickly and arrests made.

But this was 1985 and the cops, and FBI didn't have the benefit of future technology. But what they did have, particularly with the C-16 Squad led by Mouw, were a small group of informants who had a good idea of who was behind the murders. So, while much of the public and the NYPD was in the dark about who killed Castellano and Bilotti, the FBI was figuring it out pretty quickly. There were at least three, possibly four, informants feeding Mouw and his staff information over the years about Gotti and his Bergin crew. One man decided to secretly work for the FBI after he got so far into debt with the Gambino family—about $30,000—that he figured the federal government was his only way out. There was also Willie Boy Johnson, who had been a good source for years.

One of the informants, later identified by the pseudonym "Frankie," met on December 17 with Andris Kurins by a McDonald's restaurant by Myrtle Avenue in Brooklyn. As author Howard Blum said in *Gangland*, Frankie related that everyone in the Gambino family, with whom he was an associate, was being quiet. But he did say that the word was that John Gotti had orchestrated the Castellano hit and that he was going to become the new boss. Mouw and the others in the squad were skeptical about Gotti being behind things, but there had been plenty of indication that such a move made sense. Gotti knew that Castellano was prepared to split up his Bergin crew, bust Gotti down and put him under the command of another captain. Killing a boss was a move that under normal conditions and the rules of La

Cosa Nostra might get someone killed. But in the case of Castellano, he wasn't a boss who engendered much sympathy.

The negatives for Castellano were significant. He was greedy, not only in the way he treated his own men but also in his interaction with the bosses of other crime families, stiffing them out of what they believed was their cut of construction and other payoffs. Castellano had a legitimate meat business while some of the other bosses weren't so well-positioned financially. There were also rumblings that Castellano was going to become an informant, as a way of getting himself out of all of his legal jams. Then there was his affair with his maid Gloria. Castellano had been carrying on with her in his own home, flaunting the relationship in front of his wife, whom many in the mob had liked. Meanwhile, Gloria had on occasion acted disrespectful to some of the mobsters when they visited Castellano, something that intensified their dislike. Gravano said in the early planning of the murder plot that he even entertained killing her in any attempt to rush Castellano at his mansion, an idea that was abandoned.

So, for Mouw and the FBI squad, while there was the possibility of a war following Castellano's murder, it appeared that Gotti might just have been able to muster the support to pull off the coup, as the informants indicated he did. Armed with the informant leads, the FBI believed within a day or two that the Castellano homicide had been solved. The question was how they might be able to make a case that would stand up in court, and the answer for that would be a long time coming.

Meanwhile, Gotti and his crew moved quickly to consolidate their position. They set up meetings of the entire leadership and the captains of the crime family. But if there was any doubt to the police or anyone in the FBI that Gotti was now ascendant, it was quickly dispelled with the way the Gambino family Christmas Eve party shaped up at Dellacroce's old Ravenite club on Mulberry Street. Gotti was going to eventually shift his focus from the Bergin to the Ravenite and at the party, surveillance teams noticed as Gotti seemed to be the man of the hour, getting kissed by the mobsters who lined up to shake his hand.

Back in Staten Island, the only ceremony the Castellano family was worried about was the funeral for the dead boss. His family made quick work of Gloria Olarte, handing her a reported $18,000 and telling her to get out. The next matter for Castellano's family was his funeral, and things wouldn't go as easily as they did with kissing off his mistress Gloria. Because of Castellano's notoriety, the Roman Catholic archdiocese declined to allow him to have a public Mass of Christian burial. When asked why no Mass for Castellano, Cardinal O'Connor told reporters that "under normal circumstances a Catholic would be brought into church for the funeral service. I felt we could not do that in this set of circumstances."

Instances of the Church barring Masses for gangsters had happened before in mob history: Albert Anastasia was given only a graveside service at the non-sectarian Green-Wood Cemetery in Brooklyn in 1957 where his brother Salvatore, a priest, blessed the open grave. But the refusal was particularly galling for Castellano's wife and his daughter, Connie, as well as his sons. Nevertheless, the church did allow the Castellano family to hold a private memorial Mass, without his body present, at the Blessed Sacrament Roman Catholic Church on Staten Island. To keep his burial location a secret, Castellano was entombed in Moravian Cemetery, not far from his home on Todt Hill, in an unmarked grave. A priest was present for the committal service. Bilotti was also buried at Moravian in a spot marked by a modest flat marker.

About two days after the slaying of Castellano and Bilotti, the captains of the family and consiglieri, Joe N. Gallo, met at Caesar's East, a restaurant at Fifty-eighth Street and Third Avenue. Gravano later said the place was picked because he and Ed Lino owned a piece of it. Gallo presided over the meeting, sitting at the head of a long table around which the captains gathered. Gotti and DeCicco flanked Gallo, the old-timer, as he spoke. Since he was the highest-ranking member of the family with both the boss and underboss dead, Gallo was technically in charge of things. But he spoke as though he had a gun to his back, telling the group that they didn't know who killed Castellano but that an investigation was under way to find out what happened. In the meantime, said Gallo, Gotti and DeCicco would help him run things.

The Caesar's East meeting was just for show, an effort to calm the waters and tell those in the borgata that nothing was going to happen to them and that no war was going to break out. Gallo, based on the earlier approach the plotters made to him, already had a very good idea who killed the boss. But now they had to move forward and not risk more bloodshed. About two weeks after the meeting, reportedly on January 15, 1986, all of the captains again got together in the recreation room of an apartment building complex in lower Manhattan. Gotti chaired the meeting to say the time had come, with Castellano dead, to vote for a new boss.

"Frankie gets up and votes for John Gotti," Gravano recalled of the meeting. "It zips right around the room. Nobody opposes. It's unanimous."

Gotti appointed DeCicco as his underboss and kept Gallo as the aging consiglieri. He made his brother Pete a captain. Sonny Ciccone was put in charge of the dockworkers, replacing Anthony Scotto, who Gravano said Gotti didn't like, possibly because of the way he hung out with celebrities and kept publicly denying his reputed ties to the mob.

So it was done. A chain of events that got underway with a plane crash off Georgia in 1982 led to John Gotti, the kid from Brooklyn who struggled to find shoes to wear as a kid, rising to become the boss of a crime family, one of the most powerful in the American Mafia. Gotti did it with the help of his friends and never had to fire a shot himself.

CHAPTER THIRTEEN
"Shame on Them!"

WHILE MUCH OF THE WORLD HAD NO CLUE about who was responsible for Castellano's murder and had taken over control of the Gambino family, a good number of people in law enforcement figured it out right away. Gotti's name was circulated among the FBI organized crime units and their liaisons with other police agencies. The FBI informants had pretty good information and by early January 1986, word began to leak out into the public. On January 12, a full three days before the meeting of the Gambino captains in lower Manhattan, *The New York Times* ran a page one story headlined "Ex-Convict Said To Take Control of Gambino Crime Organization." The first words were the name John Gotti. "The word was passed along the street this week that Gotti is at the top," an official told the newspaper. "It was a calm transition." Details of the way Gotti and the others planned and carried out the murder were not known at that point.

The report illuminated the very telling Christmas Eve surveillance at the Ravenite club on Mulberry Street in which Gotti acted like the king of the block, the center of attention of all the mob bigshots who showed up. DeCicco was also noted to be the underboss. The Gambino family at that point was pegged as having twenty captains, about 250 made soldiers and 1,000 associates. The illicit income by conservative estimates was over $100 million a year.

Though he was baptized in Castellano's and Bilotti's blood, Gotti relished the calm that followed. With the death of Castellano, Mafia stories were all over the newspapers, and 1986 was turning out to be the year of the mob. But not all of the news was good. In fact, the New York Mafia families had much more to contend with than just Gotti's rise to power. In the Gambino stolen-car case, although the trial judge fretted about the impact of the crime boss's assassination on the jury, in the end he declined to declare a mistrial. The case would go on even without Castellano's very obvious absence. Then there was another trial in the same courthouse involving the Colombo family, whose boss Ralph Scopo was charged with shaking down construction companies. On top of those cases, the massive Pizza Connection trial, involving Sicilian and American gangsters who trafficked in heroin was grinding on and would do so for at least another several months.

Gotti himself had two legal battles looming. One of them was the racketeering case in Brooklyn where he had been indicted with the now-dead Dellacroce, Ruggiero, and others on charges they ran a corrupt mob enterprise. That particular federal case was different than the heroin drug indictment Ruggiero, Carneglia, and Gene Gotti faced, but it still was a big problem for Gotti. If convicted in that case Gotti's newly minted role could come to an abrupt end. Not long after he became boss, Gotti got involved in a battery case involving a refrigerator mechanic named Romual Piecyk who was allegedly assaulted by Gotti and a cohort during a petty street brawl in Queens sparked by a traffic dispute.

Early 1986 was a time when Gotti had a short, peaceful interregnum as boss. He held court at the Ravenite, and the money was still coming in. Yet, there was an undercurrent of violence. With Castellano's death, there were some in the crime family who saw it as an opportunity to settle scores. One of those was DeCicco, the underboss. The bad blood between DeCicco and Gus Sclafani stemmed from the latter's accusation made to Castellano that Frankie was an informant. It was never clear what the basis for that was, but DeCicco stood his ground and cleared his name with Castellano. But the damage had been done, and DeCicco needed his revenge.

It was March 10, 1986, and John Gotti had finally permitted the killing of Sclafani. As federal prosecutors would later allege, Gotti farmed out the hit to Watts. Homicide, as investigators would later allege in court filings, was not something unfamiliar to Watts. He had already played a role as a back-up shooter in the Castellano murder a few months earlier. In 1984, when a mob associate named John Cennamo was found hanging from a tree in St. Albans, Queens, investigators believed that Watts, Angelo Ruggiero, and Willie Boy Johnson had killed him on Gotti's orders. It seems as though Cennamo had been trying to convince police to investigate a murder that the Gambino family had been involved in. So, with Gotti's approval, Watts and others stabbed and shot Sclafani in the basement of the Ravenite social club, prosecutors alleged. His body was never found.

As boss, Gotti was a busy man. He had to meet emissaries from out-of-town crime families. He traveled more into Manhattan, not only for pleasure but to meet other wise guys. The meetings all came with Gotti's new territory. But Gotti also needed to show face and be in touch with his borgata and its various social clubs. The Bergin was still a place Gotti could get a daily shave and a haircut before his nightclub jaunts in Manhattan. The Ravenite was his new base, sort of a homage to Dellacroce, and he required weekly appearances by his captains. Around the other boroughs, senior Gambino captains had their own clubs and Gotti's appearance was a big deal.

The Veterans and Friends Social Club on Eighty-sixth Street in Bensonhurst was the base of Jimmy Failla, the Gambino family's respected captain who was a power in the trash-hauling industry. Many of the Brooklyn wing of the family knew to hit the Veterans and Friends to see Failla or to find others. Failla had been close with Castellano, but after the assassination swore his allegiance to Gotti. On April 13, almost four months after Gotti had been anointed boss, he planned on visiting Failla's club, one stop in his long running papal tour of social clubs and other locales. As a result, the crowd at the club that particular Sunday was larger than normal. DeCicco was there to meet with Gotti and then drive him for later appointments.

The club was a nicely appointed mob joint. It had a well-stocked bar and tables, as well as the ubiquitous espresso machine. There was also a back room for more private conversations. Bensonhurst had been a mob area for decades. Just down the street was another mob spot, The 19th Hole, a social club where powerful Lucchese crime family captain Anthony Casso hung his hat. Just a few doors from Veterans and Friends was Tomasso, the restaurant which had been bugged by the FBI.

But while there was anticipation that Gotti would be showing up at Failla's club that Sunday, there was a sudden change of plans. He wasn't going to show up because he had to stay in Manhattan. As a result Frank DeCicco would have to cut his afternoon short and drive into Manhattan to pick up the boss. It was just after 1:30 P.M. that DeCicco walked out of the club toward a four-door 1985 Buick Electra parked opposite the front door on the other side of Eighty-sixth Street. Frankie "Heart" Bellino accompanied DeCicco to the car. DeCicco never got to enter the vehicle. As he and Bellino stood near the car door on the sidewalk a remote-controlled bomb went off. The bomb, which had been under the Buick, killed DeCicco instantly and dug a two-foot-wide crater in the street. Bellino was seriously hurt but would survive. A lady walking nearby was slightly injured.

Gravano had been in the club and when the explosion occurred, he didn't think a car had exploded but rather something more catastrophic, like a boiler explosion or building collapse.

"I came out of the club and Frankie's car is in fucking flames," remembered Gravano in his book. "And there is Frankie Hearts with blood shooting out of his feet."

Gravano ran across the street to the bombed-out car and tried to help DeCicco. But he was very likely dead at that point since the bomb had done catastrophic damage, leaving a gory scene of carnage.

"I tried to pull him away. I grabbed a leg, but he ain't coming with it," Gravano recalled. "The leg is off. One of his arms is off . . . I got my hand under him and my hand went right through his body to his stomach. There's no ass. His ass, his balls, everything is completely blown off."

A police van pulled up to the scene, and Gravano and others picked up what was left of DeCicco and put him inside. They then did the same with Bellino, and the vehicle sped off to a nearby hospital. As Gravano told Maas, he ordered that Gotti be contacted immediately and told what happened. Then everybody else was to meet at Gravano's nearby club in Brooklyn, a place called Tali's.

The police couldn't immediately determine how the bomb was detonated—whether by timer or remote control. But law enforcement officials quickly expressed their belief that DeCicco was killed because of the way he had turned on Castellano and backed the plotter. The officials speculated that rivals of Gotti within the Gambino family considered him vulnerable and were openly trying to defy him.

But the truth about what happened seemed to have been foreshadowed by Gaspipe Casso when he told DeCicco that a plot against Castellano was fraught with danger. The other big bosses wouldn't stand for the killing of a sitting boss. Ultimately, Casso told his biographer and close childhood friend Phil Carlo that Gotti would have to pay a price. It was about four months after Castellano was murdered that Gigante set in motion plans to retaliate against Gotti in a meeting in Brooklyn, said Casso.

Initially Gravano had said in his biography that Lucchese boss Anthony Corallo didn't care if Castellano was killed. But, according to Casso, it was Tony Ducks who met with Gigante and after their confab it was said that Gotti had to be killed. Law enforcement officials said that Gambino captain Daniel Marino had been in talks with the Genovese family to have Gotti killed and for Jimmy Failla to be installed as the new boss with Gigante's blessing. The job, said Casso, was farmed out to Genovese soldiers in New Jersey, but they were unable to come up with a viable plan: Gotti was under too much police surveillance, and his Ravenite club was in an area of Manhattan that was too crowded. Gigante then looked elsewhere for help.

According to Casso, Gigante allegedly turned to Herbert Pate, a former cop who was an explosives expert. Pate allegedly took on the job of crafting an explosive device from military grade C-4 ex-

plosive and electrical components from toy cars. Casso said he and
Pate tested the device upstate and on the day of the blast it was Pate
who placed the bomb in a shopping bag under DeCicco's car outside the Veterans and Friends club. Then, Pate and Casso observed
the scene from The 19th Hole club down the street and waited for
DeCicco and a man they thought was Gotti to exit the club.

Casso's narrative and allegations of the bombing plot have never
been corroborated by hard evidence. In some ways, the story Casso
relates about the bombing seems a bit improbable. For instance, he
claimed Pate drove past the bomb site as DeCicco entered the car
and then detonated the device. Such a move could be risky in that
Pate's car, if his timing was off, could have caught some of the blast,
which Casso said he did, and would have been noticed by witnesses.
But Casso's claim is all that history has left us with the bombing that
killed DeCicco. Even Gravano said that it was Casso who set up the
bombing for Gigante, although he didn't know who actually carried
it out. (Pate was never charged in the killing but instead was convicted in 1988 of tax evasion, possession of firearms, and storing
and concealing explosives following a conviction for a felony. He
was sentenced to twelve years and fined $411,000.)

In his book *Gaspipe,* author Carlo said that Gotti was viewed by
some of the other bosses as a negative factor for the Mafia. He was
seen as loud and brash and constantly flaunting his power. With
Gotti's death things would go back to normal. Of course, fate played
out differently.

The other Mafia bosses couldn't help but notice Gotti's public
persona. Not only was he all over the newspaper since Castellano's
murder but his court cases kept him out front. In March, about a
month before the DeCicco bombing, Gotti finally showed up in a
Queens courtroom over the assault case involving Mr. Piecyk. The
tabloids had a field day, chronicling the case as if it were a champi-
onship baseball game.

Piecyk, the alleged victim in the case, had avoided police for
weeks as they attempted to find him and bring him to court to testify. Finally, after Piecyk was found, he was brought in for a hearing
in Queens State Supreme Court. The prosecutor had a thankless task

in trying to get his star witness to cooperate. During the two-hour hearing, the thirty-seven-year-old Piecyk was asked the key question: did he recognize the men who punched and slapped him during a traffic dispute on September 14, 1984? Piecyk's recollection failed him.

"I do not," answered Piecyk, as he glanced around at Gotti and his co-defendant Frank Colletta.

Asked if he remembered how the man who grabbed cash from his shirt pocket was dressed, Piecyk again demurred.

"To be perfectly honest, it was so long ago I don't remember," said Piecyk.

Queens District Attorney John Santucci said that his office would try to introduce Piecyk's grand jury testimony in which he had identified Gotti and Colletta. But it was clear that Piecyk had a convenient lapse of memory, so much so that one tabloid headline the next day trumpeted "I ForGotti." In the end, the case against Gotti and Colletta was dropped since the victim's fear about the new crime boss had apparently got the best of him.

Gotti's win in the assault case was the first of a number of courtroom victories that went on to burnish his image as a man who could always beat the rap as the Teflon Don. It was soon after the Piecyk case victory and the DeCicco bombing that Gotti found himself in court again in a case many had forgotten. *U.S. v. Aniello Dellacroce et al.,* an indictment out of the Eastern District or Brooklyn federal court as it is known, was easy to overlook with the looming and more publicized trials in the Pizza Connection and the Mafia Commission.

Diane Giacalone was the prosecutor in the federal case. An intense woman, she had run afoul of her male counterparts in the high-achieving world of law enforcement by sticking to her guns and refusing to defer to the FBI, which wanted a better chance to make a run at Gotti. The FBI had the benefit of months of surveillance from the Ruggiero case, and it didn't share it with Giacalone, who had to rely on other witnesses to build her case. As the case neared a trial date, many in law enforcement didn't think she had a chance against some of the more seasoned members of the defense bar. She also had very little experience doing mob cases, having only one trial in the organized crime category. Usually, the Organized Crime Strike Force, a specialized unit, handled such cases with a group of specially trained federal prosecutors. Edward McDonald, the head of the Brooklyn strike force, complained to his superiors in Washington that Giacalone's evidence was weak and that a loss by the government at trial would effectively immunize Gotti from further prosecution for crimes committed prior to 1985. Still, Giacalone was able to keep the case and go to trial.

The narrative circulating about Giacalone in news reports centered on how as a young girl walking the streets of Queens outside the Bergin Hunt and Fish Club as a Catholic school student, she spied the old men loitering out front, who seemed to razz her over being skinny. Now the girl had matured into a seasoned federal prosecutor who would be going after the very Mafiosi who once belittled her. It was a compelling part of the story: a young woman standing up against a horde of wise guys. But to make the case, Giacalone needed good evidence—something she thought she had.

Right after the Piecyk case and the DeCicco murder, Giacalone made the unexpected move of asking Brooklyn Federal Judge Eugene Nickerson to revoke Gotti's $1 million bail and hold him for the duration of her trial. The argument Giacalone made was that since the DeCicco homicide, the incentive for Gotti to retaliate was strong. She also contended that there was a strong possibility that Gotti and his crew would attempt to intimidate witnesses, something Giacalone said had occurred with Piecyk when the refrigerator repairman had received threatening telephone calls and other harassment during the pendency of Gotti's assault case.

Bail revocations aren't made without some sort of hearing, and for several days in May Judge Nickerson held a hearing in which he allowed Giacalone to bring in witnesses who could provide evidence of Gotti's mob ties and his dangerousness. One witness was Edward Magnuson, a Drug Enforcement Administration official who had an informant who seemed to have some advance but nonspecific information that something "bad was going to happen" about three or four days before DeCicco was killed. Once DeCicco died, the informant said that Gotti was "very angry" and "when he got out on bail or when the trial was over, there was going to be a war and John would take his revenge," Magnuson testified.

Gotti was being represented in the bail hearing by an aggressive attorney by the name of Bruce Cutler, who had represented the crime boss in the Piecyk assault case and was kept on for the federal case. In his bombastic style, Cutler called the government evidence a regurgitation of newspaper articles, scuttlebutt, and "comic book gossip."

However, Nickerson agreed with Giacalone and her co-counsel, John Gleeson. On May 13, Nickerson revoked Gotti's bail and said that "there was substantial evidence" that Gotti "would improperly influence or intimidate witnesses." Nickerson pointed to the Piecyk case and said there was significant evidence to "show that Piecyk received a warning not to testify" and that it was clear the warning came from Gotti or others working for him.

While he revoked Gotti's bail, Nickerson also stayed his order for a few days to give the defense time to appeal. But the appellate court decided that it wouldn't hold up Nickerson's order while the matter was on appeal and decided that Gotti had to go off to jail. Gotti had already prepared himself for the eventuality that he might have to surrender and had spent the weekend at home in which he was able to get his affairs in order and enjoy some last moments of freedom under the watchful eye of the FBI and a horde of news- papermen. Gotti showed up at the Brooklyn U.S. Attorney's Office in a tan leisure suit and brown loafers and surrendered to a few cheers from onlookers. He was overheard by one reporter saying "Ready For Freddie," a remark which some believed was a refer- ence to the undertaker character in the *Li'l Abner* comic strip

But even in jail awaiting trial, Gotti was pretty much on top of things going on in the street. He had a group of close associates— Angelo Ruggiero, Joe Armone, and Gravano—to run things and communicate with him in jail. The Gambino family rackets contin- ued to generate cash, and the family didn't miss too much of the ac- tion.

Although she had the backing of her bosses in Washington,

Giacalone did not have an easy time getting the case against Gotti and the others ready for trial. Some of it stemmed from the lack of evidence but some of the problems seemed of Giacalone's own doing, specifically, the way she handled the case of Willie Boy Johnson, one of the defendants. For years, Johnson had been a secret informant of both the FBI and the Queens District Attorney's Office, feeding information and intelligence about Gotti and the Bergin crew. But in an attempt to try and get Johnson as a witness against Gotti, Giacalone threatened him with exposure as an informant. It was an astonishing and seemingly reckless gambit. Johnson protested and pleaded that if he testified at trial that he and his family would likely be killed. The FBI also backed Johnson's bid to keep his informant status secret, for obvious reasons.

But Giacalone wouldn't budge, apparently thinking that if she exposed Johnson's status as a secret FBI mole that he might then switch sides and testify. It was a gamble that failed. Johnson refused and although Gotti told him that he didn't believe Giacalone's claim, the crime boss knew that Willie Boy would have to die at some point.

Giacalone also tried to surface another FBI informant named Billy Battista, who had been an associate and bookmaker with the Bergin crew. In the case of Battista, who was handled with agent Pat Colgan, the FBI put him up in a motel in New Jersey to keep him safe during the pendency of the trial. But Battista, knowing full well that his life was now in jeopardy, left the secret location and disappeared. He was never located, and not only did Giacalone lose a witness, the FBI had the usefulness of another informant ruined.

If the FBI and Giacalone were having trouble in their working relationship—such as it was—Gotti seemed to be able to project his power and demands outside of the confines of jail. A few weeks after Gotti was ordered to be detained before his trial, he issued an order to kill Robert DiBernardo, one of the captains who was part of the early plotting against Castellano. The message for the hit was passed from Gotti to Ruggiero, who then relayed it to Gravano to carry out. As Gravano remembered things, he was surprised, particularly since DiBernardo was earning a great deal of money for the crime family through the pornography business and had been a liaison with some union officials. Gravano liked DiBernardo and admired his business sense.

Gotti wanted DiBernardo killed because he had been talking behind people's backs or voicing what appeared to be insults. In one case, Gravano said that DiBernardo had told Ruggiero that he had "the balls to be underboss, but not the brains." Gravano maintained it was just talk and that DiBernardo, a captain without any crew of men, was essentially harmless. Gravano asked Ruggiero to see if Gotti would pull back the hit and then talk about it when he got out of jail. Nothing doing, said Ruggiero, Gotti wanted DiBernardo dead.

"What was I going to do?" Gravano said years later. "What can I do? It's an order from the boss. This was the life I chose and the boss was the boss."

As Gravano would later describe in his biography and in court, the killing of DiBernardo took place at Gravano's office on Stillwell Avenue. The secretary had gone home at 5:00 P.M., and by the time DiBernardo showed up for a meeting, Gravano was there as was his cousin Eddie Garafola and the loyal Joseph Paruta, the "Old Man" who had figured in the early planning in the Castellano hit. Gravano told Paruta to get DiBernardo a cup of coffee, and the Old Man walked over to a cabinet where a .380-caliber handgun with a silencer had been secreted. Paruta took the weapon, walked over to the back of DiBernardo and shot him in the head twice. It was that simple, said Gravano.

DiBernardo's corpse was placed in a body bag Gravano had obtained from a local Brooklyn funeral home and stored in a back room until the group cleaned up the office. Gravano then went to a local Burger King restaurant where Ruggiero had been waiting and told him that DiBernardo was dead and that they should meet at Tali's later to dispose of the body and get rid of the dead captain's Mercedes. Gravano never did find out where DiBernardo's body was taken after it was put in the back of Frank Locascio's Cadillac. As for the Mercedes, it was driven away by some young men connected to John Carneglia, perhaps to a junkyard.

However, the Gotti racketeering trial before Judge Nickerson was not going away as easily as DiBernardo did. It would just get delayed a bit. In the face of the enormous publicity that Gotti and his co-defendants were receiving, particularly after the DeCicco bombing, Nickerson decided that the trial, which was supposed to begin in late April, would be pushed back until mid-August. That should be enough time for the news coverage of the case to diminish and to allow the court to set up procedures for selecting a jury, Nickerson said.

His bail revoked, Gotti marked time in the federal lockup. But the others from the Bergin crew who had been charged in the case—including Angelo Ruggiero, John Carneglia, and Gene Gotti—remained free, each on a $1 million bond and the restriction that he avoid mob social clubs and organized crime figures. However, more troubles soon faced Ruggiero. In June 1986, he was arrested in another racketeering case, this one involving numerous defendants including the missing Robert DiBernardo, the nominal family underboss Joe Armone, James Failla, and Joe N. Gallo, on charges of racketeering.

The case was another mega indictment targeting the Gambino family and had the added twist with an allegation that the group had a source within the federal court system. Mildred Russo, the mother-in-law of Gambino associate Augustus Sclafani, had worked as a clerk in the Manhattan federal court where among her duties she docketed search warrant affidavits. Russo, who looked like a matronly sixty-six-year-old Italian grandmother was allegedly passing along to the mob information from sealed documents she was supposed to be filing. In her normal duties she worked with search warrant affidavits, which often spelled out the exact nature of the government's interest in an investigation. (The author remembers Russo at times trying to deter him from reading the search warrant affidavits, which then were matters of public record.)

While law enforcement knew from intelligence that Gotti and his crew were involved in the Castellano murder, the new indictment involving Ruggiero gave officials an opportunity to spell out their suspicions on the public record. With Ruggiero facing three indictments now, the government again moved to oppose his bail. To do that, prosecutors brought in FBI special agent William C. Noon to testify. Assigned to Bruce Mouw's squad, Noon had been deeply involved in the Gambino crime family investigations and had access to the current intelligence, including what at least six informants within the Gambino crime family had been relaying back to their handlers within the FBI.

According to Noon, the informants had said that both John Gotti and Ruggiero had orchestrated the killing of Castellano. The motive, Noon testified, was Castellano's earlier appointment of Bilotti in December 1985 as his underboss, instead of Gotti. Castellano also had learned that the bug in Ruggiero's Long Island home had given the government probable cause to place a surveillance device in his house on Staten Island, noted Noon.

As interesting as Noon's information was, none of the informants had apparently placed Gotti or Ruggiero at the scene when Castellano and Bilotti were murdered. Defense attorney Jeffrey Hoffman, who represented Ruggiero, derided the information, calling it fallacious. Hoffman noted that the fact that his client had not been charged for the murders was "proof of the pudding" of his innocence in the homicide case. To buttress Noon's testimony, prosecutors played an excerpt from a surveillance tape in which Ruggiero was heard telling the now-dead Aniello Dellacroce that their Gambino family faction "might have to go to war" with Castellano.

The Castellano evidence wasn't the strongest in the world for a bail revocation. But it actually was Ruggiero himself who turned out to be his own worst enemy. Not only did he have loose lips and an almost compulsive need to talk, Ruggiero also had a tough time keeping his temper in check during court appearances. During an earlier hearing in 1985, Ruggiero pointed his finger at one witness in what the court said was "a threatening manner." The judge saw the incident, but at the time didn't do anything about it. But at the bail-revocation hearing on June 27, before the same judge, Ruggiero vented his anger at a U.S. Marshal after the official wouldn't let him visit with his son.

"Come on, let's go, go home and celebrate with your family,"

Ruggiero said with anger and sarcasm at the marshal. "Tell them what victory you got. Go ahead and laugh. I wish it on your wife and kids what you wish on my wife and kids."

Then, as he was exiting the courtroom, Ruggiero turned to the prosecutor, pointed his finger in what officials said was a threatening manner and barked, "You first."

Judge Mark Costantino had enough. Not only had Ruggiero threatened a witness in court but he did the same to a prosecutor. Costantino revoked the bail, noting that the informant evidence Noon had testified about, as well as the Dellacroce tape, indicated Ruggiero was operating at a high level in organized crime. Ruggiero's bail was revoked. He appealed, but the appellate court was unmoved, noting "The courtroom threats in the presence of the district judge are more than enough to justify revocation of bail." Threats made before a district judge have to be taken seriously, said the court.

So now Gotti and Ruggiero are both being held in jail. Gotti's special committee to run the crime family was now missing one key man on the street, all because of Ruggiero's intemperate remarks before a judge. According to Gravano, when Ruggiero's bail was revoked Gotti was beyond angry.

"John is steaming," Gravano said later. "Blabbermouth Angie can forget being the underboss, if he ever had a chance."

Gotti picked Joe "Piney" Armone to the underboss position. But since Armone was elderly and not very tough, Gotti told Gravano to keep his hands on things but as a courtesy to keep Armone informed. That move effectively made Gravano the underboss to those members on the street. As for Ruggiero, his costly outburst was another black mark against him in Gotti's eyes.

With a trial date for Gotti coming up in the Giacalone case, Judge Nickerson had to wrestle with how to select a jury. Giacalone claimed that there was evidence that the defendants wanted "to follow jurors to their homes and then contact jurors and their families for the purpose of corruptly influencing them." To combat that, Giacalone wanted Nickerson to sequester the jury, an extreme step which would have meant that the jurors would have had to live away from home and guarded by federal marshals during the trial.

In the end, in what would be a fateful decision, Nickerson shot down Giacalone's request for sequestration.

The trial finally got underway on September 25, 1986, and with Gotti now as the lead defendant, it became a media spectacle. The courtroom of Judge Nickerson in what is now the old Brooklyn federal court house had every seat taken, with an estimated 25 percent being occupied by reporters and sketch artists (no cameras were allowed into the room). Giacalone, the prosecutor, told the jury that Gotti had killed to climb to the top of organized crime, a reference to the McBratney slaying in 1973. The prosecutor's opening statement took about ninety minutes and immediately showed that Giacalone was trying to turn her case into a tutorial on organized crime, its structure and its aims.

Giacalone used a green chalk board in the courtroom to sketch for the jury the structure of the Gambino crime family. Any seasoned cop or mob buff could see the diagram coming as she diagramed how the boss sat at the top, advised by the consiglieri, underneath whom there were captains and soldiers. At the bottom of the pyramid-like structure were eager associates who Giacalone said wanted to become made members of the crime family.

"It's organized like a business . . . and where there's money to be made, you'll find the members of the Gambino crime family," Giacalone told jurors. She said Gotti and the other defendants played their own roles over two decades in the enterprise, from hijackings, to gambling, loansharking, and murder. To be sure, some of the government witnesses Giacalone planned to call had done their fair share of crimes—murders, kidnappings, and drug dealing. Admitting such witnesses were "just horrible people," Giacalone told the jury to measure their testimony against the other proof, including wiretapped conversations.

The defendants may not have had the resources of the federal government but they certainly had an array of seasoned and top-notch criminal defense attorneys. If Giacalone acted like a professor in talking to the jury, Gotti's attorney Bruce Cutler, who had represented him in the Piecyk case, was a showman who could use props well. His voice dripped with sarcasm as he referred to Giacalone, who was dressed in a red suit, as "The Lady in Red." Picking up a copy of the indictment, Cutler tossed it in a waste basket in front of the jurors, saying, "It's garbage, that's where it belongs." Gotti, dressed in a double-breasted blue suit, a silk tie, and white handkerchief in his breast pocket, seemed taken in by the dialogue.

Cutler admitted that Gotti had a criminal past and didn't apologize for it. Gotti also didn't apologize for coming from a family of eleven surviving children that was dirt poor, said Cutler. Gotti made something of his life, and by wearing a nice suit he wasn't trying to be showy but rather to show his pride, said Cutler.

Barry Slotnick, a well-known defense attorney who a year later would be catapulted to more fame defending subway gunman Bernhard Goetz, represented John Carneglia and said the government had injected the Mafia label into the case to prejudice the jury. Giacalone's opening, said Slotnick, was like a script for a grade-B crime movie.

One of the very first witnesses for the government was Sal Polisi, a Gambino associate, who if he once had aspirations to become a made man, no longer did. Instead, he turned into a government cooperator. Polisi was a small-time thief and over time would parlay his experiences into a book and movie. But his literary ambitions caused the first of what would be many problems for the government. Giacalone had wanted to call Polisi as her opening witness but had to delay that after it became known that the mob associate had given an interview to a writer working on a book about him. That interview had been taped, and Giacalone had to provide the defense attorneys with copies of it in case there was anything said that might contradict what Polisi said on the witness stand.

Polisi finally did testify and related how he hung out with the Gotti crew in the Bergin club, sometimes gossiping or gambling and other times plotting crimes to commit. Polisi's value to the government was to set the stage and inform the jury about what went on in the club. His testimony wasn't very dramatic, but since Polisi was one of a number of informants the government had in the Gotti crew he had first-hand information about some things.

It was with the testimony of another witness that Giacalone's case started to show problems. It was part of the government's case that Jimmy McBratney had kidnapped a number of organized crime figures and had gone on to kill one of them. McBratney's own death was caused by Gotti as a favor to Carlo Gambino, and both Giacalone and John Gleeson wanted to bring in testimony of another career criminal—Edward Maloney—to prove that point. But, Maloney's information about Gotti's motive was much too tenuous and amounted to unacceptable hearsay. Said Judge Nickerson: "Far too thin."

For most of the trial, Gotti had been rather well behaved, listening closely to the testimony. But in early November as the trial was in its second month, things got testy. Victor Ruggiero, a retired NYPD detective, testified about surveillance he had done at the Ravenite social club in the late 1970s. Ruggiero wasn't the greatest witness in that he seemed evasive in giving answers on cross-examination. Suddenly, Giacalone called for a recess and for the jury to be taken from the courtroom. It was then that the prosecutor, whose case had suffered a number of nettlesome problems, told Nickerson that Gotti had been making sarcastic comments in a voice "loud enough for me to hear quite distinctly." One of Gotti's murmured comments was that ex-detective Ruggiero was testifying the way he did because the government had "threatened him."

"Your honor, it's not true," Gotti told Nickerson.

"Don't make comments," Nickerson replied.

"But it's not true, your honor . . . if anybody is making comments, it's her," insisted Gotti, pointing at Giacalone.

A thin, mild mannered jurist with a genteel, patrician demeanor, Nickerson ended the discussion with an admonition to everyone in the courtroom: "Please don't say anything the jury can overhear."

Nickerson was trying to make sure that the jury wouldn't be subjected to extraneous things that might hurt its impartiality or subject it to unwanted verbiage. But as it turned out, the mob was making an end run around Nickerson. No matter how strong or weak evidence might appear in a case—and in the Gotti trial the case seemed in trouble for the government—the end result could be unpredictable. A weak case could just as easily lead to a conviction while over-

whelming evidence of guilt could result in an acquittal, such are the
vagaries of jury deliberations. For Gotti's crew the attitude was why
take chances. Put the fix in with the jury as an insurance policy.

During breaks in the case the defendants who were out on bail
would be able to walk around outside the courthouse into Cadman
Plaza Park, at that time a bit of down-on-the heels urban greenspace
punctuated by the Brooklyn War Memorial. On one such perambu-
lation, John Carneglia was with Kevin McMahon, a young man who
Carneglia's family had adopted to save him a life of living on the
streets of Howard Beach, and they were headed toward a parking lot
opposite the courthouse. McMahon had been in court watching the
proceedings and noticed one of the jurors going to get his car.

"Oh, there is one of your jurors," McMahon said to Carneglia.
For reasons that were never entirely clear but must not have been
good, McMahon wrote down the license plate of the juror's car and
passed it along to a Gambino associate at the trial. McMahon did
that with a few other juror license plates, and before long the associate, known as "The Frog" had an insurance agent run the license
numbers through the state Department of Motor Vehicles system to
locate the names and addresses of the jurors.

Another Gambino associate who became a cooperating witness
related the same basic story as McMahon. Groups of Gambino associates would position themselves around the federal courthouse and
await word that the jurors were coming out. Jurors would be followed to their cars or else the van used by the marshals to transport
the jurors to their cars would be followed, said the witness. Once the
jurors' vehicles were identified, other associates would try and follow jurors to their homes.

While it was never entirely clear if the license plate tactic and
tailing led to any solid opportunities to compromise the jurors, the
Bergin crew learned that one of the anonymous jurors, George Pape,
was a friend of a Gambino associate named Bosko Radonjich, a Yu-
goslav gangster who, as fate would have it, was close with Gotti.
Like the other jurors in the case, Pape had sworn that he would listen to the evidence fairly and without bias. But as soon as he got on
the jury panel, according to the FBI, Pape contacted Radonjich and

said he could be a holdout juror for the right price. Pape wanted $120,000 for performing his corrupt jury service. After all, the ex-Marine had money problems and he had done his bit for his country already in the military.

As Gambino family underboss, it fell upon Sammy Gravano to try and negotiate a better price with Pape. As Gravano would later explain things, the $120,000 seemed a high price. What if the juror became ill or had to be excused from the case? Gravano said he got Pape to accept $60,000, and the payment was passed along through Radonjich. Gotti was now assured that there would be at least one holdout in the case, leading to a mistrial.

Giacalone, Gleeson, and Nickerson, as well as it seems the defense attorneys, were in the dark about the machinations going on to corrupt the jury. The case slogged on with more government witnesses whose testimony amounted to a mixed blessing for the government. James Cardinali, a thirty-seven-year-old convicted killer, testified about hijackings, murders, and loansharking, activities he tied Gotti to one way or another. But on cross-examination, Cardinali caused Giacalone one headache after another. At one point, Cardinali said he believed Giacalone had lied to him and acknowledged when questioned by Gene Gotti's attorney Jeffrey Hoffman that he would "absolutely" lie, cheat, or steal to get what he wanted. In one embarrassing moment and over the objection of Giacalone, Cardinali said that the prosecutor had told him that Nickerson treated her like a daughter, giving her anything she wanted while denying the same to defense counsel.

It didn't get much better for Giacalone the longer Cardinali stayed on the witness stand. Under questioning by Cutler, Cardinali admitted that he had told a defense investigator, "From the day I met John Gotti he did nothing but good for me. He put money in my pocket when I didn't have a dime, he put clothes on my back. He is the finest man I have ever known."

But the real cringe-worthy moment for the prosecution came with the testimony of Matthew Traynor, a man Giacalone had once considered using as a witness but didn't after she caught him in a lie. Traynor was an old heroin dealer (Gotti had plenty of those around him), bank robber, and perjurer who first approached the government to cooperate as a way of getting his sentence reduced in a bank-heist case. But when Giacalone cut him off, Traynor went to Cutler to be a defense witness, and his testimony for Gotti represented a titillating moment in the case—at Giacalone's expense.

As a woman and the lead prosecutor, Giacalone had been the butt of much contempt by the defense. When Traynor testified, the sexual innuendo came out in a way that was unexpected. Traynor said that Giacalone had tried to induce him to lie about Gotti by giving him drugs, such as Valium and codeine. During one visit to Giacalone's office, Traynor said he told her he wanted to "get laid." Giacalone, Traynor claimed, pulled out a pair of her panties from her desk drawer and told him to masturbate with them. "Make do with these," Giacalone said, according to Traynor.

Already stressed out with the way the case was going, Giacalone jumped up and protested, saying that what Traynor was saying was all lies. Not used to such courtroom histrionics, Nickerson was moved to say to Cutler and others on the defense "This case is not going to turn into any more of a circus than the defendants' attorneys have already made it."

The case finally went to the jury on March 6, 1987, about six-and-one-half months after the trial had started. It had been a tortured trial for the government, with witnesses embarrassing prosecutors and showing all sorts of credibility problems. The defense attorneys even prepared a chart showing how the main prosecution witnesses had admitting lying and the kinds of deals they got for their testimony. Privately, some government attorneys expressed doubt that the prosecution had a chance, despite the odds usually being in favor of the government in big trials.

On March 13, 1987, the seventh day of deliberations, the jury signaled it had reached a verdict. In a hushed courtroom, the Juror No. 10—the jurors were anonymous for security reasons—announced the verdict of not guilty for Gotti and all of his co-defendants: Gene Gotti, John Carneglia, Leonard DiMaria, Joseph Corozzo, Anthony Rampino, and Willie Boy Johnson. As the verdict of acquittal was read to its conclusion, Gotti and the rest of the defendants hugged their attorneys. Then, as the jurors left the courtroom, the defendants and their supporters in the courtroom applauded. Giacalone and Gleeson, the defeated prosecutors, looked glum.

A scrum of reporters was in the courtroom and fired questions at Gotti and the lawyers over the railing at the well of the room. Gotti had some pat answers.

"Shame on them. I would like to see a verdict on them," said Gotti, pointing at the empty prosecution table. Then, escorted by marshals, Gotti left to collect his belongings—he had been in custody since May—left the courthouse a free man to go back to a Howard Beach neighborhood where the trees were decorated with yellow ribbons.

Reporters did get a chance to ask one more question of Gotti before he went home: how did he beat the case. Gotti then pointed to the jury box and answered "With these people here." He was certainly right about that, although the reporters had no way of appreciating the irony in Gotti's reply.

CHAPTER FOURTEEN
Tales of the Tapes, Part 1

WITH THE ACQUITTAL IN BROOKLYN FEDERAL COURT, on top of the dismissal of the assault case involving Romual Piecyk in Queens, Gotti was quickly dubbed the "Teflon Don" in the media. He had an aura of invincibility about him. While the racketeering case in front of Judge Nickerson had been grinding on, the Mafia bosses in the other New York families had not fared well at all. On November 19, 1986, in the Commission trial taking place in Manhattan federal court, Genovese boss Anthony Salerno, Tony "Ducks" Corallo, the head of the Lucchese family, and Carmine "The Snake" Persico the boss of the Colombo family were all convicted of a range of federal racketeering offenses, including the extortion of the construction industry through the Concrete Club scheme. Their associates, Salvatore "Tom Mix" Santoro, Christy "Tick" Furnari, and Gerry Langella were convicted as well, along with union officials and Bruno Indelicato, the Bonanno associate who helped carry out the murder of Carmine Galante.

Gotti was the last of the official bosses standing, although Philip Rastelli of the Bonanno family still faced a different set of charges and had not yet been convicted. Still, as the Teflon Don, Gotti was now swaggering around town, hitting the nightclubs and laughing at the government. He was good copy for the press, and with his stylish couture and expensive night life consuming Remy Martin Louis XIII cognac, Gotti also became known as the "Dapper Don." When his son John A. got married, the reception at the Helmsley Palace, said to have cost $100,000, received media coverage as if it where a royal wedding. A fair complement of cops and agents also provided their own kind of coverage, watching the guests as they climbed the stairs inside the hotel to the ballroom.

At the FBI offices in Queens, Bruce Mouw and the rest of the special C-16 squad had sensed that the Brooklyn racketeering jury had been compromised before the verdict had been rendered. It seems that among the FBI stable of informants was a woman who was dating and sleeping with a Gambino associate. During some pillow talk, the woman learned from her lover that Gotti wasn't worried about a verdict because the jury had been compromised. But with only suspicion and no firm evidence, Brooklyn U.S. Attorney Andrew Maloney kept silent and kept his own suspicion from Giacalone and the rest of the trial team.

As would later be uncovered in the government follow-up investigation, Pape remained a stubborn holdout for acquittal. But, in a twist, Pape was apparently able to convince the other jurors that the government hadn't made its case and got the eleven others on the panel to vote for acquittal. As would later be reported, a majority of jurors had initially wanted to convict Gotti, but Pape was able to convince them to abandon their position. (Pape would later be charged federally, convicted and sentenced to three years imprisonment for his corruption.)

Gotti had good reason to feel he had won a big battle. But the war had really just begun. It was in mid-1986 that the FBI got additional authorization from Washington to conduct intensive electronic surveillance of Gotti and his haunts. Time would tell what those tapes would turn up. Even with Gotti's acquittal, Tom Sheer, a top FBI official in New York said there would likely be additional efforts to indict him. Government records show that with the acquittal in Brooklyn the FBI began to step up its efforts. Other problems also were facing the Gotti crew. The big heroin smuggling trial involving Angelo Ruggiero, John Carneglia, and others was set to begin in June in Brooklyn federal court as well, and the stakes in that case were as large as those had been in Gotti's trial.

The Ruggiero case in Brooklyn with the heroin conspiracy was basically an FBI case made from evidence gleaned from the bug in his Cedarhurst house. His big mouth and lack of impulse control got Ruggiero a stint behind bars until the trial started. Mark Reiter, having dodged one bullet with the Thelma Grant heroin case and under indictment with Ruggiero in Brooklyn, just couldn't seem to control the need to continue dealing in more heroin. From January 1980 through the fall of 1987, the Drug Enforcement Administration said that Reiter, Ruggiero, and a cadre of black heroin traffickers in Harlem worked together to move even more of the drug than the Bergin crew had done in Brooklyn. The allegations were significant because not only was Reiter tied to Gotti's crew, he was also turning out to be a major heroin connection for Ruggiero and the Harlem council of dealers, which had been established by Nicky Barnes and others to control the Harlem operation over the years. With Gotti raking in money no matter what the source, it is fair to say that Ruggiero and Reiter were feeding his avarice with cash earned from the misery drugs were causing throughout the city, particularly Harlem.

By the time Ruggiero was getting ready to stand trial on the Brooklyn heroin case, the DEA and federal prosecutors had him as a defendant in another indictment, along with Reiter, mob associate Vito Loiacono and an impressive group of black gangsters who took over Barnes's old operation including James Jackson, Raymond Clark, and over a dozen others. The government estimated that Reiter distributed about $10 million in heroin to Jackson who marketed it on the street under the brand names "Mellow Yellow, "Purple Rain," and "Murder One," the last name had an ironic meaning given that three homicides were also pinned on some of the conspirators, although not Ruggiero.

Since the Brooklyn heroin case had been indicted first, it was on deck for the first trial. In April 1987, Judge Mark Costantino began picking an anonymous jury, a practice used in other mob cases that was a way of trying to shield the jurors from publicity and possible attempts to corrupt them. Given the experience in the earlier Gotti trial, the decision to keep the jurors' identity secret was a good one. While the original indictment charged twelve people in the drug case, the indictment grew in 1985 with the addition of the brothers Anthony and Caesar Gurino, owners of a plumbing company, who were accused of being part of a conspiracy to obstruct the grand jury probe into the whereabouts of Salvatore Ruggiero's assets. The Gurinos were not accused of participating in the drug operation.

On June 1, 1987, the government and the defense gave their opening statements. Assistant U.S. Attorney Robert La Russo said the case was about drug trafficking and the substantial profit that was made from it. Although John Gotti was not a defendant in the case because there wasn't enough evidence to tie him into the trafficking, LaRusso injected his name by telling jurors that he was the boss of the main defendants: Angelo Ruggiero, Gene Gotti, and John Carneglia. Giving the jury a taste of what was to come, LaRusso said that there would be tapes made from the bug in Ruggiero's house. Even though the recordings had distracting background noise such as that of jackhammers, children's chatter, and banging pots and pans, the jury would be able to hear Ruggiero talking about the purchase of at least 100 kilograms—220 pounds—of heroin with a street wholesale value of $150,000 a kilo, said LaRusso.

The tapes were compelling pieces of evidence, so the defense in its opening sought to undercut them, claiming they were misleading fragments being used to bolster a case built on speculaton and some unsavory government witnesses. Jon Pollok, who represented Ruggiero, put forward the theory that his client tried to find the assets of his dead brother, Salvatore, so that he might secure money for his son and daughter as their inheritance, a noble task.

"The evidence will show that upon his brother's death he became consumed with overall ambition—to see that his brother's assets went to his niece and nephew," said Pollok.

"Everybody discusses Salvatore's business," Pollok said of the over eighty FBI recordings to be played at the trial. "But talking about his business and misdeeds is not a crime."

Defense attorneys took issue with the way the government wanted to use recordings sanitized of background noise and other electronic interference. Judge Costantino agreed, ordering that the original recordings should be played. Pollok made the argument to the jury that the transcripts being provided by the government of the recordings were "slanted" to mislead jurors and that the government's case was held together by "the glue of speculation and surmise."

One of the many tape recordings of Angelo Ruggiero captured him saying that the advice he had for anyone arrested who might be coerced into cooperating was "if they get pinched, tell them to lam it," meaning run away and hide. In early September, Mark Reiter, feeling the pressure of being on trial before Costantino and with another, more serious indictment looming in Manhattan federal court, took that advice to heart and disappeared. What sparked Reiter's running, alleged investigators, was a telephone call from a jailed Ruggiero who told him that James "Gator" Jackson, one of the defendants in Reiter's Manhattan drug indictment, had been moved out of the federal lockup. That was a signal, prosecutors contended, that Jackson was cooperating, all of which spelled trouble for Reiter. Since Reiter was already out on bail during the Brooklyn trial, he simply had to take off from his pricey third-floor apartment on 60th Street for parts unknown.

As the trial moved forward without Reiter, a team of DEA and FBI agents, as well as NYPD detectives, created a small task force to find the fugitive. Reiter had hid his tracks well. But, like anyone on the run, he needed to keep in touch with friends and his attorneys. Investigators pulled records of Reiter's calls and noticed numbers in California, around the upscale area of Marin County. Tracking one of the numbers, a surveillance team watched a house in the area and spotted Reiter exiting the building, which was the home of a friend. Tailing Reiter, the team followed him to a Holiday Inn motel and it was there they arrested him on November 18, 1987.

The team of investigators on Reiter's tail had come from the DEA, the FBI, and the NYPD, which was still probing the homicide of Paul Castellano. According to one member of the team, the NYPD and the Manhattan District Attorney's Office were convinced that Reiter had information about Gotti's involvement in the

Castellano hit and spent about about four days triying to convince
Reiter to cooperate. The aim of the cooperation attempt was to get
Reiter, who everybody knew was close with Gotti, to talk about
what he may have heard at the Bergin club about the crime boss's
involvement in the assassination, which at that point was still very
much an unsolved case. But Reiter proved to be a stand-up guy,
which in mob parlance meant he didn't crumble under the pressure
and refused to cooperate with the agents, even though it is unlikely
that he knew anything of value about the murder. He was then
brought back to New York after having been on the lam for about
two months. Reiter's loyalty to Gotti may have been severely mis-
placed. A few years later it was revealed that Gotti, fearing that
Reiter might cooperate, wanted him killed if he could be found.
(The same was true for Anthony Rampino, one of the shooters in the
Castellano murder. Gotti suspected Rampino as well might cooperate, and, as it turned out, Gotti's fear was justified. Rampino, after
his arrest in November 1988 on a state drug case, entertained cooperating. But after a night spent pacing a jail cell, Rampino decided
against cooperating, according to former FBI agent Phil Scala.)

In Brooklyn, the heroin case continued with a parade of government witnesses and the playing of scores of audio tapes made off
the Ruggiero bug. With eleven defendants, the case was slow going.
But by the fall, whatever had been going on in the courtroom started
to take a back seat to what the defendants appeared to be doing outside the building. If the first attempt to corrupt the jury had worked
so well in the Giacalone case, why not try it again?

Federal prosecutors in Brooklyn had already started an investigation into whether the jury in the Giacalone case had been compromised when investigators learned from confidential sources of
similar efforts in the big Ruggiero heroin case before Judge Costantino. Former FBI supervisor Bruce Mouw told the author that associates of some of the defendants—later identified in court records as
John Carneglia, Gene Gotti, Edward Lino, and Angelo Ruggiero—
carried out the same tactics Kevin McMahon had suggested in the
Giacalone case: watch the jurors at the end of the day as they re-

trieved their cars from the parking lot across Cadman Plaza Park, jot down their license plate numbers, find their identities, and then see if they could be approached.

Two private investigators were used to identify the jurors. Brooklyn federal court records later identified them as John Sewell, who failed in the task, and Victor Juliano, who apparently succeeded. According to informants, the identities of at least five of the jurors had been discovered and that one of the black jurors had been approached "and now compromised." Things got worse when one of the jurors, easily identified through his conspicuous vanity license plate, was found to have been living just a few doors away from men associated with the defendants.

The information about the jurors triggered another grand jury investigation in December into possible jury tampering. An unexpected development then occurred when one of the jurors had to be excused from serving after it was learned he was not a U.S. citizen. Two days after being removed from the jury, the now ex-juror was telephoned by a co-worker, Mel Rosenberg, who had a strange conversation about the drug case. According to court records, Rosenberg said he was a friend of Gene Gotti and offered the juror, Gary Barnes, a new BMW if he could say how the jury was feeling about the case. Since both Barnes and Rosenberg worked for a financial company, their telephone calls were routinely taped. Some of Rosenberg's initial, cryptic approaches to Barnes were recorded and proved useful for the government investigation.

By early January 1988, the government presented Costantino with evidence about the jury-tampering efforts. What followed were a series of unusual court sessions in which the government wanted Costantino to question all of the jurors and keep all of the proceedings on the issue secret and closed to the news media. Costantino decided not to question all of the jurors and then decided to allow the press access to a hearing about the tampering allegations. What transpired showed how even the suggestion of jury tampering was damaging the sanctity of the whole court process.

Costantino heard testimony from Barnes, who repeated the story about the way Rosenberg had contacted him, insisted on talking with him and then mentioned how familiar he had been with Gene Gotti. Rosenberg, according to Barnes, couched his familiarity with Gotti by saying, "I have known this kid for forty-two years, I have known his family. We are good friends," and other words to that effect. As retold by Barnes, who by that time was no longer on the jury, Rosenberg kept incorrectly stating that he had been on a jury in Queens, when in fact the case was in Brooklyn.

In further questioning of some of the remaining jurors in open court, Costantino learned some troubling information which, while not proof of any actual corruption of the jurors, raised serious questions about their ability to be impartial. One juror, Juror No. 4, told Costantino that his parents had fears, and that he wasn't sure if he could remain impartial. Juror No. 8 said he had heard of the allegations of jury tampering in media reports and after seeing that the case had so much evidence about drugs—a subject he said he couldn't be objective about because of family experiences— thought that raised a problem about his impartiality. A woman, Juror No. 12, stated to Costantino that she was not sure she could remain impartial because she had divined, from all of the delays in the case, that something fishy was going on.

"The only things is that I kind of have an idea of—on what this is all about and it is kind of changing my input as to whether I can be impartial or not," she said.

None of those sitting jurors said that anyone had actually approached them to influence their deliberations. But prosecutors asked Costantino to call a mistrial and start the case from scratch. There just weren't enough qualified jurors left to continue hearing the evidence, the prosecution said, particularly with the defense asking that jurors 4, 8, and 12 be dismissed.

Costantino had a tough decision to make: whether to scuttle the trial after so much time had been spent in court already, or continue with a depleted jury pool and risk a reversal if the trial resulted in convictions. But, then on January 19, 1988, an unusual event took place in the courthouse. The entire group of sitting judges convened an en banc hearing to consider if the governments simply made charges about jury tampering to force a mistrial because the case was going well for the defendants. Having all of the judges in a courthouse come together to hear evidence was a very rare thing for federal district courts. But it was permissible under the law, even if it had never happened in Brooklyn.

Presiding over the hearing was Judge Jack B. Weinstein, a tall, distinguished jurist who was one of the senior judges in the courthouse, having been appointed by President Lyndon B. Johnson to the bench in 1967. A former Navy submarine commander in World War Two, Weinstein loved to be in charge of things and once said he ran his own courtroom as if he was its commander. Weinstein, accompanied on the bench by eight other Brooklyn federal judges, called the case at 1:00 P.M.

"We'll hear from the government first," Weinstein said.

Brooklyn U.S. Attorney Andrew Maloney had the floor and asked Weinstein to exclude the public from the courtroom because the jury wasn't sequestered and might learn of the "sensitive" matters being discussed at the hearing. But Weinstein thought Judge Costantino had to deal with the issue of sequestration and thought it was inappropriate to exclude the public so he denied Maloney's request.

Because the hearing dealt with sealed records and a grand jury proceeding, the colloquy between the lawyers and the judge in what everybody agreed was an extraordinary hearing was a bit strained since the public was in the courtroom. But Maloney indicated for the first time on the public record that the investigation had to do with jury tampering. Since the FBI was concerned that its confidential sources might be revealed, endangering their lives, Maloney got the court to accept all documents and grand jury materials in confidence, with the judges themselves writing "Confidential" on the material because the prosecutors hadn't had time to do it before the hearing.

Turning to the defense attorneys, Weinstein said that he gathered their position was that the government essentially was trying to sabotage the trial by raising the issue of jury tampering in bad faith, thereby forcing a mistrial. Attorney Ronald P. Fischetti, who represented Gene Gotti, agreed with Weinstein's characterization but didn't want to reveal too much in such a public forum. But Fischetti said there had been nothing shown in the trial court hearing that indicated that any of the jurors had been improperly approached.

"At the hearing, your Honor, that was conducted in open court, the evidence that was submitted by the government, in our judgment, was woefully inadequate and did not reach the standard that the Court would reach in order to determine jury tampering," said Fischetti.

Fischetti also disputed the prosecution's view that the evidence against the defendant was "overwhelming," and thus provided a motive for jury tampering. There simply was nothing in the government's claims about jury tampering that indicated what a defense would be against the indictment, hence the evidence shouldn't be viewed as overwhelming, Fischetti argued.

"We have not had, if I may say, our turn at bat," argued Fischetti, stressing that the defendants didn't want a mistrial and believed they could continue with the case. The defense attorneys had made clear earlier that they would oppose any mistrial on the grounds that it would expose their clients to double jeopardy.

Weinstein and the other judges decided that the government had in good faith brought the allegation that some defendants had tampered with jurors. That ruling cleared the way for Costantino to finally decide that the government allegations of tampering compelled him to declare a mistrial. He also unsealed some of the government records that had stated one juror had been "approached and now compromised." Maloney was asked by reporters what was meant by the word "Compromised" and his answer was blunt: "Bought and paid for, in the bag."

Maloney was prepared to start the retrial immediately and also revealed that the allegations of jury tampering in the case, as well as claims about similar tampering in the Giacalone trial, were undergoing a grand jury investigation. The probes were going to get "very hot," Maloney said.

The defense attorneys stuck to their argument that any retrial would be double jeopardy since the government had caused the mistrial. The actual calling of the mistrial came after Costantino told Jurors 4, 8, and 12 that they were excused. He then replaced two of them with alternates. But that still left only eleven jurors, not the twelve normally seated in a case. Because of that, Costantino called a mistrial and thanked all of the jurors for their service. His only explanation to the now dismissed jury about what had happened to lead to the mistrial was that "serious matters came before this court."

Gene Gotti seemed incredulous about what had happened. Fischetti told reporters that his client couldn't get a fair trial now, since future jurors would be afraid to vote for an acquittal, thinking they might be accused of having been tampered with.

Ruggiero's attorney, Jeffrey Hoffman, sounded bitter, saying the government had accomplished its goal of getting a mistrial. "The government did not want the jury to vote on this case," said Hoffman. "And, as a result, the publicity caused by the unsupported charges of jury tampering allowed the government to succeed."

Costantino unsealed some of the government documents, and they alleged that Carneglia, Gene Gotti, Ruggiero and Lino "had learned the identities of at least five of the anonymous jurors for the purpose of fixing this case, and have compromised one of the jurors who is presently on the panel."

So months of trial went out the window. Ten defendants would all have to stand trial again: Oscar Ansourian, John Carneglia, Gene Gotti, brothers Anthony and Caesar Gurino, Edward Lino, Canadian gangster Joseph Lo Presti, Anthony Moscatiello, the wandering Mark Reiter, and Angelo Ruggiero. But Costantino wasn't going to have to see their faces again. He had taken senior status in December and decided to pass on handling the retrial. The case was assigned to Judge Joseph McLaughlin, one of the relatively new members of the court's bench.

McLaughlin inherited a mess and to make it more manageable he divided the case up in four parts, with Gotti, Carneglia and Ruggiero together in one major piece. Prosecutors immediately tried to get Gotti's bail revoked, but McLaughlin ruled that there wasn't enough evidence that Gotti had asked Rosenberg to approach the juror Barnes. So Gotti and Carneglia remained free, as did most of the other defendants.

Not all of the defendants had been suspected of jury tampering, and six of them, including Reiter and the Gurino brothers, thought any attempt to retry them would be double jeopardy and wanted the case dismissed. But McLaughlin ruled against them, finding that there really wasn't any way that the court could salvage the original jury for some of the defendants. Michael Coiro, the attorney who fancied himself a gangster, also saw his case severed from the rest, and he would be tried separately on several counts of obstruction of justice.

CHAPTER FIFTEEN
Tales of the Tapes, Part 2

ALFRED DELLENTASH, THE ONCE-HIGH-FLYING aviation entrepreneur and drug dealer, had found himself in a very disagreeable place after his arrest on a cocaine charge in Louisiana. Angola was the name not of the African country but rather the location of Louisiana's maximum-security prison, dubbed the "Alcatraz of the South." It had an inmate population of thousands and was said to be the largest maximum-security facility in the country. It also had a terrible reputation for violence, hard labor, and a climate that could stifle anyone.

Some authors decades earlier noted that Angola was "probably as close to slavery as any person could come in 1930," and that even hardened criminals cried when they heard they were going to be doing time there. Things may have improved by the time Dellentash arrived at Angola in January 1983 to await trial for the cocaine bust. It had a prisoner newspaper known as *The Angolite,* an FM radio station, and television programming. But no matter how Angola was spruced up, Dellentash still wanted out. So, when Bruce Mouw, supervisor of the FBI's Gambino squad sent agents down to Louisiana to see if he wanted to cooperate, well, Dellentash jumped at the idea. It was good-bye Angola and hello witness protection.

Dellentash, and to a lesser extent Wayne Debany, were important witnesses for the government in the heroin case against Angelo Ruggiero and company. True, Dellentash wasn't a major *babania* dealer—he preferred marijuana—but he had dealt with Ruggiero in filling him in on what his brother Salvatore had been doing, where his assets were, and some of the property he owned. Dellentash also was present for certain key conversations as Ruggiero tried to reconstruct Salvatore's operation and with the help of Coiro obstruct the grand jury investigation into the drug dealing. In terms of making the case, Dellentash could provide some of the glue to stitch things together. He could help prosecutors interpret some of the tapes made in Angelo's house and give important context. Dellentash also had evidence useful by the government against Ansourian.

It was no secret that Dellentash and Debany were going to testify in the Ruggiero case since the news media had publicized their cooperation just before the first trial started. Both men had much to say, but it was Dellentash who provided the prosecution and the jury with important context, laying the groundwork for the drug business Salvatore Ruggiero had set up.

According to Dellentash, it was late 1978 when he was introduced to Sal Ruggiero who along with another man wanted him to provide a plane to bring a load of heroin into the U.S. from Pakistan. Dellentash agreed to provide the aircraft and the pilot—who happened to be George Morton—and the deal was set. According to a November 2014 story about Dellentash on the website *Narratively* written by Jeff Maysh, he only knew Ruggiero by his pseudonym Steve Teri and wouldn't learn about his Mafia connections until later. But the $150,000 Ruggiero dangled in front of Dellentash was enough of an enticement to try heroin smuggling.

But according to Dellentash, the Pakistan deal fell through after the heroin supplier there got busted by Pakistani authorities. Then, recalled Dellentash, Ruggiero introduced him to a contact in the marijuana business and the three men agreed in June 1979 to attempt to fly about 10,000 pounds of marijuana into Florida. But this second venture was also star-crossed. The plane developed mechanical problems and was forced to land in Melbourne, Florida, and the load of pot was seized. A few days later, Dellentash's close friend Wayne Debany, pilot Morton, and their business partner in the drug deal were arrested for the ditched load.

While Debany was cooling his heels in a Florida jail cell, he was visited by an attorney he had never met before—Michael Coiro of New York. In their statements to the government and at trial, Debany and Dellentash said that Coiro said he was brought into the case by Sal Ruggiero, who at that point while living in Florida was actually a fugitive from New York, on the lam in three cases: heroin smuggling, hijacking, and tax evasion. Coiro was able to get bail for Debany but the defendant decided to have another lawyer represent him at trial, where he, Morton, and all the other defendants save one were acquitted.

Having dodged another bullet with the marijuana seizure, Dellentash must have been feeling invulnerable. He agreed after the acquittal of his sidekicks to team up with Sal Ruggiero and Oscar Ansourian, another mob-connected drug dealer, to bring in more marijuana loads. So, from about July 1980 through June 1981, Dellentash told prosecutors, the group flew in about twenty-eight loads of marijuana—about 2,500 pounds a load—to Millville, N.J. In his interview with author Maysh, Dellentash said his supplier was Carlo Lederer, the former Colombian drug lord, who he met at a Miami restaurant with Ruggiero. As Dellentash related to Maysh, he took some $40,000 in bribe money to spread among government officials, customs officers, and the military in places like the Bahamas and Colombia to assure he had safe passage.

Back in Millville, where Dellentash used an old World War Two–vintage hangar for his planes, the cargo was then taken by van to Westchester County, where Dellentash grew up, and distributed throughout the New York metropolitan area. Part of one load even made it to John Carneglia's junkyard in East New York. Each load, said Dellentash to the FBI, brought in $75,000, which was split between himself, Ruggiero, and Ansourian.

The marijuana business was going well until the summer of 1981 when one of the customers was arrested in Boston. It was then that the smugglers decided to suspend the flights into New Jersey until it seemed safer. By early 1982, Ruggiero, Dellentash, and Ansourian began talking about reviving the marijuana business but in the end, according to Dellentash, decided against it. It seemed that Ruggiero

owed Dellentash a great deal of money for prior marijuana ship-
ments and didn't want to pay, likely because he was a bit strapped
for cash given the demands of his fugitive lifestyle.

Ruggiero and his friends in the Gambino crime family saw more
profit potential in heroin so they called off their discussions with
Dellentash about marijuana and tried to convince him to fly in
heroin. Dellentash was reluctant to do that. It seemed too risky. Despite several meetings that were amicable, Dellentash told investigators that he didn't want to get involved at that point in shipping
heroin on his planes.

But the fact that Dellentash may have had cold feet about the
heroin trade didn't stop others in the Gambino crime family from
trying to forge drug connections. During one February 23, 1982, surveillance, FBI agents spotted John Carneglia and Angelo Ruggiero
travel to New Jersey where they visited mob-connected drug connections: Alphonse Sisca and Arnold Squitieri. Both men lived in the
high-income town of Englewood Cliffs, and it was there that Ruggiero and Carneglia were seen by FBI surveillance teams. Squitieri
was a known heroin dealer, with two convictions for heroin distribution in the 1950s, a first-degree manslaughter conviction, and one
for income-tax evasion, FBI records showed. In other words,
Squitieri had a good resume for mob life. But the fact that he had
been nabbed and convicted on drug charges was a roadblock to his
attempts to become a solider in the Gambino family. Sisca, an associate of the Lucchese crime family, was considered by the DEA to
be a major narcotics violator, with a 1973 conviction for distributing
over twenty-six pounds of heroin, which netted him a twelve-year
prison sentence.

It was unclear what Ruggiero and Carneglia discussed with Sisca
and Squitieri at their meeting. The FBI had a bug operating on Ruggiero's house, but the tapes didn't provide insight into the subject of
the meeting. But a little over a week after the Englewood Cliffs
meeting, Ruggiero and Squitieri were surveilled meeting in Queens
at a deli by the intersection of Linden Boulevard and 79th Street.
After the meeting, Squitieri and an unidentified man he was travel-

ing with got into their car, with the unknown man holding what appeared to be a package in his jacket. Was it drugs? The FBI seemed to think so.

As a fugitive, Sal Ruggiero had a lot on his plate. He not only had to live a secret life but he had a wife and two children to take care of. That he managed to do so by making money—both legal and illegal—showed how industrious and careful he could be. He had the drug business for certain. But there were also legitimate holdings Sal Ruggiero had that were held through a carefully constructed web of people who acted as fronts. He had Michael Coiro, the lawyer to thank for some of that.

As stressful as the life of a fugitive could be, Sal Ruggiero did his best to try and give some normal existence to his children. In early April 1982 he flew down to Florida with his son in Dellentash's Learjet for a Disneyland vacation. It was kind of a male bonding experience since neither Ruggiero's wife Stephanie nor the couple's daughter traveled with father and son. But Ruggiero's interest in Florida went beyond amusement. Ruggiero took another trip in April 1982 to Disney World in the Learjet to meet up with Oscar Ansourian to arrange a heroin transaction, according to Dellentash's testimony, his FBI debriefing and records of the amusement park reveal. The earlier trip by Ruggiero with his son might very well have been a reconnaissance for the heroin trip, although that will never be known. While in Florida, Ruggiero heard from Dellentash, who had some troubling news. A New Jersey State Police officer had visited Dellentash to inquire about the Learjet and its pilot George Morton. That was not a good sign, and after the cop left Dellentash contacted Ruggiero to tell him to not fly back in the jet. Things were too hot.

Ruggiero disregarded that warning and came back on the jet. He actually wasn't in any danger of being caught doing anything since he had no drugs with him. Instead, Ansourian drove the 1,500 or so miles from Florida to New Jersey with twenty-six pounds of heroin in his car. There was always the risk that Ansourian would be stopped by an aggressive highway patrol officer somewhere and the heroin possibly discovered. But that didn't happen, and the drugs got back north.

Dellentash's testimony and information wasn't the only evidence. Months of surveillance of Angelo Ruggiero's house in Cedarhurst had led to hours of incriminating recordings. One Saturday afternoon about a week before his brother Sal died in the crash of the Learjet, Angelo was visited by Gerlando Sciascia the Canadian gangster and drug trafficker who bragged that "I got thirty things of heroin. That's why I'm here." It was heroin Sciascia wanted to give to Sal Ruggiero, as much as forty kilos. When Angelo heard that he said, "Oh, yeah," with a mix of incredulity and uncertainty. "I've got to speak to my brother," said Angelo.

These conversations, which took place in the week before Salvatore's death, undercut the argument by the defense that it was only after the fatal plane crash that Angelo started to busy himself with his brother's narcotics activities. Clearly, as the Sciascia conversation showed, Angelo was working in conjunction with Salvatore as a conduit for potential sellers of heroin. There were other conversations along the same line picked up by the FBI bug, including on April 30, 1982, in which Edward Lino told Angelo about an impending heroin shipment that he wanted to give Ruggiero a first crack at. In this conversation, Ruggiero told Lino not to use airplanes to move the drugs because of government surveillance in the air. These were hardly conversations of a man unfamiliar with the drug rackets.

Yet, Ruggiero's defense attorney and the other lawyers saw the tapes as an Achilles' heel of the government's case. There were 239 recordings played at the trial, some eighty-nine picked up by the FBI bug in Angelo Ruggiero's house on Long Island. But to the defense attorneys, there was an indication in the quality of the tapes that they exploited to argue that they were tampered with by the FBI. In some cases, the playback of the recordings seemed to have the volume manipulated, the attorneys argued.

Given the worst interpretation by the government, the tapes caught Angelo talking somewhat cryptically about what appeared to be drug prices. In one case, Angelo references his brother and said,

"My brother was getting it from 135" and noted that "my brother brought him [George Sciascia] up to date about everything." In other recordings, Angelo talked about dividing up kilo loads, giving one to Sisca of New Jersey and some to Reiter, who he kept referring to as "Jew Boy."

On July 21, the case went to closing arguments with assistant U.S. Attorney Robert LaRusso saying that Carneglia, Ruggiero, and Gene Gotti were "supervisors, organizer and managers" of the heroin operation that brought in hundreds of kilos from Southeast Asia.

"They are the managers who don't take risks, who sit in their house while others do their work in the street," said LaRusso. Money was the driving force for the three defendants, and the evidence was clear in showing that, the prosecutor argued to the jury.

Ruggerio's attorney Jeffrey Hoffman, hit the tape-tampering argument hard and told the jurors that even if they didn't like his client's lifestyle, he shouldn't be convicted for that. "I ask you not to accept this terribly flawed case," Hoffman said.

Ronald Fischetti, who represented Gene Gotti, not only hit the tape-tampering issue but pointed out that not one witness could take the stand and say that Gotti was a drug dealer. Well, that was the case in the Brooklyn trial perhaps, but across the Hudson River in a different federal courtroom another jury had heard evidence that implicated the Bergin crew in heroin. Arnold Squitieri and Alphonse Sisca, the two Englewood Cliffs men Ruggiero and Carneglia had visited in 1982, were convicted of conspiring with the Bergin men, including Gene Gotti, of distributing and selling heroin.

In the New Jersey trial, the key witness was Richard Pasqua, a former heroin dealer who became a federal witness. Pasqua claimed in testimony that at one point in October 1981 Sisca had bragged he was part of the Gotti organization and that he could get as much as $3 million from John Gotti to buy heroin. Pasqua also said he bought $180,000 from Sisca and Squitieri. The evidence in the New Jersey case was of course incriminating for the Brooklyn defendants, but it was kept away from the jury in the Ruggiero trial.

In Brooklyn, the jury deliberation went on for seven days, which in a federal case is a long time. Despite hundreds of tapes, drug dealing witnesses like Dellentash, and the testimony of FBI agents, the jurors sent out a note saying they were deadlocked. At 11:45 A.M. on July 27, the jury sent a note to Judge McLaughlin that said, "After breaking yesterday, we gave serious thought to where we were heading—it amounted to nowhere." No matter how hard they tried, the jurors felt they wouldn't reach a verdict with any more deliberations.

Faced with such a note, McLaughlin called a mistrial. It was a decision that pleased no one. Carneglia seemed bitter as he told reporters, "Sure, I am upset. This case was over downstairs [in the first trial] and it's over here. Their theory is if Denver plays Washington enough times Denver might eventually win." The latter reference was to the miserable record of the Denver Broncos football team compared to that of the Washington Redskins.

"I feel empty, having been with it for so long and not having a resolution," said a downcast and disappointed LaRusso.

Gene Gotti and Ruggiero were feeling the stress of being in legal limbo, particularly Ruggiero who was still being held without bail. A few days after the mistrial was announced, the jury foreman talked to reporters and kept his identity confidential. The tapes, the foreman said, were the problem for the jurors. At one point the jurors by a show of hands voted on the reliability of the FBI tapes, and it was clear that issue was far from clear.

"Seven felt there was no tampering, and five felt the possibility existed, not that they actually did it," stated the foreman. "We didn't try to pinpoint who or what caused the tampering. We realized after seven days of replaying the tapes we were beyond the point where we could agree on the tapes."

Years later, LaRusso said that he had wanted the court to give the jurors both the tapes and transcripts of the recordings to aid the jurors in their listening. But McLaughlin decided to give the jurors the option of listening to the tapes with or without the transcripts, This, prosecutors believed caused some of the confusion with the jurors about the tapes' reliability.

After the mistrial was announced, Brooklyn U.S. Attorney Andrew Maloney said that the way the jurors seemed to accept the defense claims that the recordings were tampered with made the jury seems like gullible tourists who could eventually be sold the Brooklyn Bridge. The jury foreman didn't like Maloney's criticism and opined that he thought the government would have a hard time convincing a new jury. The foreman was also critical of the way FBI agent William Noon played the recordings in court, seeming to raise the volume in some instances to have the jurors hear what he wanted them to hear.

But Maloney was set on trying the case a third time, and McLaughlin set September 7 as a tentative trial date. The judge did cut Ruggiero a break, granting him a $1 million bail after the mistrial. McLaughlin also wanted to make sure Ruggiero didn't get involved in any mob activity while free and ordered that he not associate with his co-defendants, except when he needed to plan legal strategy. He also told Ruggiero to stay away from any alleged members of the Gambino crime family.

For whatever reason, McLaughlin was not going to handle a retrial of the Bergin crew. Instead, the case was assigned to Judge John Bartels, who at the age of ninety-one was the oldest jurist in the Brooklyn courthouse. The case would remain in a holding pattern for several months, and it was only in April 1989 that with Ruggiero becoming progressively sicker from cancer and requiring surgery that Bartels decided to sever him from the case. The court just couldn't wait the two or three months that it might require Ruggiero to recuperate. Bartels said he wanted to get the case over with and knew that Gene Gotti and John Carneglia wanted the same.

While much of the public attention in 1987 and 1988 was focused on the Gambino crime family in the heroin trial, there was much going on behind the scenes with the FBI. The Bureau didn't stop its probe into the Bergin crew and the rest of the crime family. Far from it. With Gotti very much the public face of the mob and taunting the cops with his very public persona after his acquittal in the Giacalone case, the FBI began to intensify its investigation by getting authorization from the Department of Justice to conduct extensive electronic surveillance of Gotti and his men. After all, the heroin case surveillance effectively ended in July 1982 with the FBI, but Gotti's operation continued to grow and assert itself after he became boss for all practical purposes in December 1985. Things were happening, and the FBI informants were giving Mouw and his agents plenty of ammunition to target Gotti for additional electronic surveillance warrants.

The Gotti crew was considered a national priority by the FBI, and the spigot for money was opened, although by modern standards the amounts weren't very much, perhaps $20,000 in separate disbursements, according to FBI records. By 1987, Gotti and the Bergin boys were given top priority out of New York where it was soon learned that Gotti had offices in the Manhattan garment district, namely at the companies of Lewis Kasman. The garment industry had long been a mob bailiwick, for the Gambino family in particular. The now shelved underboss Joe N. Gallo controlled the Greater Blouse Association, a trade group, along with two other Mafia families. Thomas Gambino had interests in major garment trucking companies, and mob loan sharks provided cash-strapped manufacturers with usurious loans, often leading to organized crime takeovers of a company. For Gotti, he was linked by investigators to Kasman's Scorpio Marketing and Albie Trimming companies, two garment district firms, which was a way of providing him with a source of seemingly legitimate income. Kasman, who was Gotti's confidant and considered the mob boss's "adopted son" was only too happy to accommodate him and served as an unofficial chief of staff

Mouw and his investigators in New York were, as one FBI memo stated, to be given "all manpower and support personnel that will be needed" to carry out what was planned to be a massive wiretapping and electronic surveillance of Gotti and his upper-echelon bosses. Running the investigation on the prosecution side was Brooklyn U.S. Attorney Andrew Maloney and his Strike Force chief Laura Brevetti, both of whom thought bugs and wiretaps were the way to go to get Gotti. Over time, the investigation, code-named "Hatter," focused on Gotti's haunts all around the city: the garment district, the Bergin Hunt and Fish Club, and the Ravenite Social Club. Of course, Gotti had made it easy for the FBI spies because of the way he demanded his hierarchy and captains to show up at the Ravenite. Gravano would later rail against this move by Gotti and with good reason. FBI records showed how Gotti conducted much of his business at the Ravenite in "walk and talk" conversations outside the club, away from any bug inside.

Gotti, being surveillance conscious, frustrated the agents with his outdoor way of doing business. FBI officials, according to internal agency memos, believed they weren't getting fruitful results from the electronic surveillance—"limited success" was how they characterized the results. The stage was now set for some more inventive surveillance techniques, beyond the usual wiretaps and bugs of Gotti's usual circuit.

Agents had a number of places to spy on for Gotti but needed to figure out which location was the best to plant a bug to listen to his criminal conversations. They finally settled on the Ravenite club, and it was there that the FBI black bag team entered one night and planted a listening device. But the acoustics in the club were terrible. The espresso machine would be hissing in the background, a soda machine was constantly in use, and with a number of conversations going on around Gotti, agents had a hard time discerning what was being said. The FBI team tried moving the bugging device around to different locations and even used special audio filters to take away extraneous sound. But it was to no avail.

After months of frustration, Mouw and the FBI team learned from an informant that Gotti would often leave the confines of the club and talk to captains like Thomas Gambino in a back hallway. Then, the informant discovered that Gotti would take people out of the hallway to an apartment upstairs in the building at 247 Mulberry Street. After some more discreet snooping, the informant reported back that Gotti was using the apartment of a widow, Nettie Cirelli, to hold meetings. The widow's husband had been Michael Cirelli, a Gambino soldier, and the apartment had been used by Dellacroce for discreet meetings when he was alive. So the FBI team one night, reportedly over the 1989 Thanksgiving holiday when Mrs.Cirelli was on vacation in Florida, planted a listening device in her living room, where Gotti would hold court. It was there that some of the better tapes were made of Gotti, Frank Locascio, and others in often long, drawn-out conversations about crime-family activity.

With the Gotti investigation being such a high priority, the FBI needed secrecy about the surveillance of Gotti. Even normal courthouse procedures weren't good enough. Usually, agents would troop over to the Manhattan federal courthouse, directly across the street from FBI offices, and make a presentation to the judge for wiretap or surveillance warrants. But, with so many defense attorneys around the courthouse and with FBI agents like six-foot six-inch tall George Gabriel easily spotted, the plan was to have the judge do things differently so as not to make any defense attorneys suspicious. To that end, Judge Kevin Duffy, who was the judge handling all of the wiretap and surveillance applications, walked over to FBI offices and went over the paperwork there and signed the warrants.

From late 1988 through most of 1989, Duffy kept trooping over to the FBI to read various requests to extend the surveillance authorization—something that had to be done every thirty days—as the agents continued to pick up Gotti's conversations inside the apartment. The tapes would provide the FBI with hundreds of hours of conversations from which to glean evidence for use against Gotti and his administration. But that part of the story was over a year away from developing into the public forum.

CHAPTER SIXTEEN
"Gentlemen, It's Been a Pleasure"

WILLIE BOY JOHNSON HAD LED A CHARMED LIFE for years. Not only had he been close to John Gotti, getting in the gangster's good graces and being a confidante of sorts, Johnson also did it all while being a key informant for the FBI and local prosecutors in Queens. Johnson remained in place as a key source for investigators until he was finally outed by federal prosecutor Diane Giacalone. When that happened, Johnson of course feared for his life. He was on trial with Gotti at the time and desperately told him that he wasn't a snitch. Yet, while Gotti gave Willie Boy assurances on his dead son's body that nothing would happen to him, the die was cast for revenge.

The FBI was focusing on Gotti and building a case through electronic surveillance and informants. But investigators didn't have real-time advance evidence of mob killings. On the morning of August 29, 1988, Johnson, who by that time had decided to stay away from the Gotti clique, was walking to his 1988 black Mercury outside his home in the Flatlands section of Brooklyn. He got a job in construction and was on his way to work. Suddenly, two assailants rushed up to him and started shooting.

After the first shot, which may have missed him, Johnson began running but only got a short distance before he was gunned down. A total of six rounds struck Johnson in the head, another two in the back, and one in each of his thighs. He died where he fell, blood surrounding his body. The killer or killers wanted to make sure Johnson had no chance of surviving. The assailants fled in cars and to thwart anyone's attempt to follow them threw spiked objects on the road to puncture the tires of vehicles.

The tabloids noted Johnson's tight connection to Gotti and speculated—quite correctly as it turned out—the crime boss wanted to get revenge for the way Willie Boy compromised the Bergen club activities. Gotti wasn't charged with killing, but over the years investigators pieced together what had happened. According to Gravano, Gotti farmed out the hit to Eddie Lino, the heroin dealer who by now was a captain in the crime family. But years later in an interview, Jim Hunt, special agent in charge for the DEA in New York, told the author that Lino went against Mafia protocol and in turn talked to his close friend Tommy "Karate" Pitera, a member of the Bonanno crime family, for help.

Pitera was one of the legendary killers of the modern Mafia. As a young man growing up in the Canarsie section of Brooklyn, Pitera was bullied by others because he had a high-pitched voice. Eventually, Pitera took up the martial art of karate to defend himself, hence the sobriquet in the underworld. Pitera was aligned years earlier with the infamous Three Captains of the Bonanno family—Dominick Trinchera, Philip Giaccone, and Alphonese Indelicato—who were snuffed out in May 1981 during a struggle for control of the crime family. Pitera quickly came under the wing of Anthony Spero, a captain, who headed the Brooklyn wing of the family.

Pitera soon gained a reputation as a killer who seemed to relish homicide and liked disposing of the bodies of his victims through butchery. When the DEA raided Pitera's home, they found books about homicide and dismemberment. The late author Phil Carlo wrote a biography of Pitera and said he had no qualms about placing his victims in a bathtub, stripping down, and then hacking them to pieces. Then, said Carlo, Pitera would rinse out the tub, take a shower, and get dressed. The bodies were often buried, sometimes without their heads, in a bird sanctuary on Staten Island.

As a budding, dangerous wiseguy, Pitera became close with

Lino, and according to Hunt both men carried out murders together. Lino, an accomplished killer of his own, gave the contract to kill Johnson to Pitera and another man, although he should have given it to someone in the Gambino family, said Hunt. In 1990 Pitera was arrested for, among other killings, the slaying of Johnson, and when that happened the news caused a problem for Lino. Confronted by Gravano and asked if it was true that Pitera had killed Johnson, Lino strenuously denied it, insisting he did it himself, Hunt said. As a result of his debriefing of Gravano, Gotti suspected that Lino was lying, Hunt said, but didn't care. (Pitera was convicted of several racketeering murders in 1992 but wasn't found culpable for the Johnson killing.)

Gene Gotti and John Carneglia had lived their own kind of charmed lives all throughout the two trials in the heroin conspiracy case. Two mistrials kept the case, which began with an indictment in 1983, alive for a third go-round in April 1989 before one of the oldest federal judges in the nation at the time. By the time Judge John R. Bartels was ready for opening arguments in Brooklyn federal court, the case had been split up with only Gotti and Carneglia in the courtroom. Bartels had severed Ruggiero because he was too ill, and the other defendants were to go on trial at later dates.

Defense attorneys for Gotti and Carneglia were ready to argue again, as they had done in the earlier trial, that the FBI tapes were unreliable and possibly tampered with. But Bartels wasn't necessarily going to buy that argument. He sternly told defense attorneys Gerald Shargel and Ron Fischetti that they had to prove the tapes weren't reliable.

"You will have to have some expert from M.I.T. to determine if they are bad tapes," said Bartels. "I am not going to have a false issue in this case. You will have to show which tapes are tampered with and how or I won't allow the argument to be used."

With only two defendants on trial, the case was substantially simplified and relied heavily on the tape recordings. Witnesses like Alfred Dellentash weren't needed, so that cut down on the need for lengthy cross-examination. At the close of the government's case, Bartels simplified things even more when he dismissed one of the counts of the indictment. But with the Bergin crew nothing was going to be simple, even with a markedly shorter trial of just about four weeks.

It would be a shorter trial but not without its own controversy. To quote the late, great Yogi Berra: It seemed like déjà vu all over again. On the very day of summations, May 16, 1989, the U.S. Attorney's Office got a telephone call from a lawyer representing one Walter Arnold, a resident of Kings Park, a town on Long Island. It seemed that Arnold, who was not a juror in the drug case, had received an anonymous note from someone who thought he was on the panel of jurors. The note, written by someone who claimed to be a "concerned neighbor and friend" went on to say that it appeared that Arnold was a juror on the Gotti case. The problem, said the anonymous writer, was that FBI agent William Noon, who was involved in the Gotti investigation also lived near Arnold.

"As you know Kings Park is a very small community. Our children go to the same schools, we shop in the same stores," the letter continued. "It seems improper that you be on the same jury where the head FBI agent in charge is your neighbor. In all conscience you should bring this matter to the attention of the judge, government and the court." The suspicious note had all of the earmarks of a jury-tampering attempt and years later a cooperating witness told the FBI in 2009 that the Gambino family was responsible for the note in an attempt to get the juror off the panel and replaced by an alternate who allegedly was to be bribed. The bribe money was never paid, the witness stated.

A quick inquiry found that while Arnold certainly wasn't a juror, one of his neighbors was anonymous Juror No. 9. Apparently to avoid any tampering issue, Bartels replaced Juror No. 9 with alternate Juror No. 1. That, Bartels figured, should insulate the deliberations which began on May 16.

Try as he might to have a case free of issues that had plagued the earlier two trials, Bartels actually didn't know what he was in for when he replaced the juror. On May 22, a disturbing note was sent out from the jury room stating that "one juror refused to vote" and asking for guidance from the court. In response, Bartels read the jurors the standard Allen charge, which implored jurors to reach a verdict without "fear or sympathy" and without feeling coerced.

Another note came out from the jury that stated that a juror refused to discuss the case at all. The juror in question who was causing the issue turned out to be the replacement inserted when Juror No. 9 was dismissed. Bartels, in the presence of all the lawyers, questioned the replacement juror who said that in fact he and all of the jurors had voted and that he had discussed the case with the other panel members and had voted "in my own way." The jurors all went back to deliberate but then replacement Juror No. 9 sent out a note stating he was told he could go to jail and indicated he was being coerced and that he felt his identity was known. Defense attorneys wanted a mistrial, but Bartels decided to soldier on with the case.

The next morning, after getting another jury note that indicated Juror No. 9 feared for his safety, Bartels pulled the lone juror into a private conference, with only his law clerk and a court stenographer present. It was then that Juror No. 9 told the judge about an encounter with two men in the driveway of his home earlier in the case—one black and one white—who had questioned him about being on the Gotti jury. The juror told Bartels that he didn't answer the men who then left.

While the juror told Bartels he wasn't afraid at the time, later as he became part of the jury panel deliberating, he started to worry. Bartels questioned the juror if his decision-making process was motivated by fear and the anonymous man answered "not completely, but there is some aspect of it, but not completely." Clearly, someone had done some detective work to find out where the juror lived. The situation was becoming reminiscent of what had been seen in the other trials where jury tampering had been suspected.

Ultimately, Bartels excused Juror No. 9, over the objection of defense counsel who also wanted a mistrial. But Bartels sent the now eleven-member jury back for deliberations, after they had requested some pretzels, potato chips, gum, soft drinks, cigarettes, and antacids. At 8:30 P.M. on May 23 the jury announced a verdict, convicting Gotti and Carneglia on all counts in the indictment. Questioned after the verdict by Bartels, all the jurors said that the dismissal of Juror No. 9 hadn't affected their verdicts in any way, nor had anything he said impacted the deliberations.

Fischetti and Shargel vowed to appeal. Fischetti in particular told reporters he was confident the convictions would be reversed. But any appellate process would take months and in the meantime the question was what would happen to Gotti and Carneglia, who had been released on $1 million bail. Immediately after the verdict, Bartels allowed both defendants to remain free but said that he was going to hold a hearing in about a month on a government request that their bails be revoked because they were both dangerous. The respite Bartels provided to Gene Gotti and John Carneglia gave them some time to get their affairs in order before they were sentenced on July 7, 1989, and to enjoy some time with their wives and children.

John Carneglia, for one, made the best of the time he had left as a free man. He and Gene Gotti were looking at sentences of up to fifty years in prison, although under the law in place at the time they would be out in 2018. On Father's Day in June 1989, Carneglia gathered with family and friends at an ocean-front summer home on Dunes Road in Hampton Bays. Expensive cigarette speedboats were a mode of transportation for some revelers who waded through the surf to the house where Carneglia and others had gathered. The locale is a popular place for city dwellers to vacation.

At the beach house, the group seemed like any other gathering without a care in the world. Food, drink, sun, and surf seemed to be the most important things that day. Joining Carneglia were his brother Charles and their white-haired mother Jenny. There was also Angelo Ruggiero, whose trial on the drug charges would never take place, dressed in a red tank-top shirt and pair of blue swim trunks. Ruggiero was seriously ill at this point but with a tan and sunglasses didn't look in bad shape. His wife Maria was also there and with Carneglia's other guests kept the coffeepot busy and the barbecue grill filled with chicken, sausages, and other meats. There were plenty of desserts, high-calorie cakes. The women sunbathed on lounges. If they wanted to, guests could frolic in the surf, which Ruggiero did at one point.

Carneglia's wife Helene also used a video camera to document the event, and the images would be released over a decade later during the trial of his brother Charles on racketeering. What was shown seemed benign, but there was one reference to the guest who was not there, but whose presence was unspoken—John Gotti. It was never made clear why Gotti himself never showed up at the Dunes Road house. Perhaps he had other plans or didn't want to be associated with somebody just convicted on drug charges as a way of perpetuating the myth that he had never countenanced narcotics.

With Gotti absent, John Carneglia couldn't resist ribbing the family boss, suggesting that the revelers call him up to show him what a good time he was missing. It would be cool, said Carneglia with a laugh, to get Gotti on the phone and sing, "Let Old Acquaintance Be Forgot."

"He would go crazy," laughed one of the guests.

"I'm over here with my friends. What are you [Gotti] getting hot about? It's Father's Day," was how Carneglia would respond to Gotti if he got angry.

Nobody called Gotti since any foul-tempered reply by him would only sour the party atmosphere. This was a glorious weekend— good weather, good food, and conviviality Italians knew well—why ruin it. Among the others who had shown up were Mark Reiter's son Michael, who arrived on a boat piloted by Hunter Adams, a small-time gambler who would later be useful to the mob by laundering money and doing stock swindles. Reiter himself would get caught up in the stock-market crimes which became rampant at the time and would spend some time in prison.

Another man present was John Alite, a husky street tough from Queens who was of Albanian ancestry and since not Italian wasn't eligible to become a Mafia member. Alite was close to Gotti's son, John, and both men were allegedly involved in big-time marijuana sales and terrorizing rival drug dealers in Queens. Unlike Alite, partygoer Peter Zuccaro was of Italian heritage. But Zuccaro had elected not to try and become a member of the Mafia; he didn't like the lifestyle and its treachery. Zuccaro had initially been associated with the Bonanno crime family but was "traded" so to speak, without his consent, to the Gambino clan. Over time, Zuccaro got to dislike John Gotti and his flaunting of the gangster lifestyle. So instead of trying for mob membership, Zuccaro felt comfortable doing robberies, hijackings, drug deals, and car thefts. Like Alite, Zuccaro saw it as important to show some loyalty to Carneglia. (Both Alite and Zuccaro would become government witnesses years later.)

Father's Day 1989 at the beach house was one big bash for John Carneglia, and it would turn out to be a going-away party of sorts. Two days later, he and Gene Gotti showed up in Bartels' courtroom for the beginning of three days of hearings. A key witness was the FBI agent who testified that since their arrest in June 1983 both Carneglia and Gotti had continued to do drug deals. The agent also said that both men, along with Angelo Ruggiero, had "planned, orchestrated and directed" the December 1985 slaying of Castellano.

Bartels agreed with the defense lawyers that many details about the allegations against their client were lacking. Yet the judge was still torn between his desire to be fair and his obligation to society. "I am under strong pressure from my conscience to be fair to both sides," said Bartels. But under the law, the defense attorneys had the burden of proving their clients were not a danger to the community, and on that score the government had the upper hand. Bartels revoked the bails of Gotti and Carneglia, ruling, "They have taken oaths to place their allegiance to the 'family' above the law, this country and God."

As a final accommodation, Bartels allowed Gotti and Carneglia one more night of freedom to spend with their families and pick up personal items for the trip to jail. Then, the next morning, June 29, 1989, the news media, the government, and the defense attorneys waited to see if both men would show up in court as scheduled at 10:00 A.M.

In the end they were eight minutes early. Wearing jogging suits and sneakers, Gotti and Carneglia jumped out of a sedan with tinted windows as it drove up to the Brooklyn federal courthouse at 9:52 A.M.

"Afraid we weren't going to show up?" Gotti quipped as he shook hands with his attorney Fischetti.

"How is your credibility now?" Carneglia said to his attorney Shargel, who went out on a limb to get his client the extra day of freedom.

As both men walked with their attorneys into the federal marshal's office, Gotti said, "Gentlemen, it's been a pleasure."

Sentencing on July 7 was anti-climactic. Gotti and Carneglia were already in custody, and the only question was how much of their lives would be forfeited. They had both been convicted of crimes that had a combined maximum sentence of fifty years in prison, and that is exactly what Bartels dished out. He also fined each of them $75,000.

"These are very serious crimes," Bartels said. "These defendants are tied by reliable testimony to gangland-type activities and lawlessness. Their actions tore the fabric of society."

Fischetti and Shargel had asked Bartels to show compassion, but they got none. The judge, as he did in revoking their bail, said that he had an obligation to society in deciding what the sentence should be. After hearing the fifty-year terms, both lawyers were shocked but held out hope that their appeals of the conviction would be successful. (Gotti's and Carneglia's appeals were rejected by the Court of Appeals for the Second Circuit in March 1991.)

Under the rules in place at the time of the sentencing, both Gotti and Carneglia could expect to serve twenty to twenty-five years before they would be released. Carneglia was released from prison in June 2018; Gotti released in September 2018. Their total time behind bars turned out to be twenty-nine years. They came out as old Mafia men: Carneglia, seventy-three and Gotti, seventy-one, gray haired and worn, looking more like the grandfathers they were than the mob powers they had been. Before they went away to prison, their lawyers hoped they would be treated like any other drug dealer and not because they had ties to the name Gotti. But there really was no way Bartels could ignore such a connection. He gave them both the maximum.

CHAPTER SEVENTEEN
Deaths in Harlem

THE EVIDENCE OF THE GAMBINO HEROIN CONNECTION with John Carneglia and Gene Gotti wasn't the only one investigators uncovered. Mark Reiter, while not as well-known as Carneglia and Gotti, had allegedly been involved in the narcotics trade in a way that had turned out to be more substantial than the Bergin crew but that benefited the Queens social club group nonetheless. Reiter had beat one federal drug rap in 1983. He was also indicted in the Carneglia-Gotti-Ruggiero case in Brooklyn. Yet, no matter how many times he was targeted, Reiter simply couldn't stay away from the heroin racket. Even from the time he was working with the Bergin crew, Reiter was involved in another drug operation, this one larger than the one charged in the Brooklyn case and in which he was operating with major Harlem traffickers such as James Jackson.

It was while serving prison time as a bank robber that Jackson was schooled in how to get involved in the heroin trade by a group of inmates that included a nephew of imprisoned Harlem kingpin Nicky Barnes. After getting out of prison in 1980, Jackson connected with Barnes's nephew, Eugene Romero, who schooled him in the art of drug dealing. Along the way, Jackson committed at least one homicide as he built up a $250,000 a day heroin racket. In one case, Ronald Burroughs, a drug dealer, was shot dead in the

Harlem nightclub Reflections as he danced with Beverly Ash, known as "Shamecca" and a Barnes girlfriend. In the tightly knit world of Harlem drug dealers, Ash's brother Steven also worked as a supplier of drugs who in turn allegedly got his heroin supply from Reiter.

In Harlem, thanks to the Gambino family and local syndicates run by black gangsters, drugs like heroin had turned into a scourge. In June 1982, a report submitted to Gov. Hugh Carey by former federal Secretary of Health, Education and Welfare Joseph A. Califano Jr., stated that New York City was the nation's heroin capital. The report had alarming findings: heroin-morphine emergency room visits had risen over 200 percent from 1978 to June 1981; opiate felony and misdemeanor arrests had increased 40 percent; overdose deaths were up 80 percent; Rikers Island jail inmates had a 60 percent increase in detoxification admissions.

Califano recalled that he went out with NYPD officers to visit drug locations in Harlem and his findings were compelling. In one case, a Harlem addict had feet and toes swollen together "like an elephant's hoof" after injecting heroin into his legs when his arm veins collapsed. Yet, Califano noted that new addicts had been increasing all over the city, from the Lower East Side, to Bedford-Stuyvesant and Coney Island.

Califano said the problem in New York City and State with heroin addiction was something that he believed was the fault of the federal government for not taking enough effective steps. Carey suggested that the estimated one million illegal immigrants living in the city turned to drug trafficking because they couldn't get jobs. While lowly street workers were recruited by the big dealing syndicates from the pool of unemployed—be they illegal immigrants or not—the Mafia, working in league with the black council in Harlem pumped a great deal of the heroin into the local market and into the veins of the addicts. A reliable supply was important for a business with so many addicts, and the Harlem council, such as the black racketeers were called, was always looking for a good pipeline.

In the spring of 1982, court testimony later revealed, Ash became an unreliable supplier to guys like Jackson, who finally connected with Reiter as a conduit for heroin. Since there was evidence that Reiter was dealing in heroin with the Jackson group in Harlem the same time he was heavily involved with the Gambino clan, it seems likely that some of the drugs sold to the Harlem dealers came from his Italian connections with the Ruggiero operation. Evidence of that was uncovered in the June 1982 arrest of Greco and Cestaro in possession of the heroin that investigators believed was destined for Reiter at a time he was allegedly dealing with the black traffickers. Federal investigators also believed Reiter had paid John Carneglia as much as $500,000 in August 1982 for heroin.

Things seemed to be going along smoothly with Reiter and the Harlem crowd until late Fall 1982 when, according to court documents, Reiter told his Harlem connections that Nicky Barnes had become a federal cooperating witness, something that had been going on for over two years. Federal prosecutors believed and later alleged in court filings that it was during that same meeting that Reiter told the Harlem members that as a result of Barnes's cooperation Beverly Ash and her brother Steven had to be killed.

"I got some bad news for you," Reiter allegedly told the group, according to later federal court testimony. "Your uncle is cooperating with the government and with his cooperation he could hurt a lot of people, including myself. Not only that, Shamecca [sic] knows me and Steven got drugs from me and they could also hurt me . . . You got to get rid of them."

Romero, according to investigators, always maintained that he would never kill a black man on the orders of a white man but decided to do as Reiter ordered, telling Jackson, "Man, I'm going to do what I have to do."

In December 1982, Jackson got the word to stay away from the Monarch Bar in Harlem because there would be trouble. On December 13, according to the federal court testimony of Jackson, trouble came in the form of Raymond Clark who—wearing a white mask so he would look Caucasian—said he walked with a hunchback stoop into the Monarch and shot Beverly Ash dead as she sat on a bar stool. That killing left her brother Steven, who was desperately trying to stay one step ahead of any assassins by hiding out, even refusing to attend his sister's burial. (Reiter would later tell acquaintances that he never knew Beverly Ash.)

Clark, known by the nickname "Romar," later bragged about the killing. According to Jackson's testimony, Clark later told him "That was my work, the other night up in the Monarch Bar with Shamecca [Beverly Ash]. That was me, red alert. That was my work."

Barnes learned of Beverly Ash's death from federal prosecutor Benito Romano, whose job was to prepare Barnes for his groundbreaking testimony in a number of trials. As Barnes recalled the scene in his biography, he was in the process of making himself a tuna fish sandwich, and offered to put together one for the young prosecutor, when Romano delivered the news.

"Nick, Shamecca was killed last night," said Romano. "I'm sorry."

After Romano said that Ash had been shot in the head, execution style, three times, Barnes said he broke down. Both men said nothing for what seemed the longest time, until finally Barnes composed himself. He believed that his becoming a cooperator out of revenge brought about Ash's death.

"This was a message from Reiter, from Gotti, from the mob," Barnes opined later in his biography. "They're thinking 'Nicky Barnes can make a problem for us, but we can't reach him.' So they were gonna kill all of the people I hooked up with 'em."

The traditional Italian Mafia could be brutal, but the Harlem drug council killed as much as was needed to finally get to their main target, which in this particular case was Steven Ash. One of those victims was Barry "Bones" Wilson, who had been a distributor for Steven Ash. After being tortured in a futile effort by his assailants to discover where Ash was hiding, Bones's throat was sliced with a razor and his body, wrapped in plastic bags and weighed down by barbells, was tossed off a bridge at Orchard Beach in the Bronx.

In the end, Steven Ash proved too trusting. He agreed to show up at one of the apartments the gang used as a heroin processing mill and while he was talking to Romero was shot in the head by Clark. The killers placed Ash's body in plastic bags, which were weighted down with weightlifting plates, placed in a car and then driven to the Hudson River where a few days later police discovered the floating corpse near Pier 42.

It was all business as usual in the *babania* trade. The members of the Harlem council continued to notch up homicides. Business rivals were killed or wounded around the city. Reiter, a white man and a Jew, was operating in a very precarious world. He also seemed to be playing fast and loose with the black dealers and an equal opportunity supplier he apparently was not. Federal officials believed he charged the Harlem traffickers $240,000 a kilo of heroin while only charging his white customers about $199,000 for the same amount. But what appears to have made him very useful to the council people in Harlem was the connection he had with the Mafia and the quality of the heroin he was able to supply, which proved to be very good. Evidence later developed by the DEA indicated that Reiter had a constant supply of heroin well after the Ruggiero-Carneglia-Gotti operation was taken down in 1983.

After Castellano was assassinated, the murder reverberated through the Harlem drug world. Jackson, who had become one of the preeminent heroin dealers, contacted Reiter after the mob boss's killing, apparently out of concern for what it meant for his drug supply. "Everything is going to be all right. You'll be hearing from me soon," Reiter told him, according to court records. A few weeks later, Reiter gave Jackson about a pound of heroin and agreed to reduce the price he charged Jackson from $240,000 to $200,000 per kilo and kept supplying the Harlem dealer on a weekly basis, court records show. In total, Reiter was believed by the DEA to have supplied Jackson with forty-five kilos—about 100 pounds. The heroin supplied by Reiter, according to the DEA, was spread out by Jackson's network not only in New York but also Connecticut, Virginia, and Boston.

But the Harlem dealers, as well as Reiter, with such substantial trafficking in heroin, couldn't avoid detection by the DEA. In February 1987, Jackson was arrested by federal authorities and locked up in the same local Manhattan federal jail as Angelo Ruggiero, whose bail had been revoked as he awaited trial in the Brooklyn drug case. Although he was locked up, Ruggiero still was wheeling and dealing in the heroin business. When he learned that Jackson needed money to pay for lawyers, Ruggiero intervened and, according to federal court records, Reiter agreed to help by having an associate of Jackson on the outside of jail get his hands on an eighth of a kilogram of heroin. That quantity, which amounted to about two ounces, could fetch roughly $30,000 on the street among dealers.

Being locked up in a place like the Metropolitan Correctional Center, gangsters became very attuned to what the other inmates were doing. Since he wasn't in solitary confinement, Ruggiero could talk with other mobsters, get the latest gossip, and try to do business. If a prisoner got sick or was having problems, other inmates would know. There was one particular sign everyone in the MCC became very sensitive about: the sudden disappearance of an inmate from the facility, without explanation. When that happened, the jail grapevine spread the word that the person had decided to cooperate with the government. The jailhouse telephones became busy.

On September 2, 1987, James Jackson was transferred out of the MCC. It was a clear sign that he had decided to cooperate. Ruggiero got on the telephone and called Reiter with the news and a warning. "Get a lawyer . . . 'cause the guy left the building, today . . . They know the whole story." Reiter apparently understood the message and knew that with Jackson cooperating, he was in bigger trouble, even bigger than the trial he happened to be undergoing at the moment in Brooklyn on the other heroin case. Wasting no time, Reiter was surveilled by DEA teams talking to his trusted aide Vito Loiacono at Fifty-ninth Street and Second Avenue, apparently telling him that Jackson had turned against them and to warn others in the

Harlem heroin marketplace. A few days after Ruggiero's telephone warning, Reiter left his plush Manhattan apartment, made a stop by the home of old friend Cathy Burke in Queens, and then fled the city.

According to the DEA, Reiter made his way to Florida and arranged in a telephone call to Loiacono for him to get some false identification documents and to make travel arrangements so that his son Greg could come to Florida. Reiter left New York in such a hurry that he really didn't clear out his apartment in Manhattan. He left that job to his son Greg, who apparently didn't do a good job since Loiacono found a gun and some documents inside the dwelling. Reiter kept in touch with his New York contacts through the telephone and at one point, according to investigators, got about $20,000 when Loiacono visited him in Los Angeles.

Former Gambino crime family associate John Alite, said in an interview with the author that he was a friend of Reiter's. To Alite, Reiter was head and shoulders above many of the other Gambino gangsters involved in the drug trade, "He enjoyed life," remembered Alite, who was impressed by the way Reiter associated with so many beautiful women and seemed to have a cosmopolitan flair.

"To me Mark was one of the better ones, he had class," opined Alite.

After Reiter was finally tracked down and arrested in The City of Angels, his life was no longer his own. A federal grand jury charged Reiter, Jackson, Ruggiero, and Raymond Clark and others with participation in a large heroin conspiracy run by Jackson and a host of related charges. As the investigation progressed, prosecutors filed a series of superseding indictments in the case, a total of twelve indictments in all. The final version of the indictment listed additional racketeering acts including murder—such as the killings of Beverly and Steven Ash—as well as other homicides that didn't implicate Reiter.

On top of everything was a charge of income-tax evasion, which prosecutors said was supported by the lavish lifestyle Reiter exhibited on reported wages totaling only $107,000 over a fourteen-year period. His one-bedroom apartment, which reportedly had once been planned for designer Calvin Klein, cost Reiter about $1,400 a month, which at that time was a stiff rent. It wasn't the most opulent, except for a bathroom that was encased in glass. Reiter had a speedboat valued at about $185,000 and a Mercedes 450 Sport SL, which the government seized after his arrest. He had a flashy lifestyle, as well as a wife and three children, and burned through money.

In May 1988, Reiter went on trial in a slightly smaller version of the indictment, which still accused him of being a major drug dealer and an orchestrator of two murders. The star witnesses were not only Jackson and Reiter's old minions Salvatore Corallo and Vito Loiacono but also none other than Leroy (Nicky) Barnes, the legendary Harlem Mr. Big of the heroin trade who had decided to become a cooperating witness as his only shot at getting out of prison before he died. It had been no secret that Barnes had been cooperating since the news leaked out in 1982 that he was no longer in prison but in the federal witness protection program.

When he first testified in court, Barnes stated that he decided to help the government because of his anger at the way his former friends in the drug council, which ruled over Harlem, had plundered his women and his fortune. In Reiter's case, Barnes had already been in prison when the Gotti associate allegedly started plying heroin in earnest so the ex-kingpin had only a modicum of evidence to give in court. But what Barnes did have was important. He testified how, while in prison, he helped connect Reiter to Thelma Grant and Beverly "Shamecca" Ash. Barnes also claimed that it was Reiter who hired his nephew to kill Ash and her brother as a way of sending Barnes a message.

In his biography *Mr. Untouchable: The Rise, Fall, and Resurrection of Heroin's Teflon Don,* written some years after the trial with author Tom Folsom, Barnes said that his testimony about Beverly Ash's murder was punctuated by an introduction into evidence of her mugshot.

"The prosecutor passed Shamecca's mugshot to the jury, and the jury gasped at how pretty she was. Nobody looks good in a mug shot. They didn't even see her with her good face," said Barnes.

In many ways, Jackson was as important as Barnes as a witness because he said he had worked closely with Reiter on deals and had a more current knowledge of the street and workings of the council. Jackson testified that it was Reiter who supplied him with many kilograms of pure heroin and had personally ordered the murders of Beverly and Steven Ash.

Reiter was represented by prominent Manhattan defense attorney Barry Slotnick, who a year earlier had won an acquittal for subway gunman Bernhard Goetz when he was on trial for shooting four black youths in a subway car. Slotnick tried unsuccessfully to get Reiter's trial severed from those of the other defendants, arguing that his client would be prejudiced by the allegations against the others. Slotnick also failed in an effort to argue that the prosecution violated Reiter's right against being subjected to double jeopardy. Reiter called a number of witnesses on his behalf, although the defense felt it was stymied when the trial judge, Richard Owen, rejected attempts to get the witnesses immunity for their testimony. Owen also wouldn't let Reiter's expert witness testify in an effort to challenge the veracity of various tape recordings used at trial. For Reiter and his supporters, the way Owen ran the case seemed to stack the deck against the defense.

Still the government's case was strong. Some sixty witnesses were called and 450 exhibits introduced into evidence, all of which prosecutors contended showed that Reiter supplied many kilos of heroin to the racketeering enterprise from at least 1983 to 1986 and that he ordered the murders of Beverly and Stephen Ash. On August 25, 1988, the jury convicted Reiter and his co-defendants on all counts in the indictment. For Reiter, he was convicted of racketeering conspiracy, operating a continuing criminal enterprise, heroin trafficking, and conspiracy to defraud the Internal Revenue Service. The latter charge was supported by a display of evidence about Reiter's well-heeled lifestyle at a time when his reported income amounted to almost nothing. It all meant that the forty-year-old

Reiter faced a life sentence in prison when he came up for sentencing in October.

There really wasn't much ammunition Slotnick had to try and convince Owen to give Reiter a break on the sentence. True, the case wasn't covered by the new and tougher federal sentencing guidelines, which at the time had taken away a lot of a judge's discretion. Owen had some flexibility. Slotnick made a tepid plea for leniency.

"I would also ask your honor to recognize the fact that Mr. Reiter is about to celebrate his forty-first birthday, that he is a young man, that he has a family, that he has an amicable separation from his wife, that he has children who are interested in his well-being, that he had pled not guilty, that he went to trial and a jury saw otherwise," said Slotnick. "He asks this court, if possible, to be lenient."

Owen saw things differently. Reiter, the judge said, had a long history of involvement with heroin, going back to a federal conspiracy conviction in 1972. Owen noted that on a bad week Reiter grossed $25,000 a week with the reconstructed Barnes network and when times were good pulled in $75,000. Along the way Reiter ordered the killings of Beverly and Steven Ash, Owen added, stressing that when he went on the lam when Jackson turned into a cooperating witness it was an admission of guilt.

When offered the opportunity to speak before Owen pronounced the sentence, Reiter chose to stay silent. But when Owen said that Reiter's son Greg had kept things going for his father in his absence, it was too much for him to bear.

"This is all bullshit," blurted out Reiter.

Later after calming down, Reiter said his son never did clean out his apartment as investigators claimed and again said Greg had nothing to do with drugs, "never has and never will." [Greg Reiter was murdered in October 1989 and his body was never found. In a later ruling after sentencing Reiter, Judge Owen found that there was evidence that Greg, while never shown to handle heroin, assisted his father's operation. One former Gotti associate said the murder was approved at a high level of organized crime.]

"As far as Nicky Barnes, I never met Nicky Barnes in my whole life or any kind of Nicky Barnes organization or any of that baloney," said Reiter just before he was hauled off to jail to begin the life sentence that Owen had dished out. Over the next three decades, Reiter would make various motions and legal moves to try and get his case overturned. Each try was futile, and he was resigned to spending the rest of his life in prison, dreaming about the life he once had in the Gotti universe.

CHAPTER EIGHTEEN
The Last Hurrah

THE CONVICTION OF GENE GOTTI AND JOHN CARNEGLIA, as well as that of Mark Reiter, marked a moment when the invincibility of the Gotti machine appeared to be a mirage. The verdicts had taken out three of John Gotti's trusted confederates with others—attorney Michael Coiro, the Gurino brothers—on the ropes in separate trials. Coiro would be convicted of laundering drug funds and the Gurinos would be convicted of conspiring to hide assets of Salvatore Ruggiero. The feds were chipping away at the Gambino family elsewhere and, unbeknownst to the Gambino boss, were in 1989 compiling evidence for a case against him. Gotti was fast approaching his last full year of freedom.

Of course, Gotti was looking around for scapegoats for all the troubles and found it in Angelo Ruggiero. Ever since Ruggiero's motor mouth had caused so much trouble with the surveillance tape recordings, he was in a bad way with Gotti. Although Ruggiero was terminally ill and had been effectively put on the shelf by Gotti, that didn't stop the crime boss from thinking about more severe retribution.

As Gravano remembered things, Gotti wanted to kill Ruggiero for "his fucking big mouth on them fucking tapes." No one could deny that Ruggiero's compulsive blabbering had led to so much trouble for the crime family. But for Gravano, the idea of killing a terminally-ill man was a step too far and he convinced Gotti not to do it. Instead, Ruggiero was demoted from his position as captain and ostracized by Gotti, who wouldn't even meet with his old friend. At times Ruggiero would meet Gotti's wife on the street in Howard Beach and, with tears in his eyes, try to make the case to at least get his telephone calls returned. To see a grown man in such distress was shocking to anyone watching the street-corner meetings. Yet, as far as Gotti was concerned, there would be nothing. Gotti stayed away from Ruggiero, although others in the crime family maintained contact. When Ruggiero became gravely ill and needed to be hospitalized, Gravano said Gotti couldn't even be convinced to visit the dying man.

"Everybody was begging him to go, his own brothers," said Gravano. "He wouldn't."

But Gotti's own mouth caught up with him as well. Back in 1986, carpenter's union official John O'Connor tried to shake down a restaurant in lower Manhattan known as Bankers and Brokers in the Battery City area. The place was wrecked in the process but it turned out that the location had been secretly owned by Philip Modica, a Gambino soldier. The Gambino family saw O'Connor was the one responsible for the trashing of the eatery and wanted to retaliate.

Gotti's discussion with his men over what to do about O'Connor were picked up by a bug placed in the Bergin Hunt and Fish Club by the state Organized Crime Task Force. The conversations were cryptic and not often precise. But on one of the tapes Gotti was heard saying about O'Connor, "We're gonna, gonna bust him up." It was in May 1986 that O'Connor, while waiting for an elevator in the Manhattan office building of his union was shot several times in the legs and backside, fortunately surviving the attack. It would take three years, but investigators would use the fragment of Gotti's conversations, as well as evidence from an Irish gangster named Kevin McElroy of the Westies, to bring a state indictment in 1989 against Gotti and his associates Anthony Guerrieri and Angelo Ruggiero for the attack. As it turned out, Ruggiero was the intermediary with the Westies in getting one of its members as a would-be assassin. Ironically, it was Gotti's words that got Ruggiero in trouble.

Nevertheless, Gotti's anger at Ruggiero over the narcotics tapes was understandable. His loose lips had taken down a great many mobsters and cut off Gotti from a source of tribute payments with the drug proceeds. Of course, Gotti, as boss, had other sources of income but his obsessive gambling led him to squander much of his illicit cash. Instead of putting money into companies through front men, he threw it away at the race track or on sporting events. As far as Gravano was concerned, Gotti exhibited a cruel streak in the way he treated Ruggiero, a life-long friend who grew up with him in the gutters of East New York, that was unexpected.

As ostracized as Ruggiero was, he fared better than some of the others who Gotti suspected of being informants. Take the case of Fred Weiss, a fifty-year-old Staten Island real-estate developer who was an associate of the mob for years. Weiss was accused in a Brooklyn federal indictment along with Angelo Paccione, Anthony Vulpis, and John B. McDonald of being part of an elaborate illegal-dumping scheme on Staten Island. Prosecutors said the group dumped solid waste, including asbestos and medical waste, in a landfill they had leased in 1988—state and city environmental and health regulations be damned. The scheme, said prosecutors netted them over $7 million.

The mob had been known for decades to have been in control of the waste-disposal industry, and both Paccione and Vulpis were said to be powers in the business. Paccione, according to prosecutors, was a reputed member of the Gambino family, while Vulpis was said to have mob connections. Weiss had hired as his defense attorneys lawyers who normally defended mob cases. But when he fired them and obtained a lawyer from the Legal Aid Society, which normally represents poor clients, John Gotti suspected that Weiss was cooperating with prosecutors. Gotti then did what he usually did when learning of someone turning on the mob. He ordered Weiss killed.

Joe Watts, the powerful non-Mafiosi who held great sway in the Gambino family, received Gotti's request for the hit and sought the help of Jack D'Amico, a crime family captain, to put together a team to carry out the murder, according to allegations in court records. The plan was to lure Weiss to the home of Daniel Annunziata on Staten Island and kill him. Watts, according to investigators, approached the assignment with a sense of organization: getting a team to dig a grave, another team to procure plastic wrap so that Weiss's body wouldn't foul the floor of Annunziata's garage with blood. Watts was supposed to lie in wait for Weiss in the garage where Annunziata planned to bring him, shoot him, and then kill Annunziata, claiming it was a ricocheting round that struck the home owner.

But even the best plans sometimes go awry. Annunziata never did show up with Weiss, so the businessman's life was spared. But not for long. Two days later, a group of mobsters from the New Jersey DeCalvacante family found Weiss the morning of September 12, 1989, as he walked outside his home in the New Springville section to his late-model Jeep. They fired at Weiss numerous times, striking him in the head and right arm. Two bullets also pierced the windshield of the Jeep. The killers did a good job of clearing out since no spent shells were found by police, and the shooters did the deed unseen.

The killing of Weiss was a prime example of the way Gotti policed his world. Kill the informants and when necessary kill those who crossed you, those who slighted you. The cops were stumped about what had actually happened to Weiss and wouldn't piece it together for years. Meanwhile, Gotti solidified his rule over the Gambino family, spending more and more of his time in Manhattan at the Ravenite club, feeling secure that he could talk to his leadership team without the FBI or the cops surveilling them. After all, as the espresso machine hissed, the only things discussed in the Ravenite were gossip and mob chit-chat. The real business Gotti took care of in the building hallways and the apartment three floors above the club. It all seemed so secure. Or so he thought.

About two months after Weiss was killed, November 30, 1989, to be exact, the FBI monitoring team listening in on the bug in the widow Cirelli apartment at 247 Mulberry Street picked up the first signs of pay dirt. Gotti was heard entering the apartment with underboss Frank Locascio and consiglieri Sammy Gravano. The voices were clear, and there was no distracting background noise since a radio had been turned down at Gotti's request. (He was hard of hearing in one ear.)

In the conversation that November day was the subject of the Castellano hit. Gotti said that once Castellano heard the infamous Ruggiero tapes that he would have known about the narcotics operation and started killing people. Gravano thought that Castellano would only kill Ruggiero and not Gotti. But the crime boss wasn't so sure.

At one point, to play coy, Gotti railed against Castellano, calling him a greedy "rat motherfucker" who had it coming to him.

"But, anyway, here's a guy, whoever done it, probably the cops done it to this fuckin' guy. Whoever killed this cocksucker, probably the cops killed this Paul. But whoever killed him . . . he deserved it," said Gotti.

That snippet of the conversation at first glance might not make sense. But as Gravano would remember the moment, Gotti made the remarks with a wink of the eye, a signal to those in the room that he was talking nonsense and keeping to the rule that you never talk in public about taking part in a hit.

About two weeks later, Gotti and Locascio were in the apartment and began talking about some recent murders: Robert DiBernardo, Louis DiBono, and Liborio "Louie" Milito. DiBernardo was one of the men who helped Gotti and his crew pull together and plan the Castellano hit. But by 1986, Gotti said he was told by some cohorts that DiBernardo was being "subversive," so he passed out the word that DiBernardo had to go. Gravano was the one who orchestrated the killing with Old Man Paruta.

"When DiB got whacked, they told me a story. I was in jail when they whacked. I knew why it was being done. I allowed it to be done, anyway," said Gotti.

DiBono's demise showed how petulant Gotti could be, although DiBono did antagonize the boss, and in the mob world gave him very good reason to resort to murder. DiBono was one of those Gambino family members big in the construction business, and at one time told Gotti there was up to $1 billion in dry wall contracting work to be done at the World Trade Center. DiBono seemed to dangle the prospect of a big payday for Gotti from his contracts but for months never showed up for a meeting with Gotti. The stalling made Gotti furious and by December 1989 he had decreed that DiBono was to die. (DiBono was shot dead in the basement garage of the World Trade Center on October 14, 1990.)

"Louie DiBono," Gotti said on the recordings. "You know why he is dying? He's gonna die because he refused to come in when I called. He didn't do nothing else wrong."

One of the cardinal rules of the Mafia, one drilled into new members when they were initiated, was that when your boss calls you to come, you have to drop everything and show up. No if, ands, or buts. Show up. DiBono slighted Gotti by not showing up, and for that cardinal sin had to die. In later federal court testimony in the trial of Charles Carneglia, witnesses recounted that Carneglia was tasked with the shooting of DiBono by Gotti's son John, something which the younger Gotti has continually denied.

The witness in Charles Carneglia's trial was Kevin McMahon who testified that it was himself, Carneglia, Bobby Borriello, and a man known as "Harpo" because of his bushy hair that made him look like one of the Marx Brothers, who finally caught up with DiBono as he parked in the World Trade Center garage. McMahon testified that he sat in a car as Carneglia confronted DiBono as he tried to exit his Cadillac. McMahon heard popping sounds as if someone was being hit on the head, although in reality the noise was from shots.

It turns out DiBono was shot several times, including at least three times in the head, dying in his car. McMahon said that he had only expected that DiBono would be kidnapped and brought back to Senior Gotti for a beating. A stunned McMahon, now an accessory to murder, said that Borriello, who had been Senior Gotti's driver, warned him: "Don't tell nobody, you will end up like Louis DiBono."

As Senior Gotti and Locascio talked in the apartment, the mob boss let on that he was involved in approving the murder of Lou Milito, a Gambino soldier who had been a contract killer and worked with Gravano on construction projects. As it turned out, Gravano sought permission from Gotti to kill Milito and did so on March 8, 1988, at a social club run by Louis Vallario [sic]. Milito's body was never found.

The December conversations Gotti had with Locascio strongly indicated that Gotti was aware that some of the money he was receiving was from narcotics trafficking. The subject of this part of the discussion was the apparent poverty of one of Gotti's underlings, Jack "Jackie Nose" D'Amico, and the payments Gotti was making to him. Gotti wasn't happy about paying out the money either, although he did give away money when the mood struck.

"This fuckin' cripple downstairs, Jackie Nose, I give him every week out of my pocket, every week, Frankie," Gotti told Locascio. "Every week he gets $2,000. Where do ya think I get it from . . . the mulberry bush? That junk business?"

One other bit of rambling between Gotti and Locascio in the apartment that December day involved Gravano as the subject. As captured on the FBI tapes, Gotti seemed to be having growing concerns about Gravano and the feverish pace at which he acquired interests in construction companies. To Gotti, Gravano's activity seemed to indicate that he might be trying to build his own power base, "an army inside an army," as he told Locascio.

Gotti also expressed irritation over Gravano's way of doing business and indicated that he might be responsible for a number of murders of construction business partners.

"Every fucking time I turn around there's a new company popping up. And every time we got a partner that don't agree with us, we kill him," said Gotti. "And I tell him a million times, 'Sammy, slow it down. Pull it in a fuckin' notch. Slow it down!'"

Gotti also asked rhetorically where was his share of these Gravano companies. Clearly, Gotti was annoyed at Gravano, although he realized he was a big earner for the family and a man who could be relied upon to keep the crime family on an even keel. But, as would later turn out to be the case, Gotti's words about Gravano would come back to haunt him.

But before anything else, Gotti had to contend with the impact of his own words in the old shooting of union official John O'Connor back in 1986. Manhattan District Attorney Robert Morgenthau had indicted Gotti, Anthony Guerrieri, and Angelo Ruggiero for assault and conspiracy in the O'Connor shooting and brought the case to trial in January 1990 in Manhattan State Supreme Court. (Ruggiero had been severed from the case because of illness and died a month earlier.) It was the kind of case that finally gave state prosecutors a decent chance of convicting Gotti ahead of the federal prosecutors. Morgenthau was scion of a distinguished family of public servants stretching back to the early part of the twentieth century and picked his top assistant, Michael Cherkasky, to prosecute the case. Long overshadowed by the federal government in mob prosecutions, Morgenthau's people had a chance to even the score.

A key witness in the O'Connor shooting trial was the man supposedly tasked with the job, James O. McElroy, a former member of the Westies gang who was doing a sixty-year federal prison sentence and hoped to get some leniency by testifying. On direct examination, McElroy described when he and Westies leader James Coonan went to the wake for slain Gambino underboss Frank DeCicco in April 1986. It was then, McElroy said, that he was taken into a back room of the funeral parlor and met Gotti himself.

Cherkasky, the prosecutor, asked McElroy what Gotti said and was told by the witness that the crime boss asked Coonan, "Is this the kid?" a reference to McElroy. It was then, according to McElroy, that Gotti shook his hand and said, "I would like to take you out to dinner someday."

It wasn't a very eventful meeting but later, according to McElroy, Coonan told him the purpose of the meeting was to carry out a hit for Gotti. Another meeting took place some weeks later with Angelo Ruggiero, who asked Coonan, in reference to McElroy, "Can you handle it?" to which McElroy testified that he said he could.

Those conversations were still somewhat cryptic, and McElroy said he was unclear who the target of the violence would be. It was then that later Coonan said, "We want to break this carpenters guy's legs, John O'Connor, because he messed up some guy's restaurant,"

McElroy testified. Coonan said the beating was to be done for Gotti, added McElroy.

The day of the shooting, McElroy said he and two other Westies, as well as Joseph Schlereth, a man who wanted to join the gang, went to the union building and waited for O'Connor to enter the lobby where he would catch an elevator. It was while O'Connor waited that Schlereth shot him four times in the buttocks and legs, McElroy testified.

An admitted murderer and drug user, McElroy underwent a withering cross-examination by Gotti's attorney Bruce Cutler and Gerald Shargel, who represented Guerrieri. But McElroy stuck to his story, despite Cutler's table-pounding and histrionics.

Aside from McElroy's testimony, the other key evidence in the case were the tapes made from the state task force bug at the Bergin Hunt and Fish Club. But like many surveillance tapes used by law enforcement, the recordings were affected by extraneous noise and some quality issues. Background noise like hair dryers, flushing toilets and other sounds, as well as overlapping conversations made for problems in audibility. To solve that, state officials had sent the recordings to an FBI lab for enhancement. Transcribing the tapes sometimes took as many as fifty attempts at listening to the various segments. The defense, of course, attacked the reliability of the recordings and suggested they were tampered with.

In the end, the key segment involved Gotti's voice captured on February 7, 1986, saying, "We're gonna, gonna bust him up," an apparent reference to O'Connor. Then, right after the shooting in May, Gene Gotti was heard whispering as he said, "John O'Connor's been shot four times . . . they hit him in the leg, I heard it on the news, Angelo." Ruggiero was then heard responding, "Oh yeah." Gene Gotti then chuckled, "Heh, heh."

The trial only lasted five weeks and the evidence did seem sparse. O'Connor testified for the defense and while there was no question he was shot, he simply didn't know who had it in for him and said as much on the witness stand. O'Connor acknowledged that his union had internal strife and that a rival could have shot him. On February 10, 1990, the jury acquitted Gotti and Guerreri, and upon hearing the news, Gotti clapped and then kissed Cutler. His supporters in the audience also cheered, drawing a rebuke from Judge McLaughlin who told them to button up or else risk thirty days in jail.

Out on the street, there was more adulation, and the newspaper headlines talked incessantly about Gotti being a true Teflon Don, having beaten prosecutors for the third time. In Ozone Park outside the Bergin Hunt and Fish Club, a woman told reporters, "We are happy he won. He's a good man to have on the avenue."

Prosecutor Cherkasky and his entourage exited the courtroom, with disappointment etched on their stony faces. They made a beeline to the courthouse elevator and said nothing. Later, Cherkasky admitted he was disappointed but thought the trial was fair. A few blocks away from the prosecutor's office, crowds in Little Italy cheered Gotti as he entered the Ravenite, with two women planting kisses on his face. That night, as Gotti exited the club, there were fireworks on Mulberry Street. A news photographer captured Gotti and Gravano in the doorway of the club as they beamed at the assembled crowd. Gotti's underboss Frank Locascio stood behind them, looking a bit more serious.

So what had happened? The evidence in the case didn't seem to be the strongest; the tapes were ambiguous; O'Connor, the victim, also raised a question about others wanting to do him harm. A few jurors who spoke to reporters underscored the problems. Richard Silensky told Associated Press that he didn't hear anything on the recordings that led him to believe Gotti had a role in the assault. Another juror, who preferred to remain anonymous, said, "There was nothing to connect Mr. Gotti to what happened, zilch."

Cynics could look at the result of the O'Connor case and believe that perhaps Gotti was able to reach the jury, as he had done in the previous Brooklyn prosecution led by Diane Giacalone or had been suspected in the Ruggiero narcotics case, also in Brooklyn. In fact, there was one intriguing conversation picked up on the FBI bug in which Gotti and Gravano were overheard talking about the jurors in the O'Connor case while the trial was still underway. But, according to Mouw, those conversations at the time seemed to be idle chatter, with no indication that a plan was afoot to tamper with the jury. The chatter certainly didn't rise to the level where the FBI had to tell Morgenthau that Gotti was trying to fix the jury.

Actually, there was plenty that was being uncovered in other areas about Gotti to tie him to criminal activity. If the relatively low-level assault case against O'Connor had been a failure, the FBI was gathering more evidence for what was evolving into another racketeering case against Gotti. But Morgenthau, stung by his loss in the assault case wanted another shot at Gotti, as did federal prosecutors in Manhattan as well as Brooklyn. A turf war was building, and it would take some high-level sit downs among some of the nation's biggest cops to sort it all out.

CHAPTER NINETEEN
"Number One Is In"

NEW YORK WAS A PLACE with some of the best legal minds in the country, no matter what kind of law they practiced. In terms of prosecutors, there were names known certainly around the city if not the country. Robert M. Morgenthau III, at the age of eighty-nine in 1990 was the dean of district attorneys in the five boroughs. Elected to the job in Manhattan in 1975, Morgenthau came from a family where the name was symbolic of public service. His father Henry Morgenthau Junior had served as Secretary of the Treasury under President Franklin Delano Roosevelt, and his grandfather Henry Morgenthau Senior had been the U.S. Ambassador to the Ottoman Empire during World War One. Robert himself had served as Manhattan U.S. Attorney under Presidents John F. Kennedy and Richard Nixon from 1961 until resigning in 1969.

Morgenthau had a great deal of political connections and as district attorney had a lot of clout in law enforcement. He often got his way in disputes with mayors, police commissioners, and others in law enforcement and for most of his career always seemed to prevail. Since the Castellano homicide had occurred in Manhattan and was at its essence a state crime, Morgenthau believed his office had the right to prosecute any murder indictments. As it turned out, federal prosecutors in Manhattan were also investigating the homicide as part of a possible racketeering case. At the very least, given that Morgenthau was close with then Manhattan U.S. Attorney Otto Obermaier, there could be a strong case made that both of them could work in concert on a big Gambino family indictment.

But across the East River in Brooklyn, the borough's U.S. Attorney Andrew Maloney also believed he had a strong case against the Gambino clan, particularly Gotti. The FBI squad led by Bruce Mouw had worked for many months on building a case against Gotti, particularly from the fruits of the Cirelli apartment tapes. A former West Point boxer, Maloney looked like a casting-office version of an Irish pugilist, broad in the face and with ears that had taken their share of punches. Maloney was not easily intimidated, no matter what Morgenthau's stature was.

Ever since Castellano had been killed, federal prosecutors had grappled with what to do about the case. According to mob historian Selwyn Raab, in 1987 Maloney and then-Manhattan U.S. Attorney Rudolph Giuliani had worked out an agreement that Brooklyn would handle any Gotti racketeering case while Manhattan would try and get an indictment for the Sparks homicide. After Giuliani left office in 1989, his successor Obermaier and Morgenthau proposed that there be one big racketeering trial in Manhattan, including the Sparks aspect, noted Raab.

Maloney wasn't happy with that proposal and for good reason: his office, armed with Cirelli apartment tapes, had labored long and hard on charging Gotti in a racketeering prosecution and didn't want to surrender it, especially since the Sparks shooting didn't seem that strong a part of any indictment. With both prosecution camps in disagreement, it would take a high-level meeting at the Justice Department in Washington to iron things out.

In November 1990, Maloney and his team of prosecutors, led by John Gleeson, trooped to Washington to square off against Obermaier and Morgenthau in meeting with officials at the Department of Justice. As was later reported, Morgenthau and Obermaier believed Manhattan was the best place to bring the racketeering case because it had been the venue of the Castellano hit. They also thought the judges in the Manhattan federal court were less likely to be pushed around by the lawyers Gotti and company would hire. Countering those arguments, as well as the claim that jurors in Brooklyn were more likely to be targeted for tampering, Gleeson recommended intense questioning of prospective jurors and seques- tration once the trial started. Gleeson also believed that additional murder counts found in the Brooklyn investigation would strengthen his case.

Although Morgenthau had the clout, Maloney and Gleeson's close-quarters punching won the day. Washington agreed to have Maloney and his crew bring the case to the grand jury in Brooklyn where Gleeson would obtain a sealed indictment against Gotti, Locas- cio, and Gravano in mid-December. Gotti at this time was getting in- creasingly anxious. The heroin cases, as well as other racketeering trials against senior people in the crime family, had trimmed its ranks of top people. Even Gotti had bemoaned the thin bench of new mem- bers he could bring into the fold. In one of the Cirelli apartment tapes Gotti was heard to say to Locascio "Where are we gonna find them, these kinda guys? . . . Frank, I'm not being pessimistic. It's gettin' tougher, not easier!"

Gotti also had a corrupt police source privy to intelligence opera- tions who tipped him off that the federal officials were indeed tar- geting him for another racketeering case. Tidbits had leaked out to the news media, but now Gotti had an inside source telling him trou- ble was looming. The problem was that Gotti's tipster was only privy to the Manhattan federal probe involving the Castellano hit and wasn't aware of the Cirelli apartment bugs or the extent of the racketeering case Maloney and company were putting together. Gotti, while resigned to an indictment of some sort, thought it might only pertain to the murder of Big Paul.

It was around this time, according to Gravano's testimony years later in federal court, that Gotti seemed to also grow concerned that he wasn't getting tribute money from one of the crime family's re- puted drug dealers, Patsy Conte. An executive with Key Foods, a supermarket chain, Conte was a reputed captain in the Gambino family who investigators had targeted as a suspected heroin dealer.

According to Gravano's testimony, he and Gotti talked about the large sums Conte had given Castellano, including at one point a Mercedes-Benz as a gift. Gotti wanted the same kind of consideration.

"John Gotti said that since we took over, he wasn't earning with him [Conte] in this capacity," Gravano recalled. "He told me to approach him, talk to him off the record, give him some sort of tacit approval, get some money off him. What he was doing with Paul, he should be doing with him.

"I approached Patsy Conte. I took a walk with him," Gravano continued in his testimony. "I told him I was aware of the Castellano thing. I told him that it wasn't an investigation. I wasn't investigating him for doing drugs or being in the drug business. I told him to follow my conversation. I told him that we knew that he had—Paul had earned big money from him."

A nervous Conte, Gravano continued, acknowledged that he had made payments to Castellano but said that he didn't do anything since Gotti took over, an apparent reference to drugs.

"I told him that whatever he was doing we wanted it to happen again under John," testified Gravano. "John had troubles with courts and lawyers and the administration was broke and we needed some money and I more or less gave him a tacit approval to go back and start his drug operation or whatever he was doing then. I told him I didn't want to know the details of his business. All I wanted was money for John. I told him not to approach the boss with any conversations. Just talk to me, and he accepted that conversation and left."

Gravano noted that he had lied to Conte when he told the businessman that the Gambino family administration was broke. The reality was far from that, he admitted. Gravano explained further in his testimony that in a follow-up conversation Conte said one of his associates named Cheech would have to go to Italy, a major heroin transit point, to resume the operations. Cheech later visited Gravano at the Ravenite and said that he had traveled to Italy but that his connection there indicated there was a great deal of trouble with police so more time was needed to do business, Gravano recalled.

During these follow-up conversations, Gravano said that he stayed away from hearing details about drugs, didn't want to go into the drug business and just wanted the money. In anticipation of a possible indictment that might implicate him, Gravano recalled in his book that later, in mid-October 1990, he went on the lam. As a result, Gravano said he never got any money from Conte or his people and didn't know if the drug business resumed or not. But to his mind and Gotti's mind they believed they were shaking down a drug dealer, said Gravano.

By going on the lam, the plan was if Gotti were arrested that Gravano would run things while hiding out. In anticipation of his flight, Gravano grew a beard yet kept up pretenses such as going to family parties and returning home at the usual hour without too many late nights with Gotti. When the time came for Gravano to head for the hills, he did just that, hiding with his driver Louis Saccente in the Pocono Mountains in Pennsylvania. If you like solitude, the Poconos was the place, and by the time Gravano and Saccente drove to their hideaway there was early snow on the ground.

Gravano said his idea was to stay in touch with his brother-in-law Eddie, and Gambino captains Louis Vollario and Huck Carbonaro by beeper codes and a series of public telephones. But the quiet of the mountains got to Gravano, and he said he decided to go to Florida and later to Atlantic City where he lived incognito for a while until old friends recognized him despite his full beard.

"I realized that hiding like this wasn't going to be easy," Gravano told Maas later. "I had started the process through mob lawyers to arrange phony IDs and investigate countries without extradition agreements with the United States."

Yet Gravano professed ambivalence about leaving the country or even staying on the lam. He then contacted his old Brooklyn crew and came up with the idea of converting an old warehouse in Brooklyn into an apartment for him with a small armory of weapons and a pit bull. If done right, the location would be secure, and Gravano could travel around the city in tight security. He told Gotti about the plan, and they both agreed to a meeting to firm things up about the warehouse. They decided to meet at the Ravenite on the evening of December 11, 1990.

Gravano believed the warehouse in Brooklyn would have been a good place to hide out, and he was probably right. The FBI believed he was a fugitive of sorts and needed to flush him out in the open some way to get a better chance of finding him. To do that, prosecutors issued a subpoena for Gravano to come in and provide fingerprint and handwriting samples. The subpoena was actually sent to Gravano's defense attorney Gerald Shargel. On Sunday, December 9, Bruce Mouw remembered receiving a telephone call from Shargel saying that his client would comply. That call let the FBI know that Gravano was in the area, so surveillance increased and lo and behold members of the Gambino squad got eyes on Gravano, despite his best efforts to stay incognito.

Monday, December 10, Mouw, his supervisors, and the Gambino squad had a meeting. They realized they needed to make the arrests as soon as possible. Gravano was local, but he could disappear at any minute. So could Gotti. Mouw knew that finding wise guys once they went on the lam was a labor-intensive operation with no guarantee of quick success. It was decided that the arrests would be made the next day, December 11, a Tuesday and one of the days Gotti had all of his people show up at the Ravenite. Mouw wrote in longhand on a legal pad a plan of action—he didn't trust sending anything by telephone or telex. While the New York FBI supervisors were involved, nobody remembered to tell the big bosses in Washington.

The plan was straightforward. Mouw and a few agents would watch things from their command post north of the Ravenite on Mulberry Street. Ten other agents, including George Gabriel, Frank Spero, and Matty Tricorico, would be the ones to enter the club and make the arrests. Andris Kurins and another agent would go to Thomas Gambino's building in the garment district uptown and arrest him there when the time came. Everything was to be coordinated so as not to spark any leaks. All they had to do was wait.

December was turning into a cold month in 1990. The temperatures hovered around the freezing mark and at night dipped below it, making evenings bone chilling. Anyone walking along Mulberry Street late on December 11 would have to be bundled up against the cold. The street at that hour was rather quiet at the traffic light. At 247 Mulberry, the home of the Ravenite, there was a light on inside, which indicated that caretaker Norman Dupont had opened the place up for the night.

At the command post on Mulberry Street, Mouw arrived just before 5:00 P.M. Two other agents were already inside and had their telescopes, binoculars, and two-way radios at the ready. This apartment was the nest for the FBI squad. For many months, the agents had stalked Gotti, running into dead ends in their investigation until the observation post on Mulberry Street helped them focus on the Ravenite location as the place to plant a bug. The surveillance had paid off with the bugging of Mrs. Cirelli's apartment, and the tapes that resulted had led to the federal indictment of Gotti, Locascio, Gravano, and Thomas Gambino. Those charges were still secret but wouldn't be much longer as the night wore on. Mouw and the rest of the C-15 squad waited.

The arrest team was not far away, at the corner of Mulberry and Bleecker Streets, which was about two blocks from Mouw's vantage point. Kurins was making his way to the garment district to take care of Thomas Gambino.

At about 5:23 P.M., according to records kept by Mouw, things started to happen. It was then that Frank Locascio drove up to the Ravenite. Mouw had to chuckle: Locascio was driving and his usual driver, Zef Mustafa, an Albanian associate, was tonight sitting in the passenger seat. Parking was never a problem, and both men went into the Ravenite. In Brooklyn, at about 5:40 P.M., agents had spotted Gravano getting into a car with his driver Frank Fappiano for the drive to lower Manhattan.

As Sammy Gravano drove from Brooklyn to Mulberry Street he

knew the meeting was a bad idea. Rather than have their meeting in a secluded place, Gotti had insisted that Gravano show up at the Ravenite during a night when it was certain that the FBI would be surveilling the place. In order to keep his disguise intact, Gravano decided to shave off the beard he had grown while on the lam so that cops wouldn't see what he looked like with a beard.

"The king insisted that the meeting be held in the throne room of his castle!" Gravano said later in his biography. He made very good time in New York traffic, arriving at the Ravenite at around 6:06 P.M.

Uptown in the garment district, at the very same moment that Locascio arrived at the club, Kurins and his associate met Gambino as he was exiting an office building. They weren't supposed to quickly arrest him, but follow him for a later arrest. But Kurin's sidekick jumped the gun and made the arrest. It was a wrinkle in the plan, Mouw recalled, since they were supposed to take Gambino at the same time the other agents arrested Gotti. Now, with Gambino in custody, Kurins was told to drive him in the government car to FBI offices in Rego Park, Queens, to kill time and to make sure Gambino made no telephone calls, which he did not.

It was about 6:06 P.M. that Gravano and Fappiano pulled up to the Ravenite and went inside. Two of the targets were now in place, Mouw told his crew by radio. The only missing piece was Gotti himself who was expecting nothing more than another night of adulation from his captains and soldiers as he sipped espresso laced with anisette. But across the East River in the Brooklyn federal court house, assistant U.S. Attorney John Gleeson had finished up by having the grand jury vote and approve the racketeering indictment. Gotti, Gravano, Locascio, and Gambino were now charged, although everything was still secret. Everybody just had to wait for Gotti to show up.

Around 6:30 P.M., agent George Gabriel left the Brooklyn court house after getting what was known in law enforcement parlance as "body search warrants." Assuming Gotti, Gravano, and Locascio were grabbed at the Ravenite, they could be lawfully searched without the need for a warrant. But since Jack D'Amico, Gotti's driver wasn't going to be arrested, the agents needed the special body search warrant in case he was carrying documents given to him by Gotti. The same was true for Gotti's son Junior and Gravano's sometimes driver Louis Vollario if they happened to be on the scene. It was a technicality, but Mouw didn't want to have anything screwed up.

Finally, at 6:51 P.M., Gotti pulled up in a Mercedes-Benz driven by Jackie D'Amico and entered the Ravenite. Seeing that, Mouw talked into the radio and said "Number One is in," the signal for the arrest team to start making their way to the club. The agents only had a brisk walk of about two blocks south on Mulberry. In the area were three or four NYPD officers in case they were needed to maintain the peace. Gabriel was the first one through the door and the others followed. The agents walked past a coat rack crowded with hangers by the entrance and through a front room towards a smaller back section of the club. Inside they found Gotti, Gravano, and Locascio, as well as a decidedly meek-looking group that included Joe Watts. Nobody raised a stink. The Gambino family was stunned.

As Gravano would later recall, although the others in the club were shocked by the arrest, Gotti seemed calm. He told the agents that he wasn't going anywhere until he had a cup of espresso, along with Gravano and Locascio. Gotti nursed his coffee at a small table with a white tablecloth, close to a soft drink machine. On the rear wall in back of his head were two color drawings: one of himself and another of his old mentor Aniello Dellacroce. All three men were drinking their espressos as Mouw walked through the door of the club, passed a stunned Joe Watts and Jack D'Amico, went over to the Ravenite's pay telephone and called Jim Fox to tell him everybody had been arrested.

"We cleared the club so there must have been like ten captains and ten other soldiers standing out front and there were in shock," Mouw remembered about the night. "By then they had heard the stories of the wiretaps, and as we're dragging the untouchable, the

Teflon Don, out in handcuffs you could see on their faces what they were thinking: 'Who's next?'"

"I felt pretty good," Mouw told the author about the moment. Years of work, marked by frustrations, dead ends, head-strong prosecutors, and a target who had the sympathy of the media and the public, in the end paid off. Number One was in the bag. Let the games begin.

CHAPTER TWENTY
"Cosa Nostra Needs John Gotti"

RIGHT AFTER THE ARRESTS, Gotti, Locascio, Gravano, and Gambino were taken to 26 Federal Plaza for processing. The resultant mugshots seemed to tell a great deal about the inner feelings of all. Gotti, his hair uncharacteristically unruly, had a wide, what-me-worry smile that bared his teeth, an image that was a bit over the top given the gravity of his situation. Locascio showed his teeth in a half-smile, as if he wasn't certain what to think. Gambino had a dour look with no smile. Gravano seemed the most serious, his eyes focused downward with a look of concern. He knew quite well what he now faced.

Gotti seemed jaunty as he was walked by the arrest team, including agent George Gabriel, past a gauntlet of reporters and photographers to the local Metropolitan Correctional Center jail. Meanwhile, Gravano was handled in a low-key way by agents Frank Spero and Matty Tricorico. They kept Gravano separate from Gotti and tried to exit the building through the parking garage as a way of avoiding the crush of photographers. It almost worked until one newsman got a photo of Gravano with the two agents.

Of course, Gotti was to remain defiant throughout his time at the MCC. Perhaps sensing that Gravano could be more cooperative, Spero and Tricorico unshackled him when they got to the FBI offices, offered him some coffee and then introduced him to Jim Fox, the top FBI man in New York City who shook the underboss's hand.

Once in the MCC, Gotti and company were put in separation, meaning they had no contact with other prisoners or among themselves. It seemed to be overkill, and about a month after the arrests Judge I. Leo Glasser, who had been assigned the case, ordered the three men released into the general jail population. Thomas Gambino was freed on $500,000 bail since he had not been charged with the more serious racketeering charges of murder and extortion.

Bail for Gambino was the exception in the case. Gotti, Locascio, and Gravano were held initially without bail and within a month of their confinement underwent a court hearing before Glasser to determine if they should all be detained indefinitely. But while many bail hearings in the courthouse were open to the public, Glasser agreed with a government request to keep the public and the press out after it became clear that Gleeson would play FBI tape recordings in court, tapes the defense said would be prejudicial to the defendants. From Glasser's point of view, he agreed at least for the moment, that publication of the recordings to the public might unfairly damage the defendants' right to a fair trial.

So the hearing was closed to the public. But for the defendants, this was the first time they would hear some of the evidence, and it seemed troubling to them on a number of levels. For one, they seemed to indicate that Gotti had either ordered or agreed that certain people should be murdered, notably DiBono and Robert DiBernardo. The evidence on the Castellano hit was more cryptic, but Gotti could be heard saying that the old crime boss deserved to die. The recording also captured Gotti bragging about the power of the Cosa Nostra and that he wanted certain people to be inducted into the crime family.

But the recordings that would have the most important impact were those captured on December 12 by the Cirelli apartment bug. Gotti was talking to Locascio about Gravano, and the mob boss seemed upset with his youthful underboss and indicated he thought he kept information from him. For the first time, Gravano was hearing that Gotti bad-mouthed him to another made man. Gotti complained that Gravano kept forming companies or taking them over without keeping his boss informed.

"I tell him a million times . . . Sammy, slow it down. Pull it in a fucking notch. You got concrete pouring. You got Italian floors now. You got construction. You got dry wall. You got asbestos. You got rugs. What the fuck is next?" Gotti asked Locascio rhetorically. Gotti complained that Gravano was not unlike Castellano, getting rich and not sharing anything with his boss.

In the same recording, Gotti complained that Gravano got his brother Peter Gotti involved with an informer who got Peter indicted in a windows-installation business.

"That is not the way to run the family," said Gotti. "I shouldn't break my heart."

Veteran FBI agents in the court listening to the recordings knew the impact on Gravano would be terrible. Gotti was bad mouthing him, and Gravano began to seethe. Gotti seemed to slouch deeper into his chair with embarrassment as the tapes droned on, the agents said.

Gravano had his own take on the courtroom session. He said he glanced over at Gotti, who didn't look at him but just drummed his fingers on the defense table. Gravano's eyes were glassy with anger and when the defendants were taken outside the court, he glared at Gotti, who asked him, "You're disturbed?"

"Fuckin A, I'm disturbed," said Gravano in his book. "I think we have to talk about these tapes."

But, according to Gravano, they never talked about the tapes again. Back in the MCC, Gotti seemed to turn into an abusive man. In one episode he belittled Locascio to the point of tears over a silly perceived slight centered on an orange, which Gotti thought he should have been offered first, according to Gravano. The incident started when Locascio, who was working jail kitchen duty, purloined a dozen oranges, setting aside ten for Gotti and taking one for himself and Gravano. Still, Gotti berated Locascio in front of other inmates, something which angered Gravano who pulled the crime boss aside.

"We are Cosa Nostra, we don't do that," Gravano told a seething Gotti, according to a Mafia source.

Gotti's response was to almost raise his hand to strike Gravano, who was prepared to punch out Gotti, said the source. Sensing a fight coming that he would certainly lose against a younger Gravano, Gotti walked back to his cell. Gravano and Locascio later talked and said that if they ever beat the case and got out of jail they would kill Gotti for what he had done, said the source.

Gotti dictated that Gravano and Locascio shouldn't listen to the audio tapes or their lawyers. Gotti was a control freak and it got Gravano thinking that he was being set up for failure, for a conviction that under the federal statutes could mean fifty years in prison.

It was during a visit from his brother-in-law, Ed Garafola, that Gravano said he first began thinking about cooperating and getting out from under Gotti. The way Garafola saw things, Gravano had little or no chance of beating the case. Why not decide to cooperate, said Garafola, according to Gravano.

"'I'll go with you,'" said Garafola, recalled Gravano. "'Me and you cooperate and we will go into a whole other life. Take our families and run after it is over.'"

Gravano said in his book that he was stunned by the suggestion. But later in the quiet of his cell, he began to mull over the idea of cooperation, as well as what such a life would do to his family and other ramifications. But the decisive moment occurred when Gravano, Gotti, and Locascio met with their lawyers in a strategy meeting in jail. Gravano indicated he wanted a severance, a separate trial from Gotti, so that he could mount his own defense and have a chance of saving his skin.

But Gotti, recalled Gravano, was dead set against the idea. The crime boss was more concerned than anything about what the public would think if Gravano had a separate trial. In Gotti's mind, said Gravano, he was inseparable from the image of Cosa Nostra and made a comment that sounded like something from the mind of a megalomaniac.

"'Everything has to be to save Cosa Nostra, which is John Gotti,'" the crime boss said, remembered Gravano. "'Cosa Nostra needs John Gotti. You got a problem with that.'"

Gotti seemed to think of himself as a Mafia version of French king Louis XIV, the seventeenth century Sun King. It was Louis XIV who is credited with the saying, although not without some doubt about whether he actually said it, the phrase "L'Etat c'est moi" or "The state, it is I." It was the saying of the absolute monarch, the all-wise despot. However, by this point in his travails, Gravano didn't view Gotti as a wise man to follow off a cliff. Gravano wanted to unhitch his wagon from Gotti and to do that, he needed to turn to the FBI. The first move by Gravano was to contact his wife Deborah and have her contact friendly FBI agents Frank Spero and Matty Tricorico to tell them that he wanted to chat. It was time to walk away from the King.

One event, loaded with symbolism, took place around the time Gravano was first thinking about cooperating. It was July 4, 1991, and on 101st Avenue in Ozone Park the annual fireworks display and street event was happening down the street from the Bergin Hunt and Fish Club. This was a holiday fete that Gotti had sponsored for years and had become a neighborhood institution. There were plenty of barbecued foods, drink, and of course the center-piece, the fireworks display.

Cops had taken a hands-off position with the fireworks in the past, although the pyrotechnics were illegal. But on this July 4, there was also an added note of defiance since the street fair and fire-works were also to be a show of support for Gotti. What better way to announce the King's omnipresence than the display? As the moment for the mortars, rockets, and other fireworks arrived, there was a sudden, brilliant flash of light from the rooftop launching. Something was wrong. Instead of the usual display, the fireworks all detonated at once without launching into the air. There was some kind of accident and the entire event—which usually went on for at least fifteen minutes—was over in an instant, injuring one man who was on the roof. It was a giant fizzle. A big bang and then nothing but panic on the rooftop. A metaphor of what was happening to the Gotti era.

CHAPTER TWENTY-ONE
"The Teflon Is Gone"

SAMMY GRAVANO'S DECISION TO COOPERATE with the U.S. government was one of those seismic moments in the history of organized crime. Like the murders of Albert Anastasia, Carmine Galante, and of course Paul Castellano, Gravano going over to Team America was a benchmark moment for the Mafia. It would have ramifications that were deep, wide, and continuous. He had been assumed to be the least likely person to flip but stunned everyone by the decision to do so.

Spero and Tricorico told Mouw about Gravano's intention. The squad supervisor was stunned—and happy. Prosecutor Gleeson was also floored by the news. Of course, there were questions. Was Gravano credible or was this all part of some set-up to create faulty evidence and testimony? What kind of deal did Gravano want and could the government satisfy his requests?

Finally, how would they get around the problem that Gravano already was represented by highly competent counsel—lawyer Benjamin Brafman—who was part of the defense cadre enlisted in the case?

The latter problem was easily solved. Brafman was sent a handwritten letter from Gravano that stated that he was no longer to be his attorney. As Mouw remembered it, Brafman was on vacation when his office called to read him Gravano's note. Brafman may have been incredulous, but there was nothing he could do about what was a clear signal that his client was or was about to become a cooperating witness. Once Brafman was told, the FBI had to act fast to avoid any chance of a leak to the wrong people. As reported by Selwyn Raab, agents Mouw, Spero, Tricarico, and Gabriel arrived unannounced at the MCC the night of November 8, 1991, with orders to have Gravano transferred to their custody. As reported by Raab, there was almost a monumental screw-up when one of the MCC guards thought the agents wanted Gotti.

Gravano was taken away under heavy guard and driven to a safe location, somewhere in the middle of Long Island. Mouw, Gabriel, and Gleeson also made the trip, and the two agents questioned Gravano for a couple of hours in what is known as a proffer session. This was done to make sure that the government wasn't being played for a fool by Gravano. As soon as Sammy started to talk, Mouw sensed this was the real deal. Gravano described the Castellano homicide and set the record straight, saying that neither he nor Gotti ever got out of the car the night of the shooting. As Mouw would later recall, that bit of information allowed the FBI to discount the previous statement of an eyewitness who thought he had seen Gotti at the murder scene but likely confused him with one of the alleged shooters, Vinnie Artuso, who looked a lot like Gotti. Gravano also drew a schematic map of 46th Street to show where he and Gotti waited in the car by the intersection with Third Avenue.

FBI agent Phil Scala was part of the local agency SWAT team and a member of the Gambino squad investigating the Castellano murder along with the NYPD's 17th Precinct. Without telling Scala everything, Mouw told him to get the team ready because they now had a witness who solved the Castellano murder, a case Scala was investigating. After a few hours of debriefing in the motel, the FBI swat team arrived and whisked Gravano away to a nearby field where a Blackhawk helicopter would take him to Governors Island, a former military base right in the middle of New York harbor and about 300 yards from the Brooklyn shoreline. There, the FBI had set up a special suite of rooms where Gravano and his team agent escort lived together and watched him through a couple of weeks of debriefing, Scala remembered.

A few weeks later, Gravano was flown to the FBI Academy in Quantico, Virginia. The facility would be Gravano's home for the next few months. Meanwhile, as Gravano was enroute to Quantico, Gotti was told by a talkative guard at the MCC that Gravano had been moved. The news could only mean one thing to the crime boss: his dream of a Cosa Nostra—a Gotti Cosa Nostra—for the next century was seriously in jeopardy.

In Quantico, Gravano was kept in a secure, secluded area for what would be weeks of extensive debriefings. Gravano didn't hold back. He not only set the record straight about the Castellano hit but he also told about the jury fixing in Gotti's 1986 RICO trial, an incident in which Sammy admitted being the go-between for a $60,000 bribe to a juror. Gravano also told Mouw and the others about his participation in a total of nineteen murders. While not the actual shooter in each case, Gravano said he played a role either as a back-up assassin, set-up man, planner, and a few times as shooter. As Gravano implicated himself in more crimes and filled in the gaps in the evidence, Gleeson and Maloney knew they had a strengthened prosecution of Gotti for his role as crime boss and murderer. They also knew they had a witness who was proving to be very credible.

Gravano's isolated situation at Quantico risked making him stir crazy. He could only take so many hours of debriefing a day. A former boxer and weight-lifter Gravano craved some physical activity, something to take his mind off of the long days under questioning. So, at some point during the early part of the day, Gravano was allowed to run, under guard at the Quantico athletic track. He also spent some time in the boxing ring, going a few rounds with younger agents who were likely just as fit, but not as good with the fists.

It only took two days after Gravano was whisked away by the FBI for news of his cooperation to hit the headlines. *The New York Times* said it was the highest-ranking desertion in the history of the American Mafia and that Gravano's testimony could provide the crushing blow to Gotti, who had been able to beat the rap in three other cases. What was crucial, the report stated, was that Gravano saw that the evidence against him was overwhelming and that his only option was to cooperate and hope for a greatly reduced sentence in return. The arithmetic for Gravano was fairly simple: he faced up to life in prison if he went to trial and lost with Gotti or perhaps only twenty years if he cooperated. The latter option was appealing because it would give Gravano the chance that he could see Deborah and his children as a free man.

The *Times* called Gravano's action an "apparent turning," since much was unknown about his deal and if it had been signed-off on by the government. However, Gravano's decision was what the newspaper called "the latest sign of the deterioration afflicting the five Mafia families that had flourished illicitly for more than sixty years in the New York region. In recent months, the acting boss of the Lucchese family, Alphonse D'Arco, fifty-nine, and a high-ranking capo or captain, Peter Chiodo, forty, joined the witness program and have become informers."

The Gambino crime family was in a frenzy. According to later court testimony by former captain Michael DiLeonardo, there were discussions about killing as many as three mobsters who were believed to have had contact with Gravano and might have known of his plan to become a cooperator. Such could have been the fate of his brother-in-law Ed Garafola. Nothing ever came of that plan, recalled DiLeonardo. But at some point, the home telephone of Deborah Gravano was hooked up to a monitoring device—it was unclear who did that—in the hopes of intercepting conversations she may have had with her husband and finding out where he was being sheltered as a witness. FBI technical squad members discovered the tap and disconnected it.

Try as they might, Gotti's Gambino crew couldn't get to Gravano. They would have to deal with him in the courtroom, a prospect they dreaded. While Cutler could only yell from the sidelines about how Gotti, even in custody, was going to fight the case, Maloney and Gleeson knew that with Gravano as a key witness, they were in a good position. Cutler and Shargel were prevented from being Gotti's trial attorneys because Judge Glasser had determined that they appeared to be "house counsel" to the Gambino family hierarchy. Stepping into the void was seasoned and respected Miami defense attorney Albert Kreiger. If there was any good choice for a last-minute defense counsel it was Kreiger, a nationally known expert on the art of cross-examination, a skill that could be extremely useful in handling Gravano. Kreiger also had some familiarity with the Mafia world, having represented Bonanno crime family boss Joseph Bonanno.

Much has already been written and said about the trial of John J. Gotti so it is not the aim here to retell a lot about that part of the story. Jury selection in January 1992 led to the picking of an anonymous panel to armor the case from any attempt at jury tampering, something that had haunted Gotti's earlier trials. That didn't prevent Gotti from making his own moves to try and show disrespect for Glasser. At one point when the judge threatened to have the venue changed to a different district because of the onslaught of publicity in the media, Gotti was heard to say outside of Glasser's presence, "Tell this punk, is that supposed to be a threat?" It was a comment obviously aimed at being a bit of verbal bluster to play to the public Gotti always tried to satisfy.

After about three weeks of jury selection, the trial kicked off with opening statements on February 12 with Maloney himself giving the opening statement for the prosecution. An experienced attorney, Maloney had nevertheless not been in court for some years as a trial attorney. Yet he gave what many considered a strong opening. His main point was that Gotti and Locascio would convict themselves through their own words, with help from Gravano.

"This is a case about a Mafia boss being brought down by his own words, his own right arm and in the course of it, perhaps bringing down his whole family," said Maloney. "This not a complex case . . . these defendants will tell you in their own words what it's about."

Anticipating that Gravano would come under relentless attack by the defense, Maloney didn't try to sugarcoat his key witness or make him a choir boy. "He is no different and no better than John Gotti," said Maloney, stressing that Gravano played a role in nineteen murders.

It took Maloney about forty-five minutes to give his opening statement, which for a complex racketeering case, especially one with six murder allegations, was fairly short. The defense didn't hold back, but Kreiger first had to deal with Gotti's profanity-laced conversations, acknowledging to the jury that his client was a guy from the streets who, if he had a choice, would have gone on to college and did other things with his life.

"He received his education on the streets, from the people he grew up with," said Kreiger. "He learned to speak what they speak."

Gravano, said Kreiger was the "little man full of evil." It was Gravano, Kreiger suggested who had a business motive to kill the victims—Louis DiBono, Louis Milito, in particular—and in a sense manipulated Gotti into the conspiracies. A litigator who knew the value of dramatic impact, Kreiger talked to the jurors about the nineteen murders Gravano admitted to taking part in and then noted, "There are only eighteen of you here. We don't have enough chairs to put all the victims."

Gravano wasn't the first witness called by the government. But when he was on March 2, 1992, it was one of those signature days in the history of the mob. After months of preparation, Gravano entered a hushed, packed courtroom through a door by Glasser's bench. Some saw a flicker of a smile on his face as he glanced at Gotti, who sat some twenty feet away at the defense table dressed in a double-breasted blue suit. Gravano was also wearing a double-breasted outfit—his in gray. Over a dozen federal agents sat in the first row of the spectator section, creating a buffer between the crowd and the well of the court.

Gravano recounted his life as a criminal—the nineteen murders he played roles in and his rise through the ranks of the Mafia. He identified Gotti and the Gambino family boss; Locascio as consigliere. The questioning soon turned to the charge that involved the Castellano slaying, the very man who presided over Gravano's induction ceremony in 1976.

Asked by Gleeson why Castellano died, Gravano said there were a number of reasons, including the fact that as family boss he was operating a construction company and not sharing profits with the Gambino borgata. In effect, said Gravano, Castellano was "selling out his family for his own basic businesses."

Gravano described how he, Gotti, and others plotted the hit. He also described how Gotti drove him to the parking spot across from Sparks Steak House and how they both waited for the assassination to unfold. Castellano was shot first, and then Bilotti shot from behind. Gotti drove the Lincoln sedan across Third Avenue and Gravano described how he looked down at Bilotti's body and said "he was gone."

For the FBI agents in court, the testimony was a repeat of the story Gravano had told them in his debriefings. But this was all new insight for the jury, the public, and the press. Gravano then explained how DiBernardo, Louis DiBono, Liborio Milito, Willie Boy Johnson, and another man, Francesco Oliveri, were all killed with Gotti's approval. Gravano didn't hide the fact that he had asked Gotti's permission to kill Milito because he had been bad-mouthing the Gambino family administration and wanted DiBono dispatched because he was having business problems with him. All of the hits were either okayed by Gotti, who actually came up with the demand himself to have DiBernardo killed, said Gravano.

Gotti's elevation to the head of the Gambino family came during meetings that Gravano described in detail. The final anointment of Gotti as boss came in the big meeting of captains in a lower Manhattan building. None of the captains were told who killed Castellano for the simple reason that the killing of a boss was against Commission rules and punishable by death. Gotti was recognized as boss by all the families, but the Genovese family sent an ominous warning.

"Every family sent their blessings, and they accepted it, except the Genovese family," said Gravano. Although the Genovese borgata accepted Gotti as boss, the clan warned that a Commission rule had been broken and that "some day somebody would have to answer for that," explained Gravano. It was Frank DeCicco who had to pay the price in the end.

Gotti's attorney Albert Kreiger led off the cross-examination of Gravano and focused at first on the Castellano hit. Kreiger tried to show how incredulous the notion was that Gotti and Gravano slowly drove past the assassination spot at a time when cop cars or traffic

could have ruined everything for them as they made an escape. Gravano agreed that could be the case but noted that simply didn't happen.

"It went pretty smooth," remembered Gravano.

Kreiger also asked Gravano about the taped conversation he had
with Gotti, one in which both men were heard saying they didn't
know who killed Castellano, with Gotti famously adding "maybe
the cops did it." Gravano admitted those words of denial were spoken but explained that they had agreed never to talk about their
roles.

Kreiger also tried to show that Gravano was greedy enough to
want Castellano killed since he then became bigger in construction
after the boss was gone. Gravano agreed, noting that he still continued to grow business-wise long after Castellano's demise.

The trial occupied all of March, and Gravano had in total spent
nine days on the witness stand. The case was staple fare for the news
media. Glasser's courtroom was usually packed, and celebrities made
walk-on appearances. Among them were Mickey O'Rourke, who
said he was mulling a film role as Gotti, and old TV star Al Lewis,
who played the Grandpa character in the series "The Munsters."
Lewis showed up to court wearing a wide brimmed hat and outside
for the television cameras blurted out, "The government has got no
case!" Playing off the sometimes impeccable couture of Gotti and
his retinue, *New York Newsday* ran a daily feature called "Gotti
Garb," a brainchild of editor Donald Forst. The newspaper hired a
fashion sketch artist to sit with reporter Beth Holland and draw pic-
tures of the suits—of both men and women—which were worn to
court.

The government finally rested its case on March 23, and the defense put up a few witnesses. But the foundation of the government's case seemed unassailable despite the best effort of Kreiger
and the rest of the defense team. On April 2, after a mere fourteen
hours of deliberation, the jury convicted Gotti of all the racketeering
charges against him, including the five murders, while Locascio
suffered almost the same fate, gaining a token acquittal for one
gambling charge. It was a virtual clean sweep for the government,
and at a news conference FBI official James Fox said famously

"The Teflon is gone. The don is covered with Velcro and all the charges stuck." In the background, a smile creased the face of agent George Gabriel as Fox spoke those words.

Both Gotti and Locascio were sentenced on June 24 by Glasser. Gotti, smirking, declined to address the court. However, Locascio did, saying, "I am guilty of being a good friend of John Gotti. If there were more men like John Gotti on the earth, we would have a better country." The sentences were no surprise: life in prison without parole, plus a mandatory court system assessment of $50. Gotti maintained a droll sense of humor, quipping in a courthouse holding cell about Glasser that "he sure knows how to hurt a guy with that $50 assessment."

The day John Gotti and Frank Locascio were sentenced to spend their remaining days in a prison cell was just a decade after the Learjet plunged into the Atlantic Ocean off Georgia, killing Salvatore Ruggiero and his wife Stephanie. A mere ten years had passed during which a series of fortuitous circumstances led to Gotti's brief rise to the head of the Gambino crime family. Now, Gotti was just another ambitious gangster whose string of luck had run out. It had all ended quickly.

Judy Helmey wasn't aware of the events taking place in Judge Glasser's courtroom that June day in 1992. Her father Sherman was still around but at the age of ninety didn't venture out much on the fishing boat so it was up to Judy to ease her vessel the *Miss Judy* out that morning from the dock on the Savannah River. She took it off shore with a few recreational fishermen and women to a spot some thirty-three miles out, farther east of the Learjet crash site. The water was about ninety-five feet deep and both King and Spanish mackerel were in abundance.

The catch was good and there was plenty of mackerel being pulled aboard. But the real menace to fish and man in those waters was what Judy liked to call the "toothy monster," the deadly barracuda. Torpedo shaped and with a terrifying set of razor-like teeth, the barracuda was a ferocious predator. They attack without warning and they kill for sport, like hitmen of the deep blue sea. The weak and wounded fish also made good targets. The barracuda was a creature of opportunity, sometimes waiting for other predators or humans to do the work before it selfishly cleans up.

As menacing as they are in the deep, barracuda are very good to eat. The best way to catch the "cuda" was to lure it with other fish. So, picking up a plump Spanish mackerel, Judy plunked it on the cutting board and started to slice it into small pieces. The hooks were baited with the mackerel and as soon as the lines hit the water the rapacious barracuda hit them and got snagged. It worked every time. The skin of the mackerel bait had a shine like money. The luminous scheen attracted the finned killer. A hungry predator, dazzled by the glow of the scaled skin, was blind to the dangers of the baited lines.

The one strange thing was that sometimes after the barracuda was pulled out of the water and in the throes of death on the deck of a boat, it would watch Helmey with its eyes. It was eerie, as if the fish wanted to strike and kill even when it was dying. It was very spooky and to stop the barracuda from watching with those cold eyes, Judy would put a bucket over its head. She couldn't be too careful.

With a boatload of happy anglers and their catch, Judy Helmey eased the *Miss Judy* back to shore. She would do it all again early the next morning and would be so busy that she wouldn't have time to scan the *Savannah Morning News* to catch any short item about the big New York mob boss John J. Gotti going away to the can for the rest of his life

EPILOGUE

JOHN GOTTI'S FINAL IMPRISONMENT in the high-security facility in Marion, Illinois, effectively eviscerated his ability to run the Gambino family in any meaningful way. He had to rely on various surrogates—his brother Peter and his son John—to hold the power as street bosses. That worked to some degree. Each of those two men would in turn be hobbled by separate federal prosecutions and terms of imprisonment. While his brother, son, and a few lawyers were able to visit him in prison and carry messages, Gotti's ability to control what was happening on the street was diminished. When he went through the prison gates at Marion, Gotti was effectively handcuffed and stayed that way until his death behind bars in a prison hospital bed from the effects of throat cancer on June 10, 2002.

During the period after Gotti's conviction, his son John as caretaker suspected that there were plenty of people cheating the crime family. This increased the tension between Junior Gotti and some others in the borgata. Junior's friend and fellow mobster Michael DiLeonardo, testified in a Brooklyn federal court proceeding in a case against Charles Carneglia that the younger Gotti suspected two other family members, Daniel Marino and John "Johnny G" Gammarano, were stealing construction racket funds and called both men to a meeting at a house in Brooklyn. According to DiLeonardo, Junior Gotti had two other armed family members—Charles Carneglia and Tommy "Sneakers" Cacciapoli hiding out in the house in case things went bad.

Joe Watts happened to accompany both Marino and Gammarano to the meeting and told Junior Gotti in no uncertain terms that his father had given him carte blanche to deal with the construction money, testified DiLeonardo. Junior Gotti respected what Watts told him and there was no trouble but, according to DiLeonardo, when Carneglia and Cacciapoli entered the room Watts sensed the bloodshed that had been in the offing and told Junior of the rashness of what he had planned.

In another display of dislike toward Junior Gotti, Gambino associate John Alite testified later that John Carneglia once railed against the younger Gotti, calling him a "spoiled-brat motherfucker" who he would have killed if it wasn't for his father. Incidents such as the Watts confrontation and the outburst by John Carneglia showed that Junior Gotti wasn't the diplomat in the mob world who garnered universal respect.

While his reign as Gambino official crime boss was about seventeen years, Senior Gotti only had about six years unfettered time on the street as boss before he was arrested in December 1990. His public persona, of course, persisted. He was the flashy don who reveled in all the publicity he received from an accommodating news media. When he was convicted in 1992, hundreds rioted outside the federal court in Brooklyn, overturning government cars. When he died, crowds of thousands lined the streets of Queens as Gotti's funeral procession wound its way to his final resting place at St. John Cemetery. It was as if a rock star had passed away and some of the adulation from the public appeared quite genuine. News organizations sent up helicopters and hired motorcycles to follow the processions through Queens. All of this was shown as a coda in the 2018 film *Gotti,* although it didn't do anything to impress the critics.

Gotti got to his position of power—and in his world, let's face it, he had power—through the actions of others. Gotti was ambitious and seized opportunities because he had the backing of some key people. He also lost his freedom because of the greed and mistakes of others—as well as his own. Men like Angelo Ruggiero, John

Carneglia, Gene Gotti, Frank DeCicco, Sammy Gravano, Joe Watts, and Frank Locascio, were Gotti's key allies. All of them were crucial to Gotti's seizure of power following the assassination of Castellano and the consolidation that followed.

But Gotti was not the diplomat like Frank Costello. Gotti's abrasive and abusive style with fellow Cosa Nostra members did not earn him loyalty points within the Mafia world. Even Joe Massino, the Bonanno crime boss who Gotti thought was in his pocket, came to distrust and dislike Gotti. In later years, when he was testifying as a cooperating witness, Massino would relate that Gotti and Salvatore Vitale, the Bonanno underboss, had plotted against him. Massino would also bemoan the way Gotti brought so much law enforcement attention on the mob.

The drug operation of the old Bergin crew turned out to be the Achilles' heel of the Gambino family. The FBI bugs of Ruggiero turned up strong evidence of the enormous scope of the narcotics dealings. The bugging also led the FBI to Castellano for the reason that Ruggiero and Gotti were surveilled visiting their boss on Staten Island. Those visits proved justification enough for the agency to bug Castellano's palace and bring him his own host of legal problems.

Mark Reiter, while not a Mafiosi, was his own brand of gangster who, as his federal trial showed, exploited his drug connections to the Gotti crew for his own peculiar advantage. The heroin Reiter and his Harlem connections in the trade spread largely—but not exclusively—through black communities. This drug operation also spread death by murders on the streets of Harlem and elsewhere. There may be no evidence that Gotti himself was involved in trafficking heroin, but those around him were making big money from it. The Teflon Don may have been celebrated as a folk hero to some, but his crime family spread the pernicious misery of heroin to the very "public" from which he so often sought adulation. In fact, the Mafia generally has been a big player in narcotics for decades. Gotti seemed to tolerate trafficking as an open secret and for that he bears some responsibility for the impact.

If Salvatore Ruggiero had not crashed into the Atlantic Ocean and was torn to pieces that fateful day in 1982, it is likely that John J. Gotti would not have become boss of the Gambino family as quickly as he did. The frantic scurry to find Salvatore's money and drugs triggered conversations and activity in his brother's house on Long Island just as the FBI bugs were planted. That was the catalyst, and for the government the timing couldn't have been better. But had that sequence of events not happened eventually, since Paul Castellano was held in such disrespect by so many and facing so many legal issues, he would have been removed as boss one way or another: through a prison term or a bullet from Gotti's crew. In December 1985, Gotti and his boys were there when the opportunity presented itself. They were the men who had the nerve to seize the moment. And then, faster than they expected, their moment was gone.

THE GOTTI ROLL CALL

(as of August 1, 2018)

Oscar Ansourian (Gambino associate): Ran into a load of legal troubles. After pleading guilty in the Ruggiero heroin case, Ansourian was sentenced to serve eleven years. Around 1992 he was released from prison, and in 1996 was arrested for having assorted weapons in his Queens house, some allegedly for mobsters. Ansourian pleaded guilty in 1999 to one count of withholding evidence. He died in January 2000.

Vincent Artuso (Gambino soldier): Was never formally charged with participating in the Castellano-Bilotti murders. He was convicted of federal racketeering in October 2008 and sentenced to nine years in prison. He was released in September 2016.

Judge John Bartels: After serving 38 years on the federal bench, he died on February 13, 1997, at the age of ninety-nine.

Thomas Bilotti (Gambino captain): Was assassinated with Paul Castellano on December 16, 1985, and is buried in Moravian Cemetery on Staten Island.

Anthony Cardinale (defense attorney): He is a defense attorney with an active practice in Boston, Massachusetts.

Charles Carneglia (Gambino soldier): Was convicted on federal racketeering charges in March 2009 and sentenced to life without parole. He is currently serving his sentence in the federal penitentiary in Canaan, Pennsylvania.

John Carneglia (Gambino captain): Was sentenced to a fifty-year prison terms for a narcotics conspiracy. Under the terms of the sentencing law effective when he went to prison in 1989, Carneglia was released on June 13, 2018, after serving twenty-nine years. He currently resides in Howard Beach, Queens, and Florida. He was never charged with homicide.

Anthony "Gaspipe" Casso: After being captured by the FBI, he had a truncated career as a federal witness and was remanded to the federal prison system for what is essentially a life sentence. He is currently listed in Bureau of Prison records as being in the federal prison medical center in Springfield, Missouri.

Paul Castellano (Gambino boss): Was assassinated on December 16, 1985, and is buried in an unmarked grave at Moravian Cemetery on Staten Island.

Michael Coiro (attorney): After being convicted in 1989 of helping to launder drug proceeds, Coiro was automatically disbarred. He was sentenced to a fifteen-year prison term and died in 2003. He is buried in Pinelawn Memorial Park Cemetery on Long Island.

Mark Costantino (Brooklyn federal judge): He assumed senior status in December 1987 and died in June 1990.

Bruce Cutler (attorney): He represented John J. Gotti in a number of high-profile trials but was prevented from doing so by Judge I. Leo Glasser at Gotti's last federal trial in 1992. Cutler maintains a criminal law practice in New York City.

Jack "Jackie Nose" D'Amico (Gambino captain): He was believed by law enforcement officials to have taken over as street boss of the Gambino family after Peter Gotti was incarcerated beginning in 2004. After serving time in federal prison, he is no longer believed to have much power in the crime family.

Aniello Dellacroce (Gambino underboss): He died of natural causes in December 1985 and is buried in the Cloisters Mausoleum in St. John Cemetery in Middle Village, Queens. His death precipitated John J. Gotti's move to kill Castellano.

Alfred Dellentash: Moved to California and works as a car salesman.

Frank DeCicco: He died on April 13, 1986, in a bomb explosion and is buried at Moravian Cemetery on Staten Island.

Roy DeMeo: He died in a homicide in January 1983 and is buried in St. John Cemetery, Queens.

Robert DiBernardo (Gambino captain): After years of being the Gambino family main earner in the area of pornography, he was killed with the approval of John J. Gotti in 1986. His body was never found.

James "Jimmy Brown" Failla (Gambino captain): He died of natural causes in federal prison in 1999 and is buried at Moravian Cemetery on Staten Island.

Carmine "Charley Wagons" Fatico (Gambino captain): He died on August 1, 1991 at the age of 81 and is buried in St. John Cemetery, Queens.

Daniel "Danny Wagons" Fatico (Gambino member): Died in 2006 and is buried in St. John Cemetery, Queens.

Ronald P. Fischetti (defense attorney): After representing Gene Gotti, Fischetti gained note in defending former NYPD officer Charles Schwarz, who was charged with other officers in the infamous Abner Louima police-brutality case. Fischetti won a reversal of Schwarz's conviction and ultimately saw the government dismiss the civil rights case against his client. Fischetti continues to practice law at the firm of Fischetti and Malgieri.

George Gabriel (FBI agent): Retired from the FBI and works as a security consultant in Virginia.

Anthony "Nino" Gaggi (Gambino captain): Died in April 1988 at the age of sixty-two while serving a federal prison sentence for racketeering. He was in the federal jail in Manhattan awaiting a second trial when he suffered a heart attack. His place of burial is unknown.

Joseph N. Gallo (Gambino consiglieri): After being released from prison, he died of natural causes in September 1995 at the age of eighty-three. He is buried in St. Michael's Cemetery, Queens, N.Y.

Thomas Gambino (Gambino captain): The son of crime family namesake Carlo Gambino, he pleaded guilty in 1992 to settle state charges that he was part of a group that used a cartel to control the garment trucking industry and agreed to pay a $12 million settlement. He also gave up part of his lucrative business empire. Following a 1993 conviction on federal racketeering charges, he was sentenced to five years in federal prison and was released in May 2000. Gambino, now eighty-nine, is believed to be retired and currently divides his time between homes in Lido Beach, N.Y., and Florida.

Diane Giacalone: After leaving government service, she maintains an active law practice in Manhattan.

Vincent "Vinny The Chin" Gigante (Genovese family boss): After being convicted in the late 1990s and early 2000s on various federal racketeering charges, he died on December 13, 2005 in a federal prison hospital in Springfield, Missouri, of various health complications. He was cremated at Green-Wood cemetery.

Israel Leo Glasser (federal judge): Presided at the racketeering trial of John J. Gotti and Frank Locascio in 1992 in Brooklyn federal court. Glasser, also known as I. Leo Glasser, is a senior judge in the Eastern District of New York, and still carries a caseload at the age of ninety-three.

John Gleeson (federal prosecutor): Was appointed a federal judge to the Eastern District of New York in 1994 by President Bill Clinton. He resigned his judgeship in March 2016 to join the Manhattan law firm of Debevoise & Plimpton as a partner.

Gene Gotti (Gambino captain): Was convicted with John Carneglia for heroin trafficking in 1989, and they received identical fifty-year sentences. He was scheduled for release in September 2018. He was never charged with any homicides.

John J. Gotti (Gambino boss): Died on June 10, 2002, at the federal prison hospital in Springfield, Missouri, at the age of sixty-two from the effects of cancer. He is entombed in the Cloisters Mausoleum section of St. John Cemetery, Middle Village, Queens in a crypt next to his son Frank, who died in 1980 at the age of twelve.

John A. Gotti (former Gambino acting boss, former captain): Son of John J. Gotti, and known as "Junior," he endured four federal trials in Manhattan from 2006 through 2009. In each case, the juries couldn't agree on a verdict, resulting in mistrials. Gotti's main defense was that he withdrew from the Mafia, a tactic some jurors said they found convincing. He had earlier served time in federal prison for his guilty plea in a different case. He lives with his wife Kim and their six children near Oyster Bay Cove, Long Island. In 2015, Gotti self-published an e-book, *In the Shadow of My Father,* which eventually inspired the 2018 film *Gotti,* starring John Travolta. The movie was panned by many critics and had a short theatrical run. He has continuously denied participating in any murder plots as some have alleged in court testimony.

Peter Gotti (former Gambino crime family boss): Brother of John J. Gotti, he was convicted in separate federal racketeering cases in 2003 and 2004. He is currently serving a twenty-five-year prison sentence at Butner Low Federal Correctional Institution in Butner, N.C. He is scheduled for release in 2032.

Salvatore "Sammy" Gravano (former Gambino underboss and consiglieri): Was released from an Arizona state prison in 2018 after serving a term for narcotics trafficking. He is believed to be currently living in California.

Jeffrey C. Hoffman (defense attorney): He maintains an active criminal defense practice in Manhattan.

James J. Hunt (Drug Enforcement Administration official): He was appointed special agent in charge of the Drug Enforcement Administration New York Division in 2014. He oversaw all DEA operations in New York State, until November 2018, when he hit the mandatory retirement age

Anthony "Bruno" Indelicato (Bonanno family soldier): He is currently serving a twenty-year sentence for a 2008 federal racketeering conviction. He is scheduled for release in September 2023.

Wilfred "Willie Boy" Johnson (Gambino associate): Was assassinated on August 29, 1988 on the orders of John J. Gotti. His place of burial is St. John Cemetery, Queens.

Andris Kurins (FBI agent): Retired from the FBI and is living in Connecticut.

Edward Lino (Gambino captain): Was assassinated by the so-called "Mafia Cops," Louis Eppolito and Stephen Carracappa, in November 1990, while driving along the Belt Parkway in Brooklyn.

Frank Locascio (former Gambino consiglieri): Is serving a life sentence for racketeering in Devins Federal Medical Center in Massachuseetes. He has filed numerous motions for a new trial, so far without success.

Daniel Marino (Gambino captain and governing committee member): Pled guilty in 2011 to a federal racketeering charge that he gave the "green light" to co-conspirators for the murder of his nephew, Frank Hydell, who some suspected was an informant. He was sentenced to five years in prison and released in August 2014.

Joseph Massino (former Bonanno crime boss): Following his federal racketeering conviction in July 2004 for among other things six gangland murders, he turned into a government cooperating witness. In 2013, he was freed from prison and is living in the federal Witness Protection Program.

Joseph M. McLaughlin (Brooklyn federal judge): After serving for about nine years as a district court judge, he was elevated to the U.S. Court of Appeals for The Second Circuit in 1990. He died in August 2013 at the age of eighty.

Robert M. Morgenthau (New York County District Attorney): Served as Manhattan District Attorney from 1975 until his retirement in 2009, a tenure that at the time was the longest of any New York City district attorney. After retirement he joined the Manhattan law firm of Wachtel, Lipton, Rosen & Katz.

Bruce Mouw (supervisory FBI agent): Retired from the FBI and currently serves as a special official for the Laborers' International Union of North America, Office of Inspector General, where he specializes in rooting out mob influence. He lives on Long Island.

Joseph O'Brien (FBI agent): Retired from the FBI and currently runs a private investigative firm. He lives on Long Island.

Joseph "Old Man" Paruta (Gambino associate): Old Man Paruta was a Brooklyn mob associate who was steeped in Mafia life, was close to Gravano and assisted in at least one homicide.

Gravano held a special mob initiation ceremony for a gravely ill Paruta on his death bed attended by the likes of James Failla. At one point Paruta asked Gravano to kill him to take him out of his misery. Gravano considered doing the mercy killing but Paruta died of his illness in 1986.

Thomas Pitera (Bonanno soldier): After his conviction in 1992 on racketeering charges involving six murders, he was sentenced to life in prison after a jury declined to sentence him to the federal death penalty. He is currently incarcerated at McCreary United States Penitentiary in Pine Knot, Kentucky.

John L. Pollok: Maintains an active criminal law practice in Manhattan.

Anthony "Roach" Rampino: He died in December 2010 at the age of seventy-one while serving a twenty-five-year sentence for heroin sales.

Mark Reiter (former Gambino associate): He is currently serving a life sentence without parole for a federal narcotics conviction in Schuylkill Federal Correction Institution in Minersville, Pennsylvania. He has filed numerous motions over the years to overturn his conviction or get a new trial, all without success.

Angelo Ruggiero (Gambino captain): He died on December 9, 1989, and is buried with his wife Maria at St. John Cemetery, Queens, N.Y. Maria died in 2006.

Salvatore Ruggiero (Gambino associate): Died in a plane crash on May 6, 1982, along with his wife Stephanie. The place of interment for the fragments of his and his wife's remains is unknown.

Gerlando "George From Canada" Sciascia (Bonanno family captain): He was found shot to death on a Bronx street on March 18, 1999. Hs murder, court testimony later established, had been ordered by Bonanno family boss Joseph Massino.

Gerald Shargel (defense attorney): After the big Mafia cases, he went on to develop a thriving white-collar criminal defense practice in Manhattan. He retired in January 2018.

Alphonse Sisca (Gambino crime family member): He finished serving a federal sentence in 2012. He is reputedly involved in Gambino family activities in New Jersey.

Arnold Squitieri (former acting Gambino crime family boss): Federal officials believe he served as an acting family boss in the period after John J. Gotti went to prison. He was sentenced to just over seven and a half years in federal prison in 2006 for extortion and racketeering and released in December 2012.

Jack B. Weinstein (federal judge): At the age of ninety-six, he is the oldest judge in the Eastern District of New York. He assumed senior status in 1993 and has maintained a caseload ever since.

NOTES

Chapter One: "Any Survivors?"

Details of the flight of Learjet N100TA on May 6, 1982, and its crash into the Atlantic Ocean can be found in Aircraft Accident Report of the National Transportation Safety Board, report number NTSB/AAR-83/01. Information was also obtained in telephone and email interviews with Judy Helmey as well as from her book *My Father, the Sea & Me*; telephone interviews with Bill Walsh and Edward Crittenden; contemporaneous articles in the *Savannah Morning News* and *A Guide to Georgia's Artificial Reefs*, published by the Georgia Department of Natural Resources: Coastal Resources Division. The article "Oh Captain, My Captain," which appeared in the March 21, 2017, issue of *Savannah Magazine* was also consulted.

Chapter Two: The Fulton-Rockaway Crowd

Surveillance reports described in a government prosecutorial memorandum compiled in 1983 regarding the proposed case against Angelo Ruggiero and others were made available to the author. Mark Reiter's early history was provided by a confidential news source. Early histories of John Carneglia, Angelo Ruggiero, and John Gotti can be found in *Mob Killer: the Bloody Rampage of Charlie Carneglia, Mafia Hit Man,* by Anthony M. DeStefano. A description of John J. Gotti's early criminal history and his problems with the Selective Service System can be found in FBI records available in the FBI public website area known as the "FBI Records: The Vault." His daughter Victoria described her parents' early marital life in her book *This Family of Mine: What It Was Like Growing Up Gotti.* The early years of the Fulton-Rockaway crew are described in *Mob Star: The Story of John Gotti,* by Jerry Capeci and Gene Mustain. Salvatore Ruggiero's early criminal history and involvement with drug trafficking can be found in *U.S. v. Herbert Sperling et al.* 73 CR 441, USDC SDNY, articles published about the Sperling case in *The New York Times* and the case file of *U.S. v. Angelo Ruggiero et al.* 83 CR 412, USDC EDNY. Events in the days after Sal Ruggiero's death and the search by his family and friends to find documents and money were described in the prosecutorial memorandum previously cited.

Chapter Three: "Never Mention Drugs"

Joseph Massino's telephone conversations with Angelo Ruggiero were detailed in *King of the Godfathers: "Big Joey" Massino and the Fall of the Bonanno Crime Family,* by Anthony M. DeStefano, as are attempts by the mob to find and kill Bruno Indelicato. Information about the surveillance of Angelo Ruggiero's home in Cedarhurst was obtained in an interview with ex-FBI agent Joseph O'Brien. The prosecutorial memo previously referenced was the source of details of the surveillance of Ruggiero's home and his meeting with Alfred Dellentash. Meetings and actions Dellentash took in connection with Sal Ruggiero's death are also described in the prosecutorial memo. Peter Tambone's fate and his problems with drug dealing are also described in the prosecution memo.

Chapter Four: "Angelo, Keep Your Mouth Shut"

Angelo Ruggiero's dealings with Sciascia and his efforts to keep the heroin operation going in 1982 are outlined in the prosecutorial memo. Ruggiero's dealings with Edward Lino and the substance of their conversation about heroin are also found in the prosecutorial memo. The memo also is the source of numerous other conversations and actions cited in this chapter, including those of attorney Michael Coiro, the funeral of Sal Ruggiero, the post-funeral meeting in the Ruggiero house in which drugs were discussed, the efforts to get Stephanie Ruggiero's family to go along and provide false or misleading information to federal authorities, and the Greco-Cestaro heroin arrest. Former FBI agent Bruce Mouw provided details in an interview about the funeral of Sal Ruggiero and the way the decision was made to drop the arrests in the Greco-Cestaro case to protect the confidentiality of the agency's wide probe of the Gambino family. Discussion of the Mark Reiter heroin cases can be found in *U.S. v. Mark Reiter, et al.* 848 F. 2d 336, USCA 2nd Circuit (1988), *U.S. v. Mark Reiter*, 2018 U.S. Dist. LEXIS 3864 (2018), *Mark Reiter v. U.S.,* 97 Civ. 02941 [related to 87 Cr. 132], USDC SDNY. John Alite's claim about Reiter giving John J. Gotti money from heroin sales was made in a telephone interview with the author and is contained in FBI files about his debriefings. A confidential news source raised questions in an email interview about the reliability of Alite's claim about the heroin money going to Gotti.

Chapter Five: "Take Care of Him, Nino"

Andrea Giovino's claims about her relationship with Mark Reiter and her presence at parties with Reiter and John J. Gotti are detailed in her book *Divorced from the Mob: My Journey from Organized Crime to Independent Woman,* as well as in telephone interviews with the author. John Alite and DEA agent Jim Hunt related their beliefs about Gotti's awareness of heroin dealing in separate interviews with the author. See files in *Irving Picard v. Saul B. Katz et.al.,* 11Cv 03605, USDC SDNY, a case related to the Bernard Madoff scandal for a discussion of the legal concept of willful blindness. See *Mob Star* for a description of the move of the Carmine Fatico crew to South Ozone Park and the killing of James McBratney and its aftermath with Gotti and Angelo Ruggiero. Reports that Castellano was meeting with Pizza Connection heroin defendants were related to the author by former FBI agent Charles Rooney. Historical background on the Pizza case was provided by former assistant U.S. Attorney Richard Martin. Information about FBI sources "Wahoo" and "BQ" can be found in *Mob Star*. The physical description of Castellano is captured in *Mafia Dynasty,* by

John H. Davis. History of Castellano's life in the mob and his various business interests, as well as his involvement with the murderous Roy DeMeo car-theft ring can be found in Raab's *Five Families.* The connection between the Gambino family and the Westies is discussed in *Five Families* and DeStefano's *Gangland New York: The Places and Faces of Mob History.*

Chapter Six: "I Could Give You Information"

John J. Gotti's gambling problems are detailed in *Mob Star* and *Mafia Dynasty.* The development of Wilfred Johnson as a confidential law enforcement source is in part described in Remo Franceschini's *A Matter of Honor: One Cop's Lifelong Pursuit of John Gotti and The Mob.* Bruce Mouw described to the author FBI activity surrounding the Bergin Hunt and Fish Club and his interaction with Queens District Attorney John Santucci and his staff. The raid on the Mott Street gambling house is detailed in an article in *The New York Times.* Articles in *The New York Times,* as well as *Five Families*, was the source of information about the unauthorized disclosure of FBI wiretap affidavits.

Chapter Seven: "You Are Pissing Some Big People Off"

Details of the hiring by Angelo Ruggiero of surveillance expert John Conroy through John McNally and their actions related to detection of electronic bugging were obtained in the prosecutorial memo previously cited. Ruggiero's fears about the FBI investigation were documented in the book *Mob Star.* Allegations about the August 1982 heroin deal with Ruggiero and others were obtained from the prosecutorial memo. Former FBI agent Joe O'Brien related to the author in an interview about his surveillance of Gambino family members on Staten Island. Claims by O'Brien and fellow agent Andris Kurins about the bugging of the Castellano house are found in their book *Boss of Bosses.* Bruce Mouw told the author in an interview that claims of O'Brien and Kurins that they did the actual break-in of the Castellano house were not true since case agents are not used to do such work. O'Brien related in an interview, and also reported in *Boss of Bosses*, details of the surveillance post on Staten Island.

Chapter Eight: The Junk Crowd

Details of Alfred Dellentash's activities with Angelo Ruggiero and his cooperation with federal authorities are detailed in the prosecution memorandum. The prosecution memorandum also spelled out the potential defendants in the federal heroin case, the various charges and legal considerations involved. *Mob Star* contains insight into the fears among the Gotti crew over the imminent indictment. The arrests and filing of the indictment in the drug case are detailed in *The New York Times* and *Newsday*. Gotti's being called to explain the charges and being called onto the carpet by Castellano are all detailed in Capeci and Mustain's *Mob Star*. The resulting bail hearings and bail dispositions are chronicled in *The New York Times* and *Newsday*. James Hunt was interviewed about the indictment of Ruggiero. Allegations about Mark Reiter are contained in the case files and court decisions cited in *U.S. v. Mark Reiter, et al.* 848 F. 2d 336, USCA 2nd Circuit (1988), *U.S. v. Mark Reiter*, 2018 U.S. Dist. LEXIS 3864 (2018), *Mark Reiter v. U.S.,* 97 Civ. 02941 [related to 87 Cr. 132]. Additional information about the cases involving Mark Reiter can be found in Leroy "Nicky" Barnes's book *Mr. Untouchable: The Rise, Fall and Resurrection of Heroin's Teflon Don*. The repercussions with Castellano over the heroin indictment and the surveillance tapes is described in Capeci and Mustain's *Mob Star* and Raab's *Five Families*.

Chapter Nine: "I Ain't Givin' Them Tapes Up"

The arrest of the members of the Mafia Commission was reported in *The New York Times* and Raab's *Five Families*. The arrest of Castellano is described in O'Brien and Kurins's *Boss of Bosses* and Raab's *Five Families*. Bruce Mouw provided information about Castellano's remodeling of his house after he learned of the bugging. Information about the Gambino family case handled by Diane Giacalone and the subsequent trial and acquittals comes from the

*United States of America v. Aniello Dellacroce, et al. 85-Cr-178
(EDNY)*, Raab's *Five Families*, Maas and Gravano's *Underboss*,
Davis's *Mafia Dynasty*, Capeci and Mustain's *Mob Star* and cover-
age by *The New York Times*.

Chapter Ten: "I'm Going to Blow This Motherfucker Away"

Aniello Dellacroce's death was reported in *The New York Times*.
Details of the meetings at Casa Storta and the resulting electronic
surveillance can be found in Maas and Gravano's *Underboss*. The
book *Underboss* also has a detailed recollection by Gravano about
the early stages of the planning in the plot to kill Castellano. Joseph
Watts's status in the Gambino family and the allegations against him
can be found in various court papers, including those in the case file
of *U.S. v. Joseph Watts*, S1 09 Cr. 62, USDC SDNY, in particular
document 37 titled "Notice of Enterprise Evidence."

Chapter Eleven: "Fuckin' John's Crazy"

The early history of the Italian gangsters in New York City can be
found in DeStefano's *Gangland New York: The Places and Faces of
Mob History*. The configuration of the Mafia Commission in the
days leading up to the assassination of Paul Castellano and the decision of its various members about that action is found in Maas's
Underboss. The opposition of Anthony Casso to the killing of
Castellano is found in Philip Carlo's *Gaspipe: Confessions of a Mafia
Boss*. Maas's *Underboss* gives details derived from Sammy Gravano
interviews about the planning leading up to Castellano's murder.

Chapter Twelve: "He's Gone"

The events of the day of Castellano's murder and the identities of
the alleged participants are described in a number of works: Maas's
Underboss, Sammy Gravano's testimony in *U.S. v. John Gotti et al.*
90-Cr-1951 (EDNY), Raab's *Five Families*. Bruce Mouw also described the events as they were related to him by Gravano. Events
following the Castellano assassination such as the police investigation were detailed in many newspapers but notably *The New York
Times*. The events following the Castellano murder are also outlined

in O'Brien and Kurins's *Boss of Bosses* and Raab's *Five Families*. *The New York Times* covered Castellano's funeral. The Gambino crime family meetings that led to Gotti's assumption of power were described by Mouw and by Gravano in Maas's *Underboss*.

Chapter Thirteen: "Shame on Them!"

The New York Times had coverage of the aftermath in the Gambino crime family after Castellano's murder and Gotti's assumption as the new boss role. Information and allegations about the Cenamo homicide and the alleged involvement of Joe Watts can be found in Maas's *Underboss* and *U.S. v. Joseph Watts*, S1 09 Cr. 62, USDC SDNY. The April 1986 bombing that killed Frank DeCicco was detailed in *The New York Times* and in Maas's *Underboss*. Claims by Anthony Casso about the plotting for the DeCicco killing can be found in Carlo's book *Gaspipe*. Testimony and proceedings in John J. Gotti's trial for the assault of Romual Piecyk can be found in *The New York Times* and Raab's *Five Families*. For the Giacalone trial of Gotti, Raab's *Five Families* has detailed background concerning the inside politics in the Department of Justice about the prosecution. *The New York Times* provided coverage of the Giacalone-led trial and the later acquittals. The murder of Robert DiBernardo and Gravano's involvement is detailed in Maas's *Underboss*. The indictment of Joe N. Gallo and others in the Gambino crime family case of 1986 was covered by the author for New York *Newsday* and *The New York Times*. The detailed daily coverage of the Giacalone trial was provided by *The New York Times*. DeStefano's *Mob Killer* related federal court testimony of Kevin McMahon in which he told of efforts by associates of the Gambino family to surveil jurors in the Giacalone case. The allegations of George Pape and his involvement in compromising the jury are found in *The New York Times* and Maas's *Underboss*.

Chapter Fourteen: Tales of the Tapes, Part 1

The rundown on the 1986 Commission trial can be found in *The New York Times* and in Raab's *Five Families*. Bruce Mouw provided information in an interview about the way a Gambino crime family member told a girlfriend during some pillow talk about the fact that a juror in the Giacalone case had been compromised. Information about allegations of drug dealing by Mark Reiter are contained in numerous court filings and decisions, including *U.S. v. Mark Reiter, et al.* 848F. 2d 336, USCA 2nd Circuit. News reports in *The New York Times* and New York *Newsday* provided comprehensive details of the 1987 heroin trial involving Angelo Ruggiero and others in Brooklyn federal court. Details of a special *en banc* proceeding in Brooklyn federal court on January 21, 1988, in the Ruggiero case can be found in the case files of 83-CR-412 and MISC. 88-34 (In Re Grand Jury). Allegations of jury tampering in the trial before Judge Costantino are detailed in *U.S. v Angelo Ruggiero, et.al.* 846 F. 2d 117 (2nd Circuit) and *U.S. v. John Carneglia, et al.* 83-Cr 412, EDNY, see Government's *Memorandum of Law in Opposition to Defendant's Motion to Obtain the Names and Addresses of the Anonymous Jurors.*

Chapter Fifteen: Tales of the Tapes, Part 2

For details about the life of Alfred Dellentash and his connection to the Ruggiero drug world see the article *The Man Who Got America High,* by Jeff Maysh in the November 5, 2014, posting on the website Narratively at http://narratively/the-man-who-got-america-high/. Bruce Mouw provided information about Dellentash's interview with FBI and federal officials. Details of the Angola prison in Louisiana can be found on Wikipedia. Details of the criminal cases against Arnold Squitieri and Angel Sisca were reported in *The New York Times* and the federal prosecution memo previously cited. The 1988 retrial of Angelo Ruggiero and others in the heroin case was covered by *The New York Times* and New York *Newsday*. Former prosecutor Robert LaRusso also provided information about the retrial. Details of the allegations involving the jury deliberation in the third trial of John Carneglia and Gene Gotti are found in *U.S. v. Angelo Ruggiero et al.* 928 F. 2d 1289 (2nd Circuit). The discussion of the Gotti investigation being a national law enforcement priority can be found in now-public FBI records on its website page known as "The Vault." Details of the FBI penetration of 247 Mulberry Street are found in Raab's *Five Families* and through an interview with Bruce Mouw.

Chapter Sixteen: "Gentlemen, It's Been a Pleasure"

Details of the assassination of Willie Boy Johnson are found in *The New York Times*, Maas's *Underboss,* and through an interview with DEA official James Hunt. The third retrial of the heroin case involving Angelo Ruggiero, John Carneglia, and Gene Gotti was covered on a regular basis in *The New York Times* and *New York Newsday*, as was Judge Bartels ruling on the jury-tampering issue. The Father's Day outing of John Carneglia and friends in 1989 is described in DeStefano's *Mob Killer* and was viewed in a video recording played at the 2009 trial of Charles Carneglia, in the case *U.S. v Joseph Agate*, et.al. 08-CR-76. EDNY, government exhibit 317A. The sentencing of John Carneglia and Gene Gotti was reported in *The New York Times* and New York *Newsday*.

Chapter Seventeen: Deaths in Harlem

Allegations of Mark Reiter's connections to heroin and the black drug dealers in Harlem is examined in *U.S. v. Mark Reiter et.al.* 848 F. 2d 336 (SDNY), and *Mark Reiter v. U.S.* 87 Civ. 02941 (2nd Cir.) including the brief filed by the U.S. government on the appeal that spells out the government case and statement of facts. The heroin problem in New York City and State in the period beginning in 1982 were covered in *The New York Times*. The cases of *Reiter* cited above also contain information about his trial, the murders of a number of persons, and the various witness testimonies. John Alite stated in an interview his opinion about Reiter. Information regarding Reiter's assets and lifestyle comes from government records made available to the author from a confidential source. Leroy "Nicky" Barnes's book *Mr. Untouchable: The Rise, Fall and Resurrection of Heroin's Teflon Don* give his version of his life story, his allegations about Reiter's involvement in the heroin trade, and his decision to become a government witness. Details of Reiter's sentencing before Judge Richard Owen are found in the minutes from the case file of *U.S. v. Mark Reiter, et al.*, 87 Cr. 132, SDNY.

Chapter Eighteen: The Last Hurrah

Maas's *Underboss* contains Gravano's recollections of the harsh way Gotti treated Angelo Ruggiero in the period after the various indictments. *The New York Times* reported on the way John J. Gotti targeted union official O'Connor as well as businessman Fred Weiss. Details of the Weiss murder can also be found on Wikipedia, while allegations of Joe Watts's involvement in the homicide are found in the document *Notice of Enterprise Evidence* filed by the U.S. government in *U.S. v. Joseph Watts*, 09 Cr. 62 SDNY. The bugging of the apartment at 247 Mulberry Street and the resulting tapes is detailed in Raab's *Five Families*. The killing of Louis DiBono and allegations of who was involved can be found in DeStefano's *Mob Killer* and the case files and transcripts of *U.S. v. Agate [Carneglia]*, 08-Cr-76 in the previous citation. Gotti's ramblings with Locascio over Gravano's aggressive acquisition of companies is found in Raab's *Five Families* and Davis's *Mafia Dynasty*. *The New York Times* provided extensive coverage of Gotti's 1990 trial and acquittal for the assault on union official John O'Connor.

Chapter Nineteen: "Number One Is In"

Robert M. Morgenthau's biography can be found on Wikipedia. Raab's *Five Families* is a source of much of the information about the competition between Morgenthau and federal prosecutors over who was going to prosecute John J. Gotti. Additional recordings of Gotti made at the Mulberry Street apartment are reported in *Five Families*. Gravano's discussion of how he allegedly approached Patsy Conte over getting drug money to flow to John J. Gotti can be found in a ruling by Judge I. Leo Glasser in *U.S. v. John Gotti and Frank Locascio*, 171 F.R.D. 19: 1997 U.S. Dist. LEXIS 4329. Maas's *Underboss* relates Gravano's version of his decision to go on the lam and hide out. Bruce Mouw related details of the night Gotti and others were arrested in December 1990, as did Gravano in Maas's *Underboss*.

Chapter Twenty: "Cosa Nostra Needs John Gotti"

The post-arrest events with John Gotti were detailed in Raab's *Five Families*, as well as some of Gotti's recorded statements about Gravano. The recollections of Gravano about his reaction to Gotti's criticism of him and his arguments with him in federal jail are found in Maas's *Underboss,* as was Gravano's description of his decision to cooperate with the FBI. The author witnessed the fizzling disaster of the July 1991 fireworks display near the Bergin Hunt and Fish Club.

Chapter Twenty-one: "The Teflon Is Gone"

Details of Gravano's turning into a cooperating witness are described in Raab's *Five Families,* in interviews with Bruce Mouw and in Maas's *Underboss*. Mouw and former FBI agent Phil Scala related in interviews how Gravano was secreted at various hideouts and taken to Quantico. The 1992 trial of John J. Gotti and Frank Locascio was extensively covered in *The New York Times, New York Newsday*, the *Daily News* and the *New York Post*. Insight into Gotti's comments when he was sentenced is reported in Raab's *Five Families*. Judy Helmey's activities on the day Gotti was sentenced to life in prison, and the peculiarities of barracuda, were related to the author in a series of email interviews, in between fishing charters off the coast of Georgia.

Epilogue

The testimony of Michael DiLeonardo and John Alite in the trial of Charles Carneglia can be found in DeStefano's *Mob Killer* and the case files of *U.S. v. Agate* [Carneglia] 08-Cr 76, as previously cited.

BIBLIOGRAPHY

Books

Anastasia, George. *Gotti's Rules: The Story of John Alite, Junior Gotti, and the Demise of the American Mafia*. New York: HarperCollins Publishers, 2015.

Barnes, Leroy "Nicky" and Tom Folsom. *Mr. Untouchable: The Rise, Fall, and Resurrection of Heroin's Teflon Don*. New York: Rugged Land, LLC, 2007.

Blum, Howard. *Gangland: How the FBI Broke the Mob*. New York: Simon & Schuster, 1993.

Blumenthal, Ralph and Miller, John. *The Gotti Tapes: Including The Testimony of Salvatore (Sammy The Bull) Gravano*. New York : Times Books, 1992.

Capeci, Jerry. *The Complete Idiot's Guide to The Mafia*. (2nd Ed.) New York: Penguin Group, 2004.

Capeci, Jerry, and Gene Mustain. *Gotti: Rise and Fall*. New York: Berkley, 1996.

——. *Mob Star: The Story of John Gotti*. New York: Alpha: New Edition. 2002.

Carlo, Philip. *Butcher: Anatomy of a Mafia Psychopath*. New York: William Morrow Paperbacks, 2010.

——. *Gaspipe: Confessions of a Mafia Boss*. New York: Harper, 2009.

Cowan, Rick, and Century Douglas. *Takedown: The Fall of the Last Mafia Empire*. New York: G.P. Putnam's Sons, 2002.

Davis, John. *Mafia Dynasty: The Rise and Fall of the Gambino Crime Family*. New York: Harper Paperbacks, 1993.

DeStefano, Anthony. *Gangland New York: The Places and Faces of Mob History*. Guilford, Connecticut: Lyons Press, 2015

———. *Mob Killer: The Bloody Rampage of Charlie Carneglia, Mafia Hit Man*. New York: Kensington, Publishing Corp, 2011.

———. *The Big Heist: The Real Story of the Lufthansa Heist, the Mafia, and Murder*. New York: Pinnacle True Crime, 2018.

Franceschini, Remo. *A Matter of Honor: One Cop's Lifelong Pursuit of John Gotti and The Mob*. New York: Simon & Schuster, 1993.

Giovino, Andrea. *Divorced from The Mob: My Journey from Organized Crime to Independent Woman*. New York: Carroll & Graf Publishers, 2004.

Gotti, John. Lance, Peter (Foreword). *Shadow of My Father*. Kindle Edition: Phoenix Media Productions Ltd., 2015.

Gotti, Victoria. *This Family of Mine: What It Was Like Growing Up Gotti*. New York: Pocket Books, A Division of Simon & Schuster Inc., 2009.

Helmey, Judy.*My Father, the Sea & Me*. Doraville, Georgia: B&S Printing, 1992.

Lamothe, Lee and Adrian Humphreys. *The Sixth Family: The Collapse of the New York Mafia and the Rise of Vito Rizzuto*. Mississauga: John Wiley & Sons Canada, Ltd, 2006.

Maas, Peter. *Underboss: Sammy the Bull Gravano's Story of Life in The Mafia*. New York: HarperCollins, 1997.

Mustain, Gene, and Jerry Capeci. *Mob Star: The Story of John Gotti, the Most Powerful Criminal in America*. New York: Franklin Watts, 1988.

O'Brien, Joseph F., and Andris Kurins. *Boss of Bosses: The Fall of The Godfather—The FBI and Paul Castellano*. New York: Dell Publishers, 1992.

Raab, Selwyn. *The Five Families: The Rise, Decline and*

Resurgence of America's Most Powerful Mafia Empires. New
York: Thomas Dunne Books, 2005.

Court Decisions and Cases

Michael Coiro, petitioner v. U.S. No. 90-1521, Brief for the United
   States in Opposition, On Petition for a Writ of Certiorari, United
   States Supreme Court.
Raymond Clark v. U.S., 365 F. Supp. 2d 553 (2005) (SDNY)
Herbert Pate (pet) v. United States of America, No. 89-1427,
   United States Supreme Court.
Irving Picard v. Saul B. Katz et al., 11Cv 03605 (SDNY)
Mark Reiter v. U.S., 97 Civ. 02941 [related to 87 Cr. 132] (SDNY)
U.S. v Joseph Agate, et al. 08-CR-76 (EDNY)
U.S. v. John Carneglia and Gene Gotti, 83-cr-412 (EDNY)
U.S. v. Michael Coiro, 922 F.2d 1008 (2nd Cir. 1990)
U.S. v. John D'Amico 09-Cr-62 (SDNY)
U.S. v. Aniello Dellacroce, et al. 85 Cr 178 (EDNY)
U.S. v. Joseph Gallo, et al. 86-cr-452 (EDNY)
U.S. v. John Gotti and Frank Locascio, 90-Cr-1951 (EDNY)
U.S. v. John Gotti and Frank Locascio, 782 F. Supp. 737 (EDNY
   1992)
U.S. v. Frank Locascio and John Gotti, 6 F.3d 934 (2nd Cir. 1993)
U.S. v. John Gotti and Frank Locascio, 171 F.R.D. 19: 1997 U.S.
   Dist. LEXIS 4329
U.S. Joseph Massino and Salvatore Vitale 652 F. Supp. 244
   (EDNY 1986)
U.S. v. Bosko Randonjich, et al. 92-Cr-159 (EDNY)
U.S. v Mark Reiter, et al. 848 F. 2d 336 (2nd Cir 1988)
U.S. v. Mark Reiter, et al. 87-cr-132 (SDNY)
U.S. v Mark Reiter, 2018 U.S. Dist. LEXIS 3864 (2018)
U.S. v. Angelo Ruggiero, et al. 678 F. Supp. 46 (EDNY)
U.S. v. Angelo Ruggiero, 796 F.2d 35 (2nd Cir. 1986)
U.S. v Angelo Ruggiero, et al. 83-cr- 412 (EDNY)
U.S. v. Angelo Ruggiero, et al. 846 F.2d 117 (2nd Cir. 1988)
U.S. v. Angelo Ruggiero, et al. 928 F. 2d 1289 (2nd Cir 1990)

U.S. v. Angelo Ruggiero, et al. 934 F.2d 446 (2nd Cir 1991)

U.S. v. Angelo S. Ruggiero, 06-cr-985 (EDNY)

U.S. v. John Silvestri et al. 92-mj-01645 (SDNY)

U.S. v. Herbert Sperling, et al. 73-Cr-441 (SDNY)

U.S. v. Herbert Sperling, et al. 506 F.2d 1323 (2nd Cir 1974)

U.S. v. Herbert Sperling et.al. 76-Cr-218 (EDNY)

U.S. v. Salvatore Vitale, et al. 81 Cr. 803 (SDNY 1986)

U.S. v. Joseph Watts 01-Cr-11 (EDNY)

U.S. v. Joseph Watts 93-Cr- 294 (EDNY)

U.S. v. Joseph Watts 09-Cr-62 (SDNY)

U.S. v. Lauren Watts, et al. 72 F, Supp. 2nd 106 (EDNY)

Victor J. Orena v. U.S. 956 F. Supp. 1971 (SDNY)

Government Publications

National Transportation Safety Board. *Aircraft Accident Report of the National Transportation Safety Board, report number NTSB/AAR-83/01*

Magazine and Web Articles

Jerome, Jim. *Touring Rock Stars Go to Al Dellentash When They Really Want to Get High*, October 9, 1978, *People* magazine, at People.com.

Maysh, Jeff. *The Man Who Got America High,* in the November 5, 2014, posting on the website Narratively, at narratively.com/the-man-who-got-america-high.

Newspapers and Periodicals

Daily News (NY)

New York Newsday

Newsday

The New York Times

The New York Post

The Savannah Morning News

Websites Consulted

www.biography.com

www.bop.gov

www.findagrave.com

www.ganglandnews.com

www.LOC.gov

www.nexis.com

www.wikipedia.com

www.youtube.com

www.Newsday.com

www.Proquest.com

ACKNOWLEDGMENTS

This is the seventh book I have written about organized crime and doing each has made me feel like an archeologist of La Cosa Nostra. I have had to dig back in time, sometimes decades ago, to piece together the stories. In *Gotti's Boys,* the time span covered was not as long as it was on *Top Hoodlum,* my book about Frank Costello, which went back to the early part of the twentieth century in old New York, but the amount of work was about the same. Luckily, I had some good help along the way and access to great material. As is usual in a book about the mob, some people helped me and prefer to remain anonymous. They know who they are and get my thanks.

There exist numerous court files and judicial decisions about the crimes of John Gotti and his crew. Much of that material can be found in electronic databases, including the federal PACER system of accessing files. Still, I had to dig back into some old paper court files that are kept in the National Archives, where the staff in the Northeast Region office in Manhattan assisted me. My thanks again to Kevin Reilly and Trina Yeckley of the regional office. In Savannah, Georgia, Anne Butler of the Live Oak Public Library assembled old news clips from microfilm for me.

A number of current and former federal officials provided critical assistance. Over at the Drug Enforcement Administration's New York office, special agent in charge James Hunt and his key spokesperson, Erin Mulvey, provided important historical perspective and photographs. At the FBI, spokesperson Amy Thoreson smoothed the way in setting up interviews and seeking additional photographs. Although she no longer is a full-time DEA agent, Camille Colon made some crucial introductions for me and shared some important recollections. Thanks also to Robert Cook, of the Office of The Special Narcotics Prosecutor in New York City, and retired DEA agent Robert Russello.

Among the retired FBI agents, a big tip of the hat to Bruce Mouw, who patiently shared his time in giving me crucial perspective about the Gotti years and access to public-record photographs. Former agents, Pat Colgan, Andris Kurins, Dan McCormick, and Joe O'Brien were helpful in sharing their recollections of the events in the run-up to the arrests of Paul Castellano and John J. Gotti. Another retired agent, Phil Scala, worked with Mouw and the others on the Gotti investigation and shared his recollections about the Gambino family and the events surrounding Sammy Gravano's decision to become a cooperating witness.

Former federal prosecutor Robert La Russo and retired defense attorney Joel Winograd had recollections of people and events described in *Gotti's Boys,* which they readily shared. Steadfast Bronx defense attorney Murray Richman, Andrea Giovino, and John Alite also shared information.

Since the May 1982 crash of a Learjet off the coast of Georgia, which killed Salvatore Ruggiero and his wife, played a role in getting this story going, I have to thank people who were familiar with the accident and the recovery operations. There is of course captain Judy Helmey who spent hours looking through her old records and composing emails for me that described the incident and how close her father, Cpt. Sherman Helmey, came to dying himself that day. She also told me everything I need to know about barracuda! Bill Walsh, who did the first dive to the crash site provided vivid details of the wreckage and the discovery of human remains. Edward Crittenden, whose late father was involved in the recovery of the aircraft debris, also had useful descriptions of the events.

As is always the case, I relied on the published work of a number of fellow journalists and writers: Michael Arena, Marilyn Berkery,

David Bird, William G. Blair, Ralph Blumenthal, Pete Bowles, Leonard Buder, Jerry Capeci, Maurice Carroll, Betty Darby, Walter Fee, Richard C. Firstman, Joseph P. Fried, Alan Feuer, Sean Gardiner, Robert W. Greene, Chris Hedges, Marvine Howe, George James, Peter Kerr, Don Lowery, Arnold H. Lubasch, Lawrence C. Levy, Mike McAlary, Gerald McKelvey, Robert D. McFadden, Lisa Morris, Alexandra K. Mosca, Nicholas Pileggi, Julia Preston, Selwyn Raab, Willliam M. Reilly, Tom Renner, Anthony Scaduto, Gale Scott, Alessandra Stanley, Ronald D. Smothers, Ronald Sullivan, Peg Tyre, Steve Wick.

At *Newsday,* assistant managing editor Mary Ann Skinner, Laura Mann of the newspaper's library, and my news editor Monica Quintanilla again get my thanks for their help.

Gary Goldstein, my editor at Kensington, and my agent Jill Marsal, as they always do, did much to help bring this book to fruition.

INDEX